SENSING YOUR HIDDEN PRESENCE

Toward Intimacy with God

by Ignacio Larrañaga

*Translated by John W. Diercksmeier
and Rigoberto Caloca-Rivas*

ÉDITIONS PAULINES

Originally published as *Muestrame tu rostro*
by Ediciones Paulinas-Cefepal, Santiago, Chile.

Phototypesetting: *Éditions Paulines*

Cover: *Larry Mantovani*

ISBN 2-89039-524-3

Legal Deposit –1st Quarter 1992
Bibliothèque nationale du Québec
National Library of Canada

© 1992   Éditions Paulines
          250, boul. Saint-François Nord
          Sherbrooke, QC, J1E 2B9
          Canada

Contents

Preface to the English Edition

When I wrote this book, I had no intention other than to shout, as in times past, "Listen, Israel: Yahweh our God is the one Yahweh" (Dt 6:4-9). I suppose, and I hope, that this intention continues to be valid for the English-speaking public.

God has never been, for anyone, a palpable and concrete person; instead, God is diffuse, a face of clouds that we uncover with difficulty among the traces, shadows, and silence. But today, in our technological society, the traces of God have been ever more erased, while at the same time the traces of humanity have become firm and more pronounced. Our society accepts anything that is empirically verifiable, but God is not a verifiable empirical fact, He is rather a mystery of faith.

We feel the conflict between our difficulty in expressing God with symbols and metaphors and the exact and evident formulations used to express science. We are bothered by the difference between the clarity of scientific methods of research and testing, and our analogous and deductive paths for approaching God. That is why, today, we have special difficulty in accepting the God of faith, and we have the impression of witnessing the eclipse of God.

Nevertheless, God does not need to defend His rights. On the contrary, the fate of humanity is decided here because, in the end, God is the absolute value and the ultimate meaning of our lives.

The history of secularization has demonstrated that the decline of God is indissolubly linked to the decline of humanity. The more God is reduced to silence and expelled from our lives, the more humanity is dehumanized.

Nietzsche said, "God is dead." We do not know north from south, midnight from midday, good from evil. God dies and monsters are born: absurdity, nausea, loneliness, nothingness. Without God, this world is a desolate and cold planet. After all, God is the only force capable of taking humanity out of our egocentric withdrawal and infusing us with the joy of living.

Many years ago, when Harold Macmillan, then Prime Minister of the United Kingdom, was asked where, in his opinion, could the Soviet empire begin to crack, he answered that it was not in the areas of economics or strategy, but in the area of philosophy, meaning that, after each milestone, there will always be an "and *for what?*" and after crossing the street, the citizen will always meet emptiness.

In psychological terms, the destiny/fate of an atheistic society — whether it be Eastern or Western — is suicide.

The university students of Nanterre, France, asked themselves in 1968: What is the purpose in having many things, including the ability to solve the hunger problem, if we all die of boredom?

Technology and all of the *human sciences* will be able to resolve the majority of human needs, but they will never be able to give a proper answer to the fundamental question regarding the meaning of life. When we are confronted by our own mystery, when we experience the strangeness of "being there," being in the world as consciousness, then the central question will be raised, challenging our path: Who am I? Where do I come from? Is there a future for me, and what is it? In other words, What is the ultimate meaning of my existence? These questions obligate us to make the great leap into the Absolute.

In the end, man's best friend is God. We are not treading on religious ground here, but on anthropological.

Dostoyevski said, "It is impossible to be human and not bow down; if God is rejected, before an idol we bow." When God is not the true God of humanity, something else becomes absolute in the human heart. The idol provokes and calls the heart's attention; humanity is seduced and enslaved because it is not only led to adherence but to fanaticism. Idols, then, instead of granting autonomy and freedom, absorb, enslave, and destroy humanity.

Money is the indisputable idol that dominates most human relationships; for the majority, money is the absolute value: you are worth as much as you have. *Power* is the idol that plays on human dignity and invites the individual to "be like a god"; power is what most seems like divinization because, more than any other idol, it invokes public adoration. There are other idols, such as sex, hedonism, horizontalism, permissiveness, spontaneity, secularism, and so on.

But these idols are the gods of slavery; they rob joy, engender fear, lead to loneliness, and their final goal is death. They are, then, the enemies of humanity.

We repeat: man's best friend is God.

But not an oppressor God. For many, even today, God is a threatening and demanding being who makes their lives miserable. They hold a deep dark conviction that they must be freed from this oppressive presence to be able to live joyfully and fully. And I agree. One must be freed from *that* God; that is not the God of Jesus Christ.

The God of Jesus Christ is the One who intervenes in our lives to save, liberate, and raise human life. God is always at our side to console and strengthen us in the struggle against evil that oppresses and dehumanizes us. We are able to face the mystery of life with confidence. We are not alone. Evil does not have the last word. In the infinite and inexhaustible depth of life there is goodness, acceptance, forgiveness, hope, and beauty. This God is the friend of life and of freedom, the One who accompanied Israel on the long pilgrimage through the desert.

One only needs to contemplate the life and death of Jesus and to listen to His message to be convinced that God is love, free surrender, unconditional forgiveness, grace, and mercy. Those who were Jesus' witnesses synthesized everything they "had seen and heard" in the words *God is Love*.

When the Bible makes this tremendous statement, it is not saying that God has the infinite capacity to love just as he has the infinite capacity to act; rather, it is trying to express the ultimate mystery of God, that God is love itself, the infinite irradiation of love, the unfathomable dynamic of loving, the genesis and consummation of everything that can be called love.

This is the starting point for thinking about God: God is *only love*. It is true that He is also omnipotent, but it is the omnipotence of one who is only love. God "cannot do everything". God cannot manipulate, humiliate, abuse, or destroy. God's nature of love prevents it. God can only do what infinite love can do. When we forget this, we begin to fabricate a false God, a caricature, an idol.

The God that leads to anguish, to guilt complexes and neuroses, is a false idol; he must be shaken. We must topple the omnipotent tyrant who nullifies humanity and represses our freedom, and make way for the true face of God, who is grace, liberation, joy, and strength — in a word, the Friend of humanity.

Martin Buber writes, "*God* is the most pregnant of human words. No other has been more stained or so ripped apart. Precisely because of this, I cannot set it aside. Generations of men have hurled the weight of their anguished life upon this word, or have trodden it into the ground: it lies in the dirt and carries the weight of all of them. Generations have slashed this word with their religious biases. They have killed or been killed because of it. It carries then the fingerprints and the blood of many. Where could I find a word that is like it to designate the supreme? We cannot purify or restore the word *God*. But we can — even though it is stained and torn — pick it up from the ground and stand it up in this hour of great preoccupation."

God is fire; and, although for many he may be reduced to embers, the hour has come to fan the embers into flame because, otherwise, we will die of the cold. Our happiness and our hope depend on it.

With this book, I have also wanted to lend my effort to "picking up" the word *God* and putting it on its feet in this hour of uncertainty and hope.

The Author, 1987

PREFACE

The Christian of tomorrow will be a mystic, one who has experienced something, or he will be nothing. (Karl Rahner)

Today the world needs, more than ever before, a return to contemplation... The true prophet of the Church of the future will be the one who comes from the "desert" like Moses, Elijah, the Baptist, Paul, and above all, Jesus, charged with that special radiance which only those accustomed to speaking with God face to face have. (Hortelano)

Many people fear that the process of secularization will end by undermining faith and that, as a consequence, life with God will continue to diminish until it is completely extinguished.

My personal impression is exactly the opposite. Secularization could be compared to the *dark night of the senses.* It is the most radical purification of the *image* of God. As a result, the believer of the secularized age will finally be able to live pure and unadorned faith, without its false supports.

The *image* of God is often dressed up in various attire: our fears and insecurities, our interests and systems, our ambitions, our weaknesses, ignorance and limitations; for many, God is the magic *solution* for the impossible, the *explanation* for everything we do not know, the *refuge* for the confused and the weak.

The faith and "religiosity" of many Christians is supported by these crutches.

Demythologizing continues to demolish this *imagery,* stripping away the apparel, and what begins to appear is the true face of the God of the Bible: a God who asks questions, intervenes, and challenges. He does not answer, but questions. He does not solve problems, but causes conflicts. He does not make things easy, but makes them difficult. He does not explain, but complicates. He engenders not children, but adults.

The God of the Bible is God the Liberator, the one who pulls us from our insecurities, ignorance, and injustice, not avoiding them, but confronting them and overcoming them.

God is not the "maternal womb" that liberates (alienates) us from the risks and difficulties of life. After creation, God very quickly cuts the umbilical cord, leaving us alone in the open struggle for liberation and independence, and He comes to us saying, "Be fruitful and multiply; fill the earth and subdue it" (Gen 1:28). The true God, then, is not one who alienates, but a Liberator who makes great, mature, and free individuals and nations.

This secularization, we insist, is a true dark night of the senses. From now on, faith and life with God will be a risky adventure.

This adventure of faith will consist in burning bridges, setting aside all rules of common sense and all probabilities and, like Abraham, disregarding arguments, explanations, and proofs, untying ourselves from all rational positions and, bound hand and foot, making the great leap into the abyss of the dark night, surrendering ourselves to the totally Other — God Alone — in pure and dark faith.

The contemplative of the future will need to enter the unfathomable regions of the mystery of God — without guides, without supports, without light. God will be experienced as the Other Limit; God's distance and proximity will be meditated upon simultaneously; and, as a result, there will be a feeling of dizziness which is a mixture of fascination, fright, annihilation, and dread.

The contemplative will have to run the risk of being submerged in this bottomless ocean where dangerous challenges are hidden. These, the contemplative cannot shun, but must face and accept them in their burning insistency.

Those who return from this adventure will be figures sculpted by purity, strength, and fire. Transformed by the ecstatic closeness of God, above them will appear the living and illuminating image of the Son. They will become the transparent witnesses of God.

In our day, there are certain facts that raise unsettling questions for us. For example, what does the alarming use of drugs mean? In such a complex phenomenon there is certainly evasion, alienation, and hedonism. But, according to eminent psychologists, there is also a strong, though obscure, desire for something transcendent, an instinctive search for intense feelings that are only achieved in the highest of contemplative states.

Harvey Cox spoke of "hippies" as "neo-mystics." According to his sociopsychological analysis, they take the path of humanity's profound and ancestral aspiration in order to experience, in an immediate way, the sacred and transcendent.

Another group that vehemently lives the religious experience is the movement called the "Jesus People." These are young people who did not find what they were looking for in drugs, and from this frustration there emerged — through one of those mysterious reactions — the call to an ardent attachment to Jesus Christ. They claim a personal encounter with Jesus; their life is an emotional acclamation and proclamation of Jesus; and their hedonism has been transformed into a liberating asceticism.

In the West, there has been a surprising movement toward Eastern mysticism. There are groups from every social class who, through psychosomatic means (Yoga, Zen), try to reach powerful religious experiences. They exercise a concentration of the interior faculties in order to achieve total centering.

In my opinion, for Western Christians this is a form of

substitution. Among Christians, who are not bothered about the cultivation of contemplative prayer, we are filling our cities with "gurus" imported from India or Pakistan, around whom young people gather so that, by means of mental and psychological gymnastics, they might arrive at "contact" with the transcendent God. It would seem that they have arrived at a synthesis of oriental methods and Christian theology.

The International Meditation Society of the Hindu Maharishi Mahesh Yogi already numbers 250,000 enthusiasts who can exercise transcendental meditation incessantly guided by some guru. Thousands of university students are directed to the Hindu "ashrams" or are cloistered in Zen Buddhist monasteries so that they might begin to grow in strong extrasensory experiences and immediate relationship with the divine.

These facts demonstrate that technology, consumer society, and materialism in general are not capable of drowning the profound human roots of this eternal and inextinguishable thirst for God.

* * *

Many forms, styles, and methods are taught for advancing in the experience of God: houses of prayer, desert experiences, hermitages... In Algeria, over the brilliant and burning desert, rises the oasis of Beni Abbes, to which thousands of solitary contemplatives come, arriving from all over the world, attracted by the memory of Charles de Foucauld.

The *tebaidas** are again beginning to be populated, not by fugitives from the world but by those who fight in the world and for the world, who come to purify themselves, enduring the gaze of God without blinking.

What significance is there in the fact that thousands of

---

* Translator's note: *Tebaidas* are the Arabic outposts originally inhabited by outlaws but more recently being used as desert retreat communities.

young people from all over the world come to Taizé to pray? Among them are workers and union leaders, specialists in high technology and miners. All are searching for the experience of the mystery of God. They are pulled by the "magnet" of God.

The impressive number of forms, efforts, projects, and classes for promoting the experience of God in the Church indicates that the Holy Spirit is stirring up, perhaps now more than ever before, an overwhelming desire for the highest states of contemplation, and is initiating a great parade of believers to the most profound regions of communication with God.

All of this gives us the sense that we are living at the dawn of a great contemplative era.

Within this context, and because of this context, and foreseeing the future, this book has been written. I wish to offer a means for those who want to be initiated in, or to recover, their relationship with God, and for those others who wish to advance further into the unfathomable mystery of the living God.

The Author, 1979

Chapter 1

REFLECTIONS UPON CERTAIN "GIVENS" ABOUT PRAYER

Look, I am standing at the door, knocking. If one of you hears me calling and opens the door, I will come in to share a meal at that person's side (Rv 3:20).

When we speak here of prayer, we mean a personal contact with the God who loves us; a growth in the profound and intimate intersubjectivity *in* and *with* the Lord who offers himself as a lifelong companion.

The more one prays, the more one wants to pray

All living power is expansive. On a purely human level, we aspire to unreachable heights; any goal which has been achieved leaves us like a taut bow, always dissatisfied. What is this longing? It is an endless search for a fullness which will never be.

At the center of creation, human beings are strange creatures, something like emergency cases. They possess faculties that were designed for such and such a function, and yet, when the function is accomplished or the objective attained, they feel that something is still lacking. Let us take, for example, the sexual drive or the thirst for wealth. When the desire is fulfilled, one continues to feel "hungry" and, after each successive satisfaction is attained, one is propelled in search of new sensations or new riches.

On a spiritual level, we are, according to St. Augustine, like an arrow shot toward a universal (God), toward a center of gravity that irresistibly attracts us; the closer we get to that universal, the more speed we gain. The more we love God, the more we want to love Him. The more we relate to Him, the more we want to relate to Him. Speed is proportional to His closeness to us.

Without realizing it, beneath all our dissatisfactions there is a current toward the One, the Only One capable of concentrating our strengths and calming our aspirations.

God, you are my God, I pine for you;
my heart thirsts for you,
my body longs for you,
as a land parched, dreary and waterless. (Ps 63)

There is a law of training that is valid for physical sports as well as for "spiritual sports": the more intense the training, the greater the results. If someone suddenly told me to go for a long walk of twenty miles or more, I could not do it. But if I were to start training, going out for progressively longer walks, after a few months I would have no difficulty covering twenty miles. How does one explain this? I had athletic abilities that were inactive, even atrophied, due to lack of activity. Being used, they were awakened and made apparent.

In the same way, we carry in our souls spiritual abilities that are dormant due to lack of *training*. God has planted a seed in us that is gift-power, capable of wonderful blossoms. It is a profound and filial aspiration for God. If we put this aspiration *in motion*, as it "meets" its object and nears its center, the more intense will be the desire, the greater will be its weight and, consequently, the greater will be the velocity.

Daily experience proves this. Those who have been alone with the Lord for a few days will find that, when they get back to their everyday routine, a new force pushes them more and more toward the encounter with God; prayers and sacraments have meaning because they are *full* of God. In this way, God's weight becomes heavier and will draw them with greater attraction toward Him, while the world and life in general will be "filled" with God.

We see all of this happening in the Bible. The author of the Psalms is thirsting for God like a dry land thirsting for water, like a deer longing for running streams (Ps 42). He gets up at midnight like a lover "to be" with his Beloved (Ps 119). Jesus "steals" hours from his rest and goes to the hills to "spend" the night with the Father.

Held prisoner by the SS and foreseeing his approaching death, Dietrich Bonhoeffer, the German theologian, wrote to a friend, "The day of my funeral, I want them to sing for me: One thing I ask of the Lord, to dwell in His house all the days of my life."

The law is fulfilled: the greater the proximity, the greater the velocity, as in the law of physics concerning the attraction between masses. Attraction increases in proportion to the volume of mass and relative proximity.

* * *

Few things help us sense the reality of these laws as does the description given by Nikos Kazantzakis in his novel *Saint Francis*:

> And while I was mulling all this in my mind, my body trembling, Francis suddenly emerged from the cave. He was radiant — a glowing ember. Prayer had eaten away his flesh again but what remained shone like pure soul. He held out his hand to me. A peculiar expression of joy was passing over his face.
>
> "Well, Brother Leo," he called. "Are you ready to hear what I am going to tell you?"
>
> He seemed delirious. His eyes were inflamed and as he came closer I discerned ghosts and angels in his pupils. I

21

was terrified. Could he have taken leave of his senses?

He understood, and laughed. But his fire did not subside. He came closer to tell me:

"People have enumerated many terms of praise for the Lord up to now," he said. "But I shall enumerate still more. Listen to what I shall call Him: the Bottomless Abyss, the Insatiable, the Merciless, the Untiring, the Unsatisfied. He who never once has said to poor, unfortunate mankind: 'Enough.'"

Coming still closer, he placed his lips next to my ear and cried in a thunderous voice:

"'Never enough!' That is what he screamed at me. If you ask, Brother Leo, what God commands unceasingly, I can tell you, for I learned it in these past three days and nights in the cave. Listen! 'Not enough! Never enough.' That's what he shouts every day, every hour to poor, miserable man. 'Not enough! Not enough!' 'I can't go further,' whines man. 'You can!' the Lord replies. 'I shall break in two,' man whines again. 'Break,' the Lord answers."

Francis' voice had begun to crack. A tear rolled down his cheek. I felt overwhelming compassion for Francis. I became angry. "What more does he expect from you?" I asked. "Didn't you kiss the leper?"

"'Not enough.'"

"Didn't you abandon your father and mother?"

"'Not enough.'"

"Didn't you make a fool of yourself, giving back your clothes to your father and standing naked before the whole town?"

"'Not enough.'"

"But... aren't you the poorest in the world?"

"'Not enough.'" And do not forget it, Brother Leo: God is Never Enough."

If we are honest, if we look honestly at our own history with God, we will see that we also have experienced God as an abyss that attracts and captivates, and the closer we get, the more it attracts and embraces us.

Saint Catherine of Siena wrote in her *Dialogues*:

O eternal Trinity! You are a bottomless sea into which, the more I sink, the more I find You; and the more I find You, the more I still search for You. Of You I could never say "enough." The soul which fulfills itself in Your depths, longs unceasingly for You because it is always hungering for You; it is always desirous of seing its light in Your light. Could you give me anything more than Your own self? You are the fire, always burning and never consumed. You are the fire which consumes all selfish love of the soul; You are the light beyond all light. You, the cloak which covers all nakedness; food, that with its sweetness makes all who are hungry happy.

Clothe me, eternal Trinity, clothe me with Yourself that I may live this life in true obedience and in the light of faith with which you have inebriated my soul.

The less one prays, the less one wants to pray

There is a physical malady called *anemia.* It is a particularly dangerous disease because it has no spectacular symptoms, and death comes silently and painlessly. It consists of this: the less one eats, the less appetite one has; the less appetite one has, the less one eats; and the end result is acute anemia. The individual is caught in a circle, the circle of death.

The same thing happens in the interior life. It begins when we abandon prayer for apparently valid reasons. Instead of moving from the One to the many, as *bearers of God*, the many envelops, encloses, and withholds us, filling our interior with chill and distraction.

In this way, the difficulty of centering oneself in the One and Only begins to penetrate the deepest recesses of the individual, like a long night. The more one becomes interiorly distracted, the easier it is to find excuses to abandon one's relationship with God. The desire for God diminishes as the taste for a multiplicity of things, people, events, work increases. The hunger for God diminishes as the difficulty to be content with Him grows. At this point we have begun the spiral.

Once begun, we find ourselves on a decline: as I continue to break myself away from the absolutely Other, I am being *taken* by "others." That is, while worldly things and people claim me and seem to drain meaning from my life, *God* is a word which becomes more and more devoid of meaning, ending as when we take an old dish in our hands: we look at it; we look at it again; and finally, we ask ourselves, What do I need this for? It is not useful anymore. The circle is complete, acute anemia is present, and we have fallen into the trap, the death of God in our lives.

* * *

There is also the condition known as *atrophy*, in which death comes even more silently. All life is explosion, expansion, adaptation — in a word, movement. This movement is not mechanical but internally dynamic. If dynamic tension is suffocated or stopped, it automatically ceases to be life. There is no need for an external and lethal agent to come and cause disaster. Any living being ceases to be *alive* the moment it ceases to be *movement*.

In the interior life, something similar takes place. Grace is essentially *life*, and it gives to the soul the ability to react dynamically, to move toward God to know Him directly as He knows Himself. This grace-life establishes a dynamic current between the soul and God, an interrelationship of knowledge and love.

This grace, which is a gift-power, is at the same time expansive and leavening. The same thing happens as when a woman takes yeast and puts in three measures of flour until all the dough becomes leavened. Once within human nature, this grace — because it is life — tends to conquer new areas of our spirit, gradually penetrating our faculties, dominating our selfish tendencies, and submitting them to divine approval until our entire being belongs completely to the One and Absolute. This is the brief history of gift-potency, poured into the depths of the soul.

However, if this grace stops *moving,* it also stops living. If that life does not follow an ascending and ever-widening path, it automatically takes the route of death due to atrophy. There also is *sclerosis* in the life of the spirit. If the "tissues" of the inner faculties are not exercised, hardening and rigidity soon take over. If one prays very little, it becomes difficult to pray. Sensing the difficulty, prayer is abandoned altogether, according to the law of least resistance. And gift-power is inhibited; its vitality takes the path of inactivity, immobility, and death.

I have the impression that, among Christians, there are some who have had a powerful call to a profound life with God, and that call is languishing due to an oft-repeated story: they stop praying, abandon acts of piety, underestimate the sacraments, put aside personal prayer, saying that they have to search for God in humanity; and in looking for God, they have abandoned God.

Essentially, they are dominated by a kind of frustration, and they do not even know why. To me, the explanation is very clear: there, deep within themselves and beneath their consciousness, they are suffocating that powerful *call*, which is *given* to some and not to others. A life which could have flourished remains only a possibility.

The more we pray, the more God is God-within-us

God does not change. He is definitively complete and, therefore, immutable. He is unalterably present in us and does not admit various degrees of presence. What does change is our relationship with Him, according to the degree of our faith and love. Prayer makes this relationship more intimate, an intimate penetration of the I-Thou produced through affective experience and joyful knowledge, and resemblance and union with Him becomes more profound day after day.

It is like having a candle in a dark room. The more light we get from the candle, the better we can see the room, which becomes more "present" even though it does not actually change.

We all experience the feeling that when our prayer is more profound, God *is* closer to us, more present, evident, and alive. And the more the glory of the face of God shines upon us (Ps 31), the more events have new meaning (Ps 36) and history is filled with Him. In a word, the Lord becomes *vividly present in everything.* There is no game of risk or chance; there is a pilot who directs events with a steady hand.

When we have "been" with God, He becomes more "Someone" through whom and with whom we overcome difficulties and defeat repulsions; we face hard times with joy, and love blossoms everywhere. The more we "breathe" God, the more we want to be with Him; and the more we "are" with God, the more God becomes Someone. The circle of life is opened up.

As the contemplative advances in the mysteries of God, God stops being an idea that needs clarifying and begins to be freedom, humility, joy, and love. Gradually, God becomes an irresistible and revolutionary force that draws all things from their places. Where there was violence, He brings gentleness; where there was selfishness, He brings love; God completely changes the "face" of the individual.

However, the process does not end here. As the contemplative lets himself be taken, God brings together everything that is good in the person and He becomes the "all good." God "takes the place" of a loving spouse, a good brother, a solicitous father, a thousand acres of property, or a wonderful palace (Mt 12:46-50; Lk 8:19-21; Mk 3:31-34). In a word, God becomes the great reward, a feast, a banquet (Ex 19:5; Jer 24:7; Ez 37:27). "You are my Lord" (Ps 16). "In your name they rejoice all day long" (Ps 89).

This is what the psalmist means when he says, "You are a richer joy than all their corn and new wine" (Ps 4). The "corn and wine" symbolize all the compensations, emotions, and joys for which our human hearts long. For the contemplative who has "tasted" how good is the Lord (Ps 34), God "tastes" like an inebriating wine, more pleasurable than all of the fruits of the earth.

The less we pray, the less God is God-within-us

The less we pray, the more God vanishes into the distance. He slowly becomes a meaningless and lifeless "idea." No one wants *to be, to relate,* or *to live* with an idea; nor does it stimulate us in times of struggle or challenge. This is how God stops being Someone and is diluted to the point of being a distant and absent reality.

Once we get trapped in this spiral, God slowly stops being reward, happiness, joy... and is "worth" less and less. And the crisis approaches. We do not turn to God, because He has become a word that "says" almost nothing to us; we would rather try psychological help, or simply let ourselves be carried away by the crisis.

While this process of disenchantment is going on, the serpent called selfishness assails the person, and the appetites of the "old man" again seek recognition. And why is this? As the center of gravity starts failing and enormous vacuums in the interior are created, human compensations present themselves as defense mechanisms, according to the physical law of displacement. And to what end? To cover the empty spaces and to prop up the building; this building is called the *meaning of life* or *life project*.

The less we pray, the less God makes sense to us; and the less sense God makes in our life, the less we turn to Him. At this point, we are trapped in the spiral of death.

If we stop praying, God ends up being a "nobody"

If we stop praying for a long period of time, God "dies!" — not in Himself, because He is essentially living, eternal, and immortal, but He dies in our hearts. God "dies" like a withered plant we have neglected to water.

Once we have abandoned the source of existence, we soon come to *existential atheism.* Those who are in this situation may not have formally questioned the intellectual problem of the existence of God. Perhaps they continue to believe or feel that the "hypothesis" of God still has validity; but the fact is that they manage to live as if God did not exist. God is no longer a close, concrete, and living reality. God is no longer the Easter Strength that used to move them from their selfishness on a constant "exodus" to a world of freedom, humility, love, and commitment. Most of all, the unmistakable sign of the "death" of God is that the Lord no longer brings happiness to the heart.

It happens, sometimes, that the emptiness of God weighs as heavily as a corpse. This is why people argue, question, and discuss prayer as never before, its nature, and the need for it. This may be a good sign. It may mean that God's shadow does not let them live in peace.

Naïvely, these individuals ramble on and on about new forms of prayer, saying that we must demythologize the concept of God; that personal prayer is a waste of time, an egoistic and an alienating waste; that we live in secular times in which the religious element is outdated; that traditional forms of prayer are just subjective games; and so on. Prayer is criticized and intellectualized, and this is a bad sign.

Prayer is *life,* and life is simple — not easy — and coherent. When it stops being life, we turn it into a huge problem. We ask, for instance, how should we pray today? To me, this question makes no sense. Do we ask, how should we love today? We love — and pray — the same way people did 4,000 years ago. Facts of life have their roots in the immutable essence of our being.

When a Christian experiences an emptiness of God due to the abandonment of prayer, he or she feels the need for self-affirmation by getting involved in various activities, such as politics. This may be justified by beautiful theologies but, deep within, people are trying to give meaning to their lives, trying to cover over this emptiness by doing things and basing them on texts from Scripture.

This is not the case for everyone, but it is true for many. They never talk about eternal life, the soul, or God; rather, they speak about suffering and social injustice. Sociological studies tell us that most priests like this end up as lay people. Some of them will say that they have done this in order to live a more authentic life, as Christians and as human beings. But, if they have been unable to love "in" religious life, they will continue to be unable to love "outside," and they will never find the real meaning of their lives.

I am aware that our relationship with God can be an escape from reality. This book, however, tries to show that the true liberators and the truly committed people in the Bible were those capable of withstanding God's gaze in silence and solitude. And, certainly, not a sweet God, but one who makes us uncomfortable, who moves away and pushes the "worshipper" down the hill of patience and humility toward the adventure of the great liberation of the masses. If contemplation does not end in this, it will be anything but prayer. Escape and prayer are mutually exclusive terms.

* * *

What will happen to the life of Christians in whom God has grown weak? They will certainly continue to talk "about" God, but they will be incapable of speaking "with" God. Their words will be bronze trumpets: they will make noise but will carry nothing with them, neither message nor life nor fire. Believers will never see on their foreheads the radiance of God (Ex 34:29). The faithful will say, We were looking for a prophet but we have found a professional. Those who are hungry and thirsty for God will find a dry spring. These Christians in whom God has grown weak will not raise the dead or heal the sick. Definitely, they will not be those "sent" by God.

Those who have not taken God seriously will not take anything seriously; deep within, they are a frivolous people. Nothing will be important to them, neither the poor, the sick, the oppressed, nor even friends. They will only be important to themselves. It is more comfortable and less committing for us to deal with our own selves than with Someone who meets us and unmasks everything we have, do, and are.

When a group of Christians analyzes the causes for the crisis in prayer, the following is frequently mentioned: *the fear of God*. In what sense? Their thinking is more or less like this: if I take God seriously, my life has to change. God will challenge me not to confuse charism with my own desires, to be open to this brother or sister whom I can't get along with, to put an end to useless diversions, to accept this burden, to end that friendship, to be less worldly, to do more penance, to practice more obedience; in a word, He is going to make me like a drawn bow. God is something serious. So I opt, rather, for being distracted with respect to Him. This is foolishness.

* * *

Once God has been displaced, life is like a flower whose leaves have been stripped off. Nothing makes sense and Nietzsche's description in *Thus Spoke Zarathustra* comes true:

Have you not heard of that madman who lit a lantern in the bright morning hours, ran to the marketplace and cried incessantly: "I seek God! I seek God!" As many of those who did not believe in God were standing around just then, he provoked much laughter. "Why, did He get lost?" said one. "Did He lose his way like a child?" said another. "Or is He hiding? Is He afraid of us? Has He gone on a voyage? or emigrated?" Thus they yelled and laughed.

The madman jumped into their midst and pierced them with his glances.

"Whither is God?" he cried. "I shall tell you. We have killed Him — you and I. All of us are his murderers. But how have we done this? How were we able to drink up the sea? Who gave us the sponge to wipe away the entire horizon? What did we do when we unchained the earth from its sun? Whither is it moving now? Whither are we moving now? Away from all suns? Are we not plunging continually? Backward, sideward, forward and in all directions? Is there any up or down left? Are we not straying as through an infinite nothing? Do we not feel the breath of empty space? Is not night and more night coming on all the while? Must not lanterns be lit in the morning?..."

Here the madman fell silent and looked again at his listeners; and they too were silent and stared at him in astonishment.

We have let God "die," and absurdity, nausea, anguish, loneliness, and nothingness have been born... Simone de Beauvoir wrote that, having suppressed God, we have been left without the only intermediary who was really worth the bother. Life becomes a "useless passion," an "absurd bolt of lightning between two eternities of darkness."

Frequently, I have asked myself this question: What would the end be like for those who have lived as if God did not exist? Since death is the highest moment in the meaning of life, when they become aware that there is no hope left, that they have just a few weeks of life left to them, to whom do they cling? To whom do they offer sacrifice? Where do they hold on? They have no support.

Chapter 2

LIKE ONE WHO COULD SEE
THE INVISIBLE

[Moses] held to his purpose like someone who could see
the Invisible. (Heb 11:27)

During the past few years, throughout the entire world,
there have been explorations, inquiries, and evaluations of
prayer. There is talk about a crisis, the abandonment of
prayer, and the difficulties encountered in attempting to
communicate with the transcendent God.

Nevertheless, in this general examination, people have
come to the conclusion — with unusual unanimity — that
prayer is on the decline due to a profound crisis of faith.
They emphasize that the center of this crisis is not the
intellectual questioning of faith but, rather, the living out of
that faith. It is, therefore, an existential crisis of faith. The
most serious inquirers have arrived at the conclusion that
the core of the problem is not one of forms of prayer. The
root of the crisis is not in *how* to express ourselves in prayer
but in *what* to express.

Since we are searching for something practical, we will
be concerned in this present reflection only about the
essential act of faith, which, in the Bible, is always *adherence
and unconditional surrender to God*. We will also analyze the
difficulties encountered in this act of faith, especially when
the silence of God and the discouragements that constantly
threaten the life of faith take place. These difficulties, which

are inevitable and normal for anyone who tries to live God's way, seem to be increasing today due to certain ideologies that we shall also analyze.

With these reflections, we will advance in our task of exploring the *mystery of prayer*, which is nothing more than putting this same faith *in motion*. Finally, we will look for some means to help us overcome discouraging and difficult situations, although we know there are no easy answers.

1. THE DRAMA OF FAITH

Opening the Bible and contemplating the movement of people toward God in an ever-deepening purification of their faith, we vividly see how difficult the path is that leads us to the mystery of God, the path of faith! And not only for Israel, but most of all for ourselves. Day after day, we see that dismay, unfaithfulness, and crisis wait for us around every corner. And all this without forgetting that faith in itself is darkness and uncertainty. That is why we speak here of *drama*.

And so, entering this tunnel, we should remind ourselves of Jesus' challenging invitation: "Try your hardest to enter by the narrow door" (Lk 13:24).

The test in the desert

At different times, the Second Vatican Council presents the living out of faith as a pilgrimage (*Lumen Gentium* 2, 8, 65). Moreover, it is presented to us as a parallel to Israel's journey through the desert. That march certainly was a trial by fire for Israel's faith in God. Nevertheless, even though it is true that Israel's faith was strenghthened by that experience, the pilgrimage itself was filled with worship and blasphemy, submission and obstinacy, fidelity and desertion, acclamation and protest.

All of this makes it a real symbol of our relationship

with God. We, too, are "on the road" and, most of all — and this is what we wish to emphasize — it is a symbol of the failings and perplexities that all people suffer in their ascent to God, even more concretely in their life of faith. Few people, perhaps no one, have been spared such failures, as we shall see by taking the Bible in hand.

* * *

When the right moment came, God was present in the midst of human history; He entered it to wound, to free, to make equal. Moses, God's friend and the leader of His people, confronts Pharaoh, gathers the scattered people, and puts them in motion toward the land of freedom. Coming out of Egypt, they begin the great journey of faith. But with the first steps, the crisis of faith begins curling like a snake around their hearts. Doubt wells up in their throats and cries out, "Was it for lack of graves that you had to lead us out to die in the desert?... Did we not tell you as much in Egypt? 'Leave us alone,' we said, 'we would rather work for the Egyptians! We prefer to work for Egyptians than to die in the desert'" (Ex 14:11-12). There is a preference for security over freedom. In the midst of the confusion, Moses alone keeps faith alive: "Do not be afraid! Stand firm, and you will see what Yahweh will do to rescue you today... Yahweh will do the fighting for you; all you need to do is to keep calm" (Ex 14:13-14).

With these words, the faith of the people was revived again, and with their own eyes they contemplated wonders never before seen by anyone. Suddenly, a strong wind from the south began to blow, opened the waters and divided them in two. And the people crossed as if between two walls. In the meantime, the Egyptians were overtaken and sank like lead to the bottom of the sea. In the face of such a spectacle, "the people put their faith in Yahweh and in Moses, his servant" (Ex 14:31) and sang a triumphal song (Ex 15:1-23). Nevertheless, once more they needed a "sign" to recover their faith. "Blessed are those who have not seen and yet believe" (Jn 20:29).

The pilgrimage advanced for three days into the desert of Shur. The desert again tested the faith of the people. The silence of the land, and sometimes, the silence of God filled their souls and they were afraid. They ran out of provisions. What would they eat? And, like birds of prey, discouragement, homesickness, and stubbornness came upon the people. "Why did we not die at Yahweh's hand in Egypt, where we used to sit round the flesh pots and could eat to our heart's content! As it is, you have led us into this desert to starve this entire assembly to death!" (Ex 16:3).

The people succumbed to the temptation of nostalgia and "began to weep again. 'Who will give us meat to eat?' they said. 'Think of the fish we used to eat free in Egypt, the cucumbers, melons, leeks, onions, and garlic!'" (Num 11:5).

Moses, whose faith remained unshaken because he spoke daily with God "as with a friend," told them, "I will have nothing to do with your murmurings, you are complaining against God. But I tell you that in the morning you shall see the glory of the Lord, and your complaints will turn into ridiculous voices" (cf. Ex 16:5-9).

And the next day, in the evening, quail came up and covered the camp; and in the morning, dew lay all around the camp. And when the dew had disappeared, there, on the surface of the entire wilderness, lay a fine, flake-like substance, fine as hoarfrost on the ground, and morning after morning, the people ate of it (Ex 16:13-16).

The pilgrimage advanced toward Rephidim under a red-hot sun, on a sea of shimmering sand. And as they went forward, depression and temptation again disturbed their souls; the persistent temptation to stop, to abandon the journey, and return to their old security, even if it were as slaves in Egypt. The people murmured against Moses, saying, "Why did you bring us out of Egypt... only to make us, our children and our livestock die of thirst?" (Ex 17:3).

At this moment, a nagging doubt destroyed the memory of all wonders, gnawed at the foundations of their faith, and emerged in that dreadful question. "Is Yahweh with us, or not?" (Ex 17:7). The doubts had reached their peak. This is why this place is called Massah (because of their protest against God) and Meriba (because they challenged God). This was the great trial in the desert on their journey to Canaan.

Few people of God have been spared some difficult test. The way of faith has always been rough and difficult; in our day, the difficulties have increased. Today, the Church is going through a new desert. The dangers that waylay pilgrims are the same as those of long ago: discouragement caused by God's "disappearance," the appearance of new "gods" that demand worship, and the temptation to put an end to the hard journey of faith and return to comfortable and "fertile Egypt."

Intellectual difficulties

Humanity has lived for thousands of years under the power of the blind forces of nature, forces that were made into gods. In order to resist these divinized forces, people created magical rituals. Although the Bible is a purification of those concepts and magical customs, in our past there are still reminders of that enchanted world, many of which we have attributed to the God of the Bible.

Technology has replaced those beliefs and customs. Science explains that which previously was attributed to mythical divinities, or was considered to be the exclusive attribute of God. And here is where the danger lies: in the confusion of magic with the supernatural, in destroying one or the other without separating the wheat from the chaff, and in coming to the conclusion that everything that is not science-technology either does not exist or is just a projection of our helplessness and fear.

* * *

It is true that, in times past, many phenomena of nature were explained by identifying them with God. Now, by stating that every natural phenomenon can be explained with proper scientific methods, we are unconsciously forgetting all about God. The more our mind gets rid of those divine explanations, the more our conscious life is gradually emptied of God's presence. Many people simply sense it, while others say it openly: science will end up explaining everything that is explainable and, in the future, God will be an unnecessary "hypothesis."

Nevertheless, neither technology nor even the socio-psychological sciences will ever be able to give a complete answer to the fundamental and unique question of humanity: the meaning of life. Only when men and women accidently confront their own mystery, when they experience the dizziness, the strangeness of "being there," in the world as a conscious being and as a person, only then will they ask themselves fundamental questions, such as, Who am I? What is the reason for my existence? What is the source of this existence? Is there a future for me? What kind of future?

Today, there are no emotional campaigns filled with arguments pro and con about God. We simply have set Him aside; God has been abandoned as a useless object. This is *practical atheism*, which is more dangerous than philosophical atheism, since it subtly penetrates the mind and its thought processes.

* * *

Our theological knowledge does not resist the cosmic and anthropological vision given to us by the sciences. Investigations into the origins of humanity and the world differ from scriptural data, though we believe today that the Bible does not intend to give scientific explanations.

Unable to avoid it, we sense the contrast between our difficulty to express God with signs and symbols, and the clear, evident, and direct expression of the sciences. The clarity of scientific methods of investigation confuses us, in contrast to our ways of knowing God.

If we have not nurtured a personal faith consistent with scientific discoveries, secularization becomes, without a doubt, a purification of the *image* of God. But many people do not succeed in recognizing this useful and necessary process; they enter the realm of "secularity" and end up in a worldly secularism in which their faith in God is agonizingly debated to death.

As a result of these facts and ideas, there emerges a "horizontalism," an ideology that weakens faith and causes problems for our serious commitment to God. It says that any effort directed to that which does not belong to this world is "alienation." Life with God is a waste of time; any religious "pursuit" is a waste of time; celibacy is hurtful and absurd; the only valid activity is human progress; the only sin is alienation.

* * *

The destructive atmosphere thus described has penetrated the souls of many who, in the past, had been bound to God in a powerful covenant by an unconditional faith in Him.

I have the impression that the new people of God have again been stopped at Meriba and Massah, where faith has descended to its lowest level and, as before, we can already hear cries and struggles. Today, faith is for many an "intolerable language. How could anyone accept it?" (Jn 6:66).

After the confusion, maturity will come; that is to say, a coherent and living synthesis, personally developed, and not simply taken from some manual of theology; a synthesis in which the advances of science and a deep friendship with God are fused. In the meantime, this period that we are presently going through will help us to purify our image of God. Faith, as Martin Buber says, is an adherence to God, not an adherence to the image we have formed of God, nor an adherence to the faith in the God that we have conjured up, but an adherence to the living God.

Existential difficulties

Immediacy, efficiency, and speed are accepted as the criteria for life in our society. By contrast, the life of faith is slow and demands superhuman faithfulness; its progress varies and cannot be verified by methods of exact measurement. Consequently, we feel deceived, confused, and as if we were lost in a jungle.

Today, under the influence of the psychological and sociological sciences, the criterion of subjectivity predominates. Those things that were "objective" — truths of faith, moral norms, or ideals, for example — have lost their reality and value, freely opening the doors to subjective and instinctive values. What is popular today is the emotional, the affective, and the spontaneous.

The result is the total devaluation of certain criteria, such as self-control, asceticism, self-denial, and self-improvement, which are indispensable elements in our journey to God. These concepts and words are even repulsive to many people. Others believe that they are harmful to the development of one's personality.

The norm adopted by some coincides almost completely with the ideals of a consumer society: enjoy life to the utmost, consume as many things as you can, satisfy yourself completely, follow the ideal, "let us eat, drink, and be merry!" Of course, this is not said in so many words. We say: we should avoid repression and encourage spontaneity; let us not go against our nature; we need to preserve authenticity.

We don't know what to do with silence. Consumer

society has created a variety of industries to provide distraction and entertainment in order to save people from "loneliness" and their fear of emptiness. In this way, the object is made to fit the subject. People can't stand established norms, so they open the doors to spontaneity, the daughter of subjectivity.

* * *

We live in the new desert. The path to God is riddled with difficulties. Temptations have changed their names. Today, the temptations are horizontalism, secularism, hedonism, subjectivity, spontaneity, and frivolity.

How many pilgrims will get to the Promised Land? How many will abandon the difficult journey of faith? Do we also have to come to the conclusion that only a remnant is going to arrive at total fidelity to God? Which and where is the Jordan River that we will cross in order to enter the land of freedom? Once again, the horizon is filled with questions, silence, and darkness. This is the price of faith.

We are living a time of purification. Faith is a flowing river. The impurities are lodged in the riverbed, but the current keeps moving.

2. CONFUSION AND SELF-SURRENDER

In the Bible, faith is an act and an attitude that embraces the whole person: profound confidence, fidelity, intellectual assent, and emotional attachment. It embraces one's entire life, committing one's entire life history with all of its projects, all that emerges from the individual, and all that surrounds him.

Biblical faith, in its normal development, is composed of the following elements: God initiates communication with us. Then, God speaks a word and we surrender ourselves unconditionally. God tests that faith. We become confused and waver. God reveals Himself once more. We fulfill the plan outlined by God, participating deeply in God's own strength.

This is the faith that caused Abraham to "live in my presence" (Gn 17:1), an expression loaded with heavy meaning: God was the inspiration of his faith; God was also his strength and ethical norm; above all, God was his friend. "Abraham put his faith in Yahweh and this was reckoned to him as uprightness" (Gn 15:6). With these words, the author wants to indicate that Abraham's faith had exceptional merit, that it conditioned, comprised, and transformed his entire life as well.

A story of fidelity

The New Testament presents Abraham as the prototype of faith, precisely because in him, more than in any other believer, the dramatic alternatives of faith were fulfilled. He is the true pilgrim of faith.

God gives an order to Abraham, which is at the same time a promise: "Leave your country... for a country which I shall show you; and I shall make you a great nation" (Gn 12:1-4). Abraham *believed*. What did it mean for him to believe? It meant handing over a blank check, trusting against common sense and the laws of nature, surrendering blindly and without calculations, breaking with all established patterns, and, at the age of seventy-five, "to set out" (Gn 12:4) toward an uncertain land "without knowing where he was going" (Heb 11:8).

However, this confident self-surrender cost him a great deal and led him into a state of great inner tension, which is not separate from confusion and perplexity. In a word, God put Abraham's faith to the test.

The years pass and the promised son does not come. God keeps Abraham in continual suspense — like a TV soap opera that ends every night precisely at the moment we expect the climax to be shown — promising a son to

Abraham on six different occasions (Gn 12:2; 15:5; 17:16; 18:10; 21:23; 22:17). But dozens of years pass and the son does not arrive. During this period, Abraham lives the *story of fidelity*, in which afflictions alternate with hopes, like the sun that appears and disappears among the clouds. It is the story of hope, "though there seemed no hope" (Rm 4:18), resisting the rules of common sense and the laws of physiology (Gn 18:11), making a fool of himself in front of his wife: "So Sarah laughed to herself, thinking, 'Now that I am past the age of childbearing, and my husband is an old man, is pleasure to come my way again?'" (Gn 18:12).

Loneliness begins knocking at the door of Abraham's heart. He has to bear the painful separation from his nephew, Lot (Gn 13:1-18). In spite of the victories against four kings and the increase of riches and servants, in his heart, faith begins to grow feeble and anguish gains more ground day after day.

There comes a moment when his faith almost fails completely. And in the midst of deep dismay, he complains to God, saying, "What use are your gifts, as I am going on my way childless?... Since you have given me no offspring... a member of my household will be my heir" (Gn 15:2-4). At that moment, God renewed the promise.

But Abraham's faith, at this moment, sinks into a deep crisis: "Abraham bowed to the ground, and he laughed, thinking to himself: 'Is a child to be born to a man one hundred years old, and will Sarah have a child at the age of ninety?'" (Gn 17:17). As an answer, God took Abraham outside of the tent to a beautiful starry night, and told him, "Look up at the sky and count the stars if you can. Just so will your descendants be" (Gn 15:5).

It happens all the time. When faith fails, we need a "sign," something to hold on to. God, understanding and compassionate, gives a sign considering the emergency of the weakness which is overcoming Abraham's faith. "'Lord Yahweh,' Abraham replied, 'how can I know that I shall possess it?'" (Gn 15:8). And God, "when the sun had set and it was dark," took the form of a "flaming torch passing between the animals' pieces" (Gn 15:17). Abraham was 100 years old when his son Isaac was born to him (Gn 21:5).

The trial by fire

We see that, as a result of these events, Abraham not only completely recovered his faith, but also definitively solidified it; he deepened it to the point of living permanently in intimate friendship and relationship with the Lord, according to what had been said to him: "Live in my presence, be perfect" (Gn 17:1). We can picture him as a man used to this testing, immunized against any possible doubt, master of great maturity and inner strength. "Abraham planted a tamarisk at Beersheba and there he invoked the name of Yahweh" (Gn 21:33).

God, seeing Abraham with such determined integrity, submits him to a final trial by fire, one of those dreadful "nights of the spirit" about which Saint John of the Cross speaks. Let us take a look at the greatness and serenity with which Abraham overcomes the test:

> It happened some time later that God put Abraham to the test.
> "Abraham, Abraham!" he called. "Here I am," he replied. God said: "Take your son, your only one, your beloved Isaac, and go to the land of Moriah, where you are to offer him as a burnt offering on a mountain which I shall point out to you." (Gn 22:1-2)

In my opinion, in this episode, biblical faith climbs to its highest summit.

To be able to understand the content and quality of Abraham's faith, in its exact dimensions, we have to remember that undertaking a heroic act might even be attractive when the act has meaning and logic, as might be the case, for example, in giving one's life for a noble and beautiful cause. But to submit oneself to an absurd mandate, either one needs to be crazy or the reasons for such submission must definitely surpass our concept and norms of heroism.

Let us put ourselves in Abraham's place, to explore the impulses and motives of this great believer. Abraham had always hoped to have a child. He is old and no longer holds the hope of any offspring. Nevertheless, one day God promises a son to him. Because nothing is impossible with God, Abraham believes. Many years of hope and despair go by, and finally the child who shall be the trustee of the hopes and promises comes: now Abraham can die in peace. But at the last moment, God asks him to sacrifice the boy.

A demand as cruel and irrational as this might easily destroy a lifelong faith. The most elementary common sense would have convinced him that he was the victim of a hallucination. But Abraham *believes* once again. This believing implies self-surrender and unlimited trust.

There is an unconditional disposition of abandonment and of giving oneself up with infinite confidence, being absolutely certain that God is almighty, good, just, wise, contrary to any evidence of common sense; it is like tying our own hands and feet and allowing ourselves to fall into an abyss — because He will not let us hit bottom. In my opinion, this is the definitive essence — and the highest moment — of biblical faith.

Now let us see Abraham's approach, which is filled with peace, greatness, and tenderness:

Early next morning, Abraham saddled his donkey and took with him two of his servants and his son Isaac. He chopped wood for the burnt offering and started on his journey to the place God had indicated to him. On the third day Abraham looked up and saw the place in the distance. Then Abraham said to his servants, "Stay here with the donkey. The boy and I are going over there; we shall worship and then come back to you."

Abraham took the wood for the burnt offering, loaded it on Isaac, and carried in his own hands the fire and the

45

knife. Then the two of them set out together. Isaac spoke to his father Abraham, "Father?" he said. "Yes, my son," he replied. "Look," he said, "here are the fire and the wood, but where is the lamb for the burnt offering?" Abraham answered, "My son, God himself will provide the lamb for the burnt offering." And the two of them went on together.

When they arrived at the place which God had indicated to him, Abraham built an altar there, and arranged the wood. Then he bound his son and put him on the altar on top of the wood. Abraham stretched his hand and took the knife to kill his son.

But the angel of Yahweh called to him from heaven. "Abraham, Abraham!" he said. "Here I am," he replied. "Do not raise your hand against the boy," the angel said. "Do not harm him, for now I know you fear God. You have not refused me your own beloved son." (Gn 22:3-13)

In this account, faith and self-surrender take on a particular hue. *God will provide* is like a background melody that brings meaning to it all. It is very significant that this story ends with the verse: "Abraham called this place 'Yahweh provides,' and hence the saying today: 'On the mountain Yahweh provides'" (Gn 22:14).

Hope against all hope

Israel's history is another example of "hope against hope." During the long centuries, from Sinai until "the completion of time" (Gal 4:4), God appears and disappears, shines like the sun and hides behind the clouds; there are thundering theophanies and extended periods of silence. It is a long journey filled with hopes and disappointments. God had wanted the history of Israel to be the history of an experience of faith. In both Israel's history and our own life of faith, we often find the silence of God, the testing of God, the dark night.

Israel was taken out of Egypt and sent on an unending

pilgrimage to a better land. It was a long journey, filled with sand, hunger, thirst, sun, suffering, and death. A land "flowing with milk and honey" was promised to them; but the price would be a prolonged struggle filled with defeats, humiliations, blood, and tears. And in the end, it provided neither milk nor honey but was a hostile land that they had to cultivate with a great deal of difficulty.

There was a time when Israel was convinced that either God did not exist or He had abandoned them completely, and that the nation had been swept from the face of the earth. It was the year 587 B.C., when Nebuchadnezzar's warriors succeeded in breaking down the resistance of Jerusalem, which had fought the invaders for eighteen months. Finally, the city fell — and the vengeance was dreadful.

Jerusalem was ransacked, destroyed, and burned. The famous Temple of Solomon fell to the ground, ablaze, and the Ark of the Covenant disappeared forever. All the inhabitants of Jerusalem and most of the people of Judah were taken and deported to Babylon under the eyes of their conquerors, on a march of a thousand miles, wrapped in dust, humiliation, and disaster.

These are the "dark nights" on the path of faith. In the midst of that darkness, we too are tempted to abandon God, because we feel abandoned by Him. But, after a while, once we have cleansed our eyes of the dust, His face will appear more radiant than ever. The prophets Ezekiel and Isaiah give evidence of this.

Apart from the imperial context of the kingdom of David and Solomon, the life of Israel is an insignificant story of the alliance of twelve tribes, a nation assailed by successive waves of Egyptians, Assyrians, Babylonians, Macedonians, and Romans. It was as if it were better not to trust in their God anymore, or to think of their God as a "laughing stock." Nevertheless, along this path of deception and darkness, God led Israel from the delusions of earthly grandeur to a truly spiritual grandeur: true faith in the true God.

Boredom and suffering

For those who attempt to live a total faith in God, the crisis that the prophet Elijah suffered on his pilgrimage to Mount Horeb is a moving and impressive example.

Elijah was a prophet who was tempered by his struggles with God, like a wild animal tamed along the Cherith River. He ate a piece of bread brought by the ravens, and he drank from the river. He confronted kings and revealed the hidden intentions of the powerful. He confused and beheaded the worshippers of Baal near the river Kishon.

We would not expect any failings from a man of such conviction and courage; nevertheless, they were present — and they were many! Queen Jezebel was notified of how Elijah had put all of the priests of Baal to the sword, and she sent an emissary to announce to him that the next day he too would be killed by the sword. (Jezebel is the one who introduced the worship of foreign gods to Israel.)

When the prophet Elijah heard the announcement, he began the arduous march to Mount Horeb, symbol of the soul's ascent, along the path of faith, to God.

> He was afraid and fled for his life. He came to Beersheba, a town of Judah, where he left his servant. He himself went on into the desert, a day's journey, and sitting under a furze bush wished he were dead. "Yahweh," he said, "I have had enough. Take my life; I am no better than my ancestors." Then he lay down and went to sleep. Then all of a sudden an angel touched him and said, "Get up and eat." He looked round and there at his head was a scone baked on hot stones, and a jar of water. He ate and drank and then lay down again. But the angel of Yahweh came back a second time and touched him and said, "Get up and eat or the journey will be too long for you." (1 Kgs 19:3-8)

The prophet's deep depression is surprising. His words sound like those of Jesus: "My soul is sorrowful to the point of death" (Mt 26:38; Mk 14:34). According to Saint John of the Cross, for those who have taken God seriously and who live in His presence, these depressions have the characteristics of true suffering.

There is no one who, sooner or later, more or less intensely, does not suffer from these purifications which, basically, are waves of darkness, clouds that cover God, as if the weight of one hundred atmospheres were pressing down upon the soul. John of the Cross adds that if God were to withdraw His hand from us, we would die.

3. THE SILENCE OF GOD

In their day-after-day search for the Lord, what disturbs most people who walk in faith is the silence of God. Miguel de Unamuno, the Spanish philosopher-poet, said, "God is He who has always been silent from the very beginning of the world; and this is the root of the tragedy."

Where have You hidden

Our eyes were designed to possess, that is, to search for reality. When they end up mastering the world of perspective, figure, color, and dimension, the eyes are satisfied. They have fulfilled their purpose; they have arrived at reality.

Our ears, by their internal structure, are meant to apprehend the world of sound, harmony, and voices. When they achieve their objective, they are stilled and satisfied.

And so on, with all of the different powers that make up the human structure: intellectual, intuitive, visual, auditory, sexual, affective, neurological powers, and so on. Each power has its own functioning mechanisms and objective. Once its objective is achieved, the power rests. Otherwise, it remains restless. In summary, all our powers and our entire being are structured for possession.

But therein lies the *mystery*: we put all the mechanisms into action and, one by one, they reach their goals; they are satisfied, and yet we ourselves are left unsatisfied.

What does this mean? It means that we are something *more*, more than the sum of all these powers. The specifically constitutive element of human beings is some other power, that is, a superpower that exists and supports the others.

Let me explain. Because we are an image of the Invisible and an echo of the Silent One, we possess restless and uneasy strengths that emerge, long for, and aspire toward their center of gravity, where they will adjust themselves and rest, waiting to get within sight of the "finish lines."

Every act of faith and deep prayer is an attempt at possession. Those inner forces are put to work by the mechanisms of faith. The believer, lifted by a powerful force, approaches the Universal, to possess it and thus find rest. And, at any given moment of prayer, reaching the threshold of God, just when the believer has the impression that the Object is in sight, God vanishes, as in a dream. God becomes absence and silence.

And the believer is always left with a feeling of frustration. This subtle disappointment that results from the "closeness" of God is intrinsically inherent to the act of faith. From the combination of human nature and God's nature comes the *silence of God*: we have been born to possess an infinite object and, because it is beyond time, our traveling in time must necessarily be in *silence* and *absence*.

The life of faith is at once an adventure and a misfortune. We know that the word *God* has a "meaning." But, as long as we remain on the way, we will never possess Him physically or control Him intellectually. The "meaning" will always be silent, covered with the veil of time. Eternity will be the lifting of this veil. Meanwhile, we are pilgrims who are always searching for Him and never "finding" Him.

John of the Cross admirably expresses the silence of God with these verses:

Where have You hidden,
Beloved, and left me moaning?
You fled like a stag,
after wounding me;
I went out calling You, and You were gone.

The experience of faith, the life with God is this: an exodus, a constant "going out calling Him." And here is where the eternal odyssey of the seekers of God begins: the long monotonous history, capable of overcoming all resistance. In every moment, in every attempt to pray, when it seems that the figure of God is within sight, "You were gone": the Lord wraps Himself in the mantle of silence and remains hidden. It seems like a perpetually unsteady and inaccessible Face, as It appears and then disappears, gets closer and then far distant, or as It forms and then vanishes.

Henri de Lubac is quoted as saying:

Why is it that the soul, when it has already found God, keeps feeling as if it had not found him? Why the feeling of a profound absence even in the most intimate presence? Why that invincible darkness of him who is all light? Why that immeasurable distance before him who penetrates everything? Why is it that all things betray us: they have hardly shown us God and, then, they keep him away from our sight?

The universe around us is filled with enigma and questions. Each day, our ears are assaulted by the sounds of pain and human desperation. We see death, mutilation, unemployment, injustice, and war. What is God doing? Isn't He a Father? Isn't He Almighty? Why is He silent?

It is a stubborn and intolerable silence that slowly undermines even the strongest resistance. Confusion enters the picture. And you begin hearing voices from everywhere asking, "Where is your God?" (Ps 42). This is not sarcasm or the formal argumentation of an intellectual atheist.

The believer is confused because of the enveloping and

disturbing silence of God; and, little by little, a vague feeling of insecurity leads the individual to question everything: Is this real? Am I creating it? Is it all true? And the believer remains in the midst of the churning waters, disturbed by the silence of God. And what is said in Psalm 30 comes true: "You turned away your face and I was terrified."

The prophet Jeremiah experienced, with terrible sharpness, this silence of God. The prophet says to the Lord, "Realize that I suffer insult for your sake... Why is my suffering continual, my wound incurable, refusing to be healed? Truly, for me you are a deceptive stream with uncertain waters?" (Jer 15:15-18).

The ultimate victory

What happened to Jesus in the final moments of His agony? It was something that had all of the characteristics of a disturbing crisis due to the *silence of God*. In that moment, the Father was, for Jesus, the "Silent One." Jesus, nevertheless, reacted to this by magnificently distinguishing between *feeling* and *knowing*.

In order to examine and ponder this crisis, we must take into consideration certain physical and psychological premises.

According to experts in this field, Jesus had lost almost all of His blood by this time. The primary effect of the bleeding was complete dehydration, a phenomenon wherein the individual does not suffer acute pain but rather a depressed and choking sensation. As a result of this, Jesus was overcome by a burning thirst that He felt not only in His throat but in His entire body, a thirst like that experienced by bleeding soldiers on the battlefield. Nothing in the world can alleviate this thirst except a complete blood transfusion.

Furthermore, as a consequence of this loss of blood, Jesus was overcome by a high fever that, at the same time, gave rise to a delirium tremens, which in this case and in psychological terms is a type of mental confusion: it is not a fainting but a loss, more or less, of consciousness with regard to identity and surroundings.

Apart from all this, and placing ourselves on a more intimate level, we must take into consideration that Jesus, obedient to the will of the Father, was dying in the fullness of His youth, at the beginning of His evangelizing mission, abandoned by the crowds and His disciples, betrayed by one, rejected by another, without fame or honor, apparently without results, with a feeling of failure (Mt 23:37). His psychological state is reflected in the prayer of the psalmist:

> Save me, O God, for the waters
> have closed in on my very being.
> I am sinking in the deepest swamp
>   and there is no firm ground.
> I have stepped into deep water
>   and the waves are washing over me.
> I am exhausted with calling out, my throat is hoarse,
>   My eyes are worn out with searching for my God.
>   (Ps 69)

What is more, in every human being there are levels deeper than the physical and psychological. These two levels could be bypassed in the case of Jesus. But there, in the area of the spirit, Jesus was able to maintain an admirable serenity throughout His Passion.

Nevertheless, at a certain point in His suffering, the described circumstances dragged Him to a state of disturbance and confusion. A crisis? A loss of emotional stability? We do not know how to classify or describe it. A momentary *night of the soul*? An extreme level of aridity? A fear upon finding Himself faced with the abyss?

One thing is true. Suddenly, all the lights went out in Jesus' sky, as if a total eclipse of the sun were taking place. Around Him, from east to west, He saw nothing, heard nothing, no one breathed. Absence, emptiness, confusion, silence, and darkness unexpectedly came over Jesus' soul like a wild and ferocious beast. Nothingness? Absurdity? Was His Father also among the group of deserters?

It was the trial of the Just One. Unjust people judged Him unjustly and condemned Him. This was to be expected. Nevertheless, at the right moment, the Father would speak up for the Son, tipping the scales in His favor. But, when the decisive moment came, no one spoke up for the Son. Had the Father been sitting next to Pilate and Caiaphas on the tribunal? Was the Father also outside the door, simply watching the condemned man pass?

And then, to whom did He turn? All frontiers and all horizons had been closed off. So then, was "reason" against the Son? Had Jesus been an intruder rather than a messenger? A dreamer? Had everything been worthless? In the end, was everything going to vanish in a psychedelic nightmare, in a deceptive mirage?

The "Son of Man" floated over a limitless abyss like someone lost and shipwrecked. Beneath His feet, nothing. Above His head, nothing. "Father, Father, why have you forsaken me?" It was the silence of God that had fallen upon His soul like a ton of bricks.

Nevertheless, all that was a *feeling*. But faith is not *feeling*; it is *knowing*.

Jesus was never as magnificent as in the last moments of His agony. He opened His eyes. He shook His head like someone awakening and shaking away a wicked nightmare. He soon overcame that horrible moment. The awareness of His identity emerged from the haziness of the "delirium" and took possession of His entire being. And thus calmed, He fought the last battle: the battle for certainty as opposed to evidence, for *knowing* as opposed to *feeling*. And from this ultimate struggle arose the ultimate victory.

Without words, He said, Dear Father, I cannot *feel* You, I cannot *see* You. My inner senses tell me that You are far away, that You have become a mist, a fleeting shadow, immeasurable distance, cosmic emptiness, nothingness. Nevertheless, in spite of all these appearances, I *know* that You are *here, now, with me*; "into Your hands I commit my spirit" (Lk 23:46).

In the midst of darkness, Jesus leapt into the abyss, knowing that at the bottom, the Father was waiting for Him with open arms. And He was not mistaken. It was a glorious end. The Father did not save Him from death, but immediately rescued Him from its power.

Those defeated by the silence

Among the great variety of experiences produced by the silence of God, we are today able to distinguish three very different groups, especially among those completely committed to God. The first group is the *defeated.*

These people completely abandon the life with God and arrange their lives as if God did not exist. For many years they forced themselves to live their faith. They awoke at midnight, prayed to God, and God did not answer. They got up in the morning, pleaded with the Lord, and they felt that He was far away or simply absent. Every attempt to pray ended in failure. A thousand times, they felt like throwing the whole thing overboard. A thousand times, they reacted against this temptation, thinking that, after all, the only thing that gave meaning to life was God. They never formally dealt with the intellectual problem of God's existence. They were afraid of finding nothing more than an empty tomb.

Today, they are lost. They seem to be in a peculiar and contradictory situation: on the one hand, they wish that God were an *actual and living* reality, but they "feel" that He is dead. To themselves, they do not deny God, even less so in front of others. They would like to believe. But they lack the strength even to lift their heads. They are convinced that there is nothing they can do.

They left the Church structure or are in the process of

doing so. The particular symptom of these people is aggres-siveness, typical of all frustrated people: compensatory violence. They seem bitter. They "need" to destroy. This is the only way they can justify themselves and their defeat. They violently, and without just cause, criticize the general structure of the Church: institutions, authority, formation programs, social teaching, and so on.

They do not speak against God. On the contrary, they keep silent. But, it seems to me, they practice psychological transference; that is, when they attack the Church so obses-sively, underneath, they are doing so to God, even though they consider Him to be a nonexistent enemy, a hallucina-tion who has watered down their enjoyment of life. Their deception and frustration, then, is directed against God Himself.

I have heard some of these people make some of the most incredible statements: I am almost forty years old; I must begin to live but I cannot return to my childhood to begin again to make plans or to dream. You only live once, and this once I made a big mistake... I have wasted the best years of my life and I can't get them back...

Hearing these and similar statements, one cannot help but feel a reverent sympathy for such people.

Those disturbed by the silence

For many years, they held the torch high. It had been a prolonged honeymoon in which God was one long *celebra-tion*. During those years, ideals floated on the wind, self-de-nials became liberty and riches, and these people seemed to lack nothing in the world. It was a golden age.

The years passed and the night of silence began to oppress them. The strength of youth disappeared like money in an overdrawn account. At this time, the Lord was no longer the celebration of the past. Life continued and, as if by osmosis, enthusiasm drained away. During this time, they never received a single gift from on high, not a single one of those graces that mark, affirm, and confirm us in faith and give us certainty. Routine invaded their days like an invisible cloud.

That night of silence was long, very long. Fatigue began to weaken these pilgrims. They continued to drag themselves along almost until they did not even have the desire to continue. It was — how does one say it — a sensation somewhere between disenchantment, weakness, and failure, as when someone says, I do not have the wings for such flights. But the more exact word for defining the situation is *disturbance.* "You turned away your face and I was terrified" (Ps 30).

The desire for the Lord died and was substituted by apathy. They abandoned the effort at personal prayer; they took part in the sacraments more out of habit than hunger; they participated in only a few community prayers. The emptiness of God was substituted with strong doses of compensation. To avoid the feeling of failure, they launched themselves into activity, which they labeled "apostolic," and, according to the law of equality, the greater the interior emptiness, the greater the activity.

The typical symptom of this group, besides disenchantment, is *nostalgia.* Without trying and without being able to avoid it, these people return to the time of their first love, the years in which the desire for the Lord was clothed in beauty and meaning.

This I remember
  as I pour out my heart,
how I used to pass under the roof of the most high,
  used to go to the house of God,
among cries of joy and praise,
  the sound of the feast. (Ps 42)

Even in the rush of this activity, a voice that cannot be silenced follows and pursues them. It is the ancient reproach of the Lord: "I remember your faithful love, the affection of your bridal days" (Jer 2:2).

They would give every one of their professional successes to recover that first love, that living enchantment of the past that they once felt for the Lord. What they feel most is that they have lost their happiness. And there, far away, in some lost region within themselves, they carry the belief that apart from God there is no happiness. And they are always ready to begin again on the road of return to this source. The majority of those disturbed by the silence of God end, sooner or later, by recovering their first love.

The confirmed

A long and painful history weighs heavily upon the shoulders of the confirmed. They have seen everything in their lives: marches and countermarches, crises, falls, and more falls. But a basic fidelity covered fleeting failures with a mantle. And the "Silent One" was shaping, hardening, carving, and confirming the ones who had surrendered themselves to light and darkness.

From the beginning, He gave them the grace to perceive that, on the journey of life, God and God alone could give meaning and solidity to their life project. And, for years without end, they raised their uninterrupted cry to the Lord God. "Your face, Yahweh, I seek; do not turn away from me" (Ps 27). "Do not turn away from your servant" (Ps 69, 87, 101). "Let your face shine on your servant" (Ps 31). "They will live in the light of your presence" (Ps 89). "Let your face shine on us and we shall be safe" (Ps 80).

But what was the secret recipe that rooted and confirmed these believers in faith? It was a profound and universal *spirit of surrender*. Not resisting but *delivering themselves*: that was the key to their confirmation. God was the "Silent One" for them, too. But they never became impatient, irritated, or scared; they never demanded a guarantee of credibility, a sign they could *see*, or crutches so they could walk. Without offering resistance, they delivered themselves, over and over again, in silence, to the silence.

They spent long periods of aridity and dryness. They did not let themselves be beaten by this. In the midst of the densest darkness, they remained firm. They received unexpected blows, which cut down their tree to the very roots. They were not disturbed, however. They surrendered, in silence, to the silence.

The crisis came. For long periods of time, the skies remained mute and the world appeared to be governed by absurdity and fate. They were not confused by this, nor were they disheartened, but, rather, tied hand and foot, they let themselves be carried by the river of silence and darkness, sure of sailing in the sea of God. The compass, that guided their sailing, was certainty.

Like Abraham and other people of God, those confirmed in faith began by burning their bridges; that is, leaving behind securities, such as common sense and probability. They continued by ignoring explanations that did not explain and evidence that dit not satisfy them and, folding their arms and closing their eyes, they delivered themselves over and over again to the "Absolutely Other," incessantly repeating *Amen!* Just like the *poor ones of God*, they surrendered themselves without support, in complete darkness, with unconditional trust, to their God and Father.

And so, they remained forever confirmed in the certainty of faith.

Strength in silence

Today, we have a prominent exponent of this faith of surrender: Thérèse of the Child Jesus. From her, we have these words of pathetic and almost superhuman greatness:

The most absolute aridity and even surrender were my dowry. Jesus as always, remained asleep in my little boat.

59

This is great comfort for all of us, to know that someone of such high esteem has lived, smiling and peaceful, this surrender of faith, despite the absolute silence of God.

This testimony gains a renewed grandeur when it is finished with these words:

It could be that [the sleeping Jesus] will not awaken until my final rest in eternity. But this, instead of saddening me, gives me the greatest comfort.

This fragile woman was of the same mold as Abraham. As we shall see later, some people pass through the world with the comforts of God. But many others see God as a torture. Only surrender — absolute faith — transforms torture into sweetness. Thérèse of Lisieux belongs to this class of people. Her statements a few days before dying leave us dumbfounded, and she shines above many men of the Bible who asked God for a "sign" in order to have the security that God is God. This saint refuses that "grace."

I do not wish to see God on earth... I prefer to live in faith.

With simple words, she sketches for us a beautiful metaphor for the mystery of faith:

I think of myself as a baby bird covered with down. I am not an eagle; I only have the eyes and heart of an eagle, but, in spite of my extreme smallness, I dare to stare at the divine sun, at the sun of love, and in my heart I feel all of the hopes and dreams of an eagle. The little bird would like to fly toward the sun which fascinates the eye...

What will become of that bird? Will it die of pain, seeing itself so weak? Oh, no! The little bird does not even feel sorry. With courageous surrender it wants to continue staring at the divine Sun. Nothing would be able to frighten it, not even the wind or rain. And if dark clouds come to hide that star of Love, the little bird does not budge; it knows that beyond the clouds, its Sun continues to shine, that the splendor cannot be darkened even for a moment.

This is the final mystery of faith. We have been designed for an infinite Objective. But the design has been distorted by a disaster that makes the original objective difficult to attain.

We are sparrows, but we have the hearts of eagles. This is the terrible and contradictory mystery of humanity: to be at one and the same time sparrow and eagle; to have the eagle's heart and the sparrow's wings.

What are we to do? I know that I cannot fly that high. I will not even attempt it. I will not even trouble my wings to surrender myself to the wind: that wind which is God. He will do the rest. I know that I am not an eagle, but I also know that if I surrender myself to God, He will be able to give me the powerful wings of the eagle. Is anything impossible with God? I know that I am a pile of ruins and failures; but I also know that if I surrender to God, He will be able to transform me into a magnificent mansion. He is power and grace.

If God is wrapped in a mantle of silence or is hidden behind the clouds, "with courageous surrender" I will continue to gaze, although I may see or feel nothing. Although a thousand voices may assault me, speaking to me of illusion, I know that He is behind the silence and I will stubbornly and peacefully continue to search for Him. And although God is "asleep" in my boat, for as long as I live, it does not matter. I know that He will "awaken" on the great day of eternity.

You believe that the moon shines now because the clouds have disappeared. You are mistaken. The moon has been shining for an eternity. (Ancient Proverb)

4. TOWARD CERTAINTY

They were like two *old friends*. Between the two of them, they were carrying on a memorable epic. Fighting elbow to elbow in a singular battle, without giving or taking refuge, they had gathered together an oppressed people. Then they took them to the land of the free, which is the desert. And, walking over the golden sands, they began marching toward a far-off and almost impossible dream. They treated each other with the camaraderie of two war veterans. The two were God and Moses.

But God had been an invisible "comrade." However, because Moses was an ardent contemplative, he had desired to see God's face for a long time. And once, when he was overcome by anxiety, he brought forth this prayer, which he had kept secret for so long: "Please show me your glory." And the Lord answered him:

> "I shall make all my goodness pass before you... but my Face you cannot see for no human being can see me and survive." Then Yahweh said, "Here is a place near me. You will stand on the rock, and when my glory passes by, I will put you in a cleft of the rock and shield you with my hand until I have gone past. Then I will take my hand away and you will see my back; but my face will not be seen." (Ex 33:19-23)

In this wild and almost cosmic scene, the whole mystery of faith is admirably revealed: as long as the battle of life continues, it is impossible to look upon the Lord face to face. It will only be possible to get a glimpse of Him from the fleeting traces, moving from the effects to the Cause, walking along the path of deductions and analogies, in shadows, indirectly; in short, "from behind."

The dark night

John of the Cross never tires of saying, over and over again in different ways, that faith "is the habit of a *dark and certain soul.*" I have always thought of John as the great *doctor of faith* because if he is the master and guide on spiritual paths, he is especially so on the nighttime paths of faith. Among the many thoughts that are developed in his books concerning this subject, the following words from his *Ascent of Mount Carmel* might be taken to be a synthesis of those ideas:

> Faith is the substance of things to be hoped for and these things are not manifest to the intellect, even though its consent to them is firm and *certain.* If they were manifest, there would be no faith. For though faith brings certitude to the intellect, it does not produce clarity, but only *darkness.*

I will try to explain these two concepts that, like a backbone, constitute the essence of faith: *dark* and *certain.*

* * *

This is called — using a complicated name — the *cognitive process.* The mystery of faith is taken from this.

Impressions and sensations of different objects enter the human mind through the channel of the senses. In reality, the mind is a filter or netting. Essentially, from each object detected by the senses, the mind takes that which the object is in itself, and also separates that which the object has in common to all other objects of its class. That is, it deduces a common idea of all objects and, as a consequence, arrives at a universal. It is a task of *universalization.* Let us take a concrete example.

I see a chair here; there, I see another chair that is different from the first; there is another chair that does not look anything like the other two in design or size. And so on. Fifty chairs of fifty different shapes enter my mind. Now the work of the mind begins. The mind puts aside the particular characteristics of the fifty chairs, or rather, of the images of the chairs, and picks out what is common to all fifty: a universal idea of chair. From now on, I will be able to recognize a chair.

Does the same thing happen in the process of knowing God? In truth, no. The Lord is not clothed in colors or smells, does not have measurement, cannot be apprehended by the senses. God cannot *enter* the laboratory of the mind and submit to analysis and classification. Because of this, God will never be an *object of the intellect,* because there is nothing in the mind that has not passed through the senses. The Lord is an *object of faith.* Only faith can "understand" Him properly.

So then, God will never take part in our little game. He will always be *outside,* transcendental; He is *above* the normal processes of human knowledge. He is in another orbit. God is *something else.*

I mean, God is not to be "understood" analytically because He will never be part of our gymnastics of syllogisms, premises, and conclusions of induction and deduction. God is "understood" on one's knees: praising Him, welcoming Him, living Him. The "overtaking" of John of the Cross is not to be understood in the intellectual sense — that is not possible — but in the actual sense. To conquer (intellectually) God? In this sense, God is unassailable. The difficult and necessary thing is to be conquered *by* Him.

Because it is not possible to intellectually "overtake" Him, then God is *mystery.* This does not mean that He is *something mysterious,* but rather that He is inaccessible by intellectual power: as the Bible says, we will never be able to look at Him face to face.

Henri de Lubac once wrote that in every sense, God is totally different. A process which brings us to other beings or other truths will not be able to bring us to Him, just as representations, sufficient for other beings, are not capable of representing Him.

Even after logic has demanded that we affirm that God exists, His mystery remains intact. Reason does not reach Him. Dialectic and representation cannot cross the threshold.

But even before any dialectic or representation, our spirit affirms that He who might be reached by dialectic and representation is beyond all dialectic and representation.

And this affirmation, moving from darkness to light and from light to darkness, remains standing.

This beautiful concept of de Lubac's underlines the "gift" of faith before, here, and beyond all dialectic and representation. The true believer surrenders in darkness, and only then begins to understand the mystery — and certainty is born.

Saint Augustine in *Contra Adimantum* says:

"Do you think you know what God is? Do you think that you know what God is like? He is nothing you imagine, nothing your thought embraces. O God, You who are above every name, above all thought, beyond every idea and every value, O Living God."

Because of this, human words will never be "messengers" of the real essence of God. Words carry and transmit images of the realities we live, hear, and feel. God, being out of reach of the senses, will never be understood by us in terms of our language. Every word referring to God will have to be in the negative: in-finite, in-visible, in-comprehensible, un-created, un-named... Words cannot convey Him; that is, the Lord is greater than anything we can imagine, dream, desire. He truly is the In-comparable One.

God is *understood* in faith. More than an intellectual object, He is the object of contemplation. It is very well to become involved in the things of God. But, originally, the act of faith consists in approaching "mystery" in the darkness of night. John of the Cross says:

To attain union with God, a person should advance neither by understanding... nor by feeling... but by belief... For God's being cannot be grasped by the intellect... or any other sense... The most that can be felt and tasted of God in this life is infinitely distant from God...

What is Your name?

The writers of the Bible did not dare to define or describe, let alone name, God. To define is, in some way, to contain something; and the Lord God is uncontainable. One's *name*, for the Semitic people, equaled the person; and to name is, in a certain sense, to apprehend and measure the essence of the person; and God is immeasurable.

Everything that the Bible does with respect to God is part of a very complex game: it ignores and avoids giving Him a name. Instead, the Bible makes use of a roundabout way of referring to God: "the God of Abraham; the God of Isaac; the God of Jacob." Following this same style, Paul speaks of "the God and Father of our Lord Jesus Christ." The most adequate way of representing or pointing to God would be this: *The One* who was revealed by the patriarchs; *The One* who was revealed in Jesus Christ. To refer to God, one only needs the pronoun, not the name.

Because of this, the Israelites could not utter the name of Yahweh. Beneath this minor detail lies a great deal of depth: the transcendence of the God of Israel.

* * *

Therefore, for the Israelites, there were three inter-changeable and identical questions: Who are You? What are You? What is Your name? It is within this context that the following biblical scene is to be understood.

Fleeing from the fury of the Pharaoh, Moses has taken refuge in the land of Midian and watched over the sheep of his father-in-law. God said to him, "Bring my people the Israelites out of Egypt."

Moses then said to God, "Look, if I go to the Israelites and say to them, 'The God of your ancestors has sent me to you,' and they say to me, 'What is his name?', what am I to tell them?" God said to Moses, "I am he who is" (Ex 3:13-14).

God has not avoided Moses' question; He gives Moses the only answer humanly possible. God could not have a *name*! He is the unnameable. We cannot classify Him. We cannot qualify Him. The most impressive words will not be able to contain Him. He is not within the sphere of spoken vocabulary but within that of Being. Could we ever channel a roaring river with a single shovel?

This is the meaning of the mysterious and dramatic episode of the nighttime battle between Jacob and the angel of God. In the morning, Jacob asks, "Please tell me your name." And the answer of God, always evasive: "Why do you ask my name?" (Gn 32:25-33).

The same answer is given to Manoah: "Why ask my name? It is a name of wonder" (Jgs 13:18). God is the One who cannot be named. God is always "something else." He is deeper than the deep, wider than space, and higher than the heavens: He is something other than heavenly melodies. He is not sound, but Being.

In the profound night of faith, when the soul, like a blind and thirsty land, bows humbly before the divine activity and accepts the Infinite Mystery, like the soft rain that falls, floods and feeds... only thus, surrendered and receptive, will the soul begin to "understand" the Unintelligible.

Analogies, traces, and symbols

Traveling at night, without the shining stars, how will we avoid being devoured by fear? Where will we hold on so as not to succumb to distress? What signposts, what pointers will we use to know that we are on the right path? Where is God? How do we contemplate Him, even "from behind"?

The Bible offers us images and symbols. The Invisible is made visible through the forces of nature, the written word, and historical events, which are an invitation for us to dive into the divine waters.

God often takes the form of fire, a very appropriate sign for making Himself visible by virtue of the brilliance with which He lights the darkness, and because of the energy of His heat by which He tempers, joins, or gives life. On Mount Horeb, Moses is fascinated by the burning bush that is not devoured by the fire (Ex 3:2). On Sinai, the mountain burns but is not consumed (Ex 19:18). God is a fire that does not destroy but purifies.

And so, by way of the path of deductions and traces, we struggle to discover the Being and Face of the Lord.

We only need to poke a little bit beneath the skin of humanity to discover that we are measured in terms of infinity. Who dug such a deep well? Who put this fire here that always burns yet never goes out? From where did this hunger come which all the food in the world cannot satisfy? And that thirst that cannot be quenched by all of the waterfalls in the mountains? Although no one says anything, underneath everything there *must be* a source of life, a first cause, and a final goal.

And that shiny mirror which is the world?... Behind such beauty there exists Beauty; behind so much life there is Life; behind so much tenderness there is Love.

And so we climb from creature to Creator, from the effects to the Cause, but always by a blind path, guided by means of analogies and deductions, groping, in shadows, in faith.

In spite of all this, in the fullness of time (Eph 1:10), God showed Himself with signs and words of salvation. His mystery, however, remained hidden and veiled in silence.

Through the Word, that veil was drawn aside and the mystery of Christ "was made known to me by a revelation" (Eph 3:3). However, the profound and ultimate reality of mystery is still trapped and hidden in words and signs, and we contemplate the "glory of the Lord" only "like mirrors" (2 Cor 3:18).

From now on, throughout the centuries, the destiny of the Church is to discover, ever more clearly, that mystery, until the veil is completely drawn back. In each stage of her history, the Church advances toward the heart of the mystery, in an ever deepening growth, penetration, depth, and clarity of the mystery of Jesus Christ.

Revelation is an *historical* event, in the sense that it is produced in the *past.* But revelation is not completed in the past; it continues unfolding throughout history. That is, the knowledge of the mystery of Christ did not end with the writing of the Scriptures, but rather is enriched and deepened with the contemplative contributions of all times and all cultures. History is nothing else but an advancing toward the interior of the Word.

The great leap into the abyss

The "adult" believer is the one who believes, *surrendering* him or herself. We could, then, speak of an *adult faith.* In order to understand it, we begin by presenting some ordinary concepts from everyday common speech. A *child* is essentially a dependent being who needs support from someone else to walk, eat, live. An *adult* is capable of standing alone, without being supported by anyone else; alone, the adult can live, earn a living, create a family...

Applying these ideas to the case at hand, *childish faith* would be that which necessitates support, security, reassurances. *Adult faith* is that which, without support, reaches out, runs every risk, trusts, allows, and surrenders. We are delivered into the abyss, void of all security, evidence, and reassurance. Adult faith is that which is done standing and alone.

The person who, in order to believe, needs security and defenses, has the faith of a child. It is as if someone were to come up and say: It appears that what you believe is contrary to common sense; it is against the laws of the universe and it is contrary to reason. But calm down. I bring you reasons why what you believe is not so crazy. With these arguments, you will be convinced that what you believe is not contrary to reason, nor reason contrary to faith; I am going to present to you an orderly argument, proving to you that miracles are possible because the One who created the laws of nature can break them and, finally, that the fundamental truths of faith can hold up to the doubts of science... Calm down, and you may believe in peace.

This faith is childish because, in order to take a single step, crutches are needed. It is good that the believer intellectually probes the material of faith; but, a faith that needs reassurances to soften the fright of the leap is not faith. In itself, radically speaking, the mature act of faith is to take the leap without any crutches.

The "adult" in faith overcomes all distance and all limitations inherent to faith, leaving them to themselves; the "adult" gives up all the intellectual handholds that give weight to arguments, and takes the great leap into the abyss, in the fullness of night, surrendering to the *Absolutely Other*. It is a leap into the abyss because the believer surrenders "reason" and lets himself fall into the depths that are Mystery.

The believer always has the feeling of running a risk. It is not rational thought but blind and "irrational" feelings that overpower the believer and "say" things such as: Look, you bet everything on a Someone, and what if you lose the bet? The believer is left without any solid handle, without any empirical proof, without any explanation that really explains, without any evidence that settles the question... This is the abyss into which the believer makes the leap — and not just once, but forever.

This is the great moment of faith. This is the radical act that underlies faith's merit and transforming value. It is only meritorious to believe in light when we are in darkness. I believe that behind this silence, You breathe. I believe that behind this darkness, Your Face is shining. Although everything is turning out badly for me, although bad luck follows me, I believe that You love me. Although everything appears to be fate, although it seems that absurdity rules the world, and we see hatred and sadness, that evil triumphs and good fails, although sadness reigns and the dove of peace has been killed, although we feel like dying... I believe; I surrender to You. Without You, what meaning would there be in life? You are eternal life.

This is the faith that moves mountains and gives believers an indestructible solidity. With this "leap," the gift of faith is understood to be *gift*. Without a doubt, faith from God is *gift*, the primary gift. But, it seems to me, there is also a beautiful and basic act of giving on the part of the believer. In pure darkness, the believer leaps into the arms of the Father, who is not seen, without having any other motive or security than His Word. There is great gift (and merit) on the part of the believer, in the act of faith. And, we repeat, it is the greatest act of love.

Walter Kasper, in his book *Jesus the Christ*, writes:

> Faith does not mean merely accepting something as true, but neither is it merely trust...
> Believing means saying "Amen" to God, holding fast to him and taking him as our ground. Believing means allowing God to be wholly God, and that means recognizing him as the sole ground and meaning of life... Faith is existence in receptivity and obedience.

71

Transfigured night or certainty

If it is true that the act of faith involves the whole person (feelings, thoughts, and behavior), it is nevertheless an act of the will because it deals with a real "holding fast."

With this surrender, the believer opens the way, in a single stroke, for the entire night of faith, and gives up that radical incapacity of our intellect to "dominate" God intellectually. The believer surrenders, leaps over all mental processes, above the problems of formulas and content... and "reaches" God, and thus, the Lord becomes certainty.

The security that rationality could not give us is given by the One who *is the content of faith,* on condition that it has been *accepted* through a "freely given" and unconditional surrender.

And so the night of faith is *conquered* and, without ceasing to be night, is transfigured, taking the form of light, or better, taking the place of light; that is certainty. Pope Dionysius, in the third century, called faith a *dark ray*: a beam of darkness that penetrates the world and "illuminates" everything, not with sight or evidence but with the securities that come from within and are something other than clarity. There is no clarity in faith but there is security ("dark and secure"). This certainty is not a product derived from evident truths, but one that proceeds from surrender itself. Likewise, the psalmist tells us that "even darkness to you is not dark and night is as clear as the day" (Ps 139).

And so, God, transformed into light (certainty) for the adult believer, leads and precedes the caravan of believers through the desert of life, walking in light and hope. And, so that the people are not disturbed by the darkness of night, God will take the form of fire to give them light (cf. Ex 13:21-22).

* * *

We are now able to classify faith as *certainty*. Because faith is the first gift of God, certainty is the *first grace* from the Giver of all graces. Nevertheless, looking at certainty as a human phenomenon, we are searching here for the original sources of that certainty.

John of the Cross discovers for us, in immortal verses, how the night of faith is transformed into the light of day:

> ... with no other light or guide
> than the one that burned in my heart;
> this guided me more surely than the light of noon.

Certainty ("more surely") does not come from the traces found in nature, nor from philosophical arguments, but from the inner structure of faith itself ("that burned in my heart"). Without believing, nothing is understood. Without surrendering, nothing is believed. And no one surrenders without making a real decision. The one who surrenders does not suffer from intellectual problems with faith. Security is found in life.

The believer begins by not being afraid of the darkness or resisting the silence. Seduced by the voice of the One who calls us out of the deep and brilliant darkness, we reach out, overcoming the puzzles and insecurities of travel in an unknown land. Just as the stars illuminate the night at midnight, so the semi-veiled light of God's face gives light to the path of the believer. There is, furthermore, another "light and guide": that which "burn[s] in the heart."

The confluence of these two lights (though the night continues to be dark) makes our march in faith more sure, stronger, as if we were walking in the brightness of the noonday sun. It is a bright and mysterious night, something like a wedding night: we surrender, confess, affirm; without seeing, we see; without feeling, we are sure; we surrender the keys and are united in an eternal covenant, a transfigured alliance. All insecurities disappear in that moment, and the earth, the sky, the sea, and everything under the sea, everything is covered with certainty, a certainty as serene as a summer evening, and we are confirmed forever in faith.

In reality, certainty is born out of life. It is the fruit of the heart, not of the mind.

For I know well...

Once more, it is John of the Cross who gives us the link between darkness and certainty in his *Song of the soul that rejoices in knowing God through faith.* Here are a few verses:

> For I know well
> the spring that flows and runs,
> although it is night.
> That eternal spring is hidden,
> for I know well where it has its rise
> although it is night.
>> I do not know its origin, for it has none.
>> But I know that every origin has come from it,
>> although it is night.
> Its clarity is never darkened,
> And I know that every light has come from it,
>> This living spring which I long for,
>> I see in this bread of life, although it is night.

The deep mystery of faith is precisely in those two contradictory expressions that run through, alternate, and dominate the stanzas: *I know well* (certainty) *although it is night* (darkness). The act of faith consists of the unifying and contrasting force that ceases to be a paradox the moment one begins to live it.

Chapter 3

STEPS TO THE ENCOUNTER

Reveal Your Presence,
And may the vision of Your Beauty be my death;
For the sickness of love
Is not cured
Except by Your very Presence and Image.

John of the Cross

In writing these chapters, I have especially in mind those Christians who do not have certain guidelines at their disposal by which to feed and channel their deep hopes and aspirations.

Wanting to make this as easy as possible, I have arranged these guidelines in a practical order so that, without needing any help, these persons can make their pilgrimage toward the infinite mystery of God, transforming their lives in love.

Meaning of this chapter

Patience, constancy, and hope will be like three guardian angels that will accompany us on this path, not allowing the night of desolation to take us by surprise.

We need *calm.* Anyone dominated by interior distraction, lacking wholeness due to agitation and nervousness, cannot achieve a transforming union with God. In order to calm this nervousness, we have collected a series of exercises that are easy to practice.

We need *peace.* Anyone loaded down with aggression, inner resistance, and deep-seeded rejection is not able to enter the temple of peace which is God. In order to calm the soul, we must put together a process of profound purification, with practical exercises in surrender.

Furthermore, we need *interior unity.* Great waves assault us in our spiritual sailing: distraction, dryness, aridity... What are we to do? Here, we will point out practical methods for overcoming these squalls.

In order to take the first steps, we are going to lean on the *word* as a bridge between the soul and God. As practical means we will propose vocal prayer, spiritual reading, and the like.

There are other things that, apparently, are secondary and yet play an important role in the results to be gained from prayer. Where, when, how to pray? Posture, breathing... We give practical guidelines for concrete problems.

Prayer is not easy

In my opinion, one thing that prejudices us and throws us off is the assurance that prayer is easy, as easy as conversing with our father, mother, or a friend. I agree that it may be easy to say a prayer out loud, to join in the prayers of the faithful, to say some ejaculations, or to take part in some superficial communication with God.

But to explore the deep mysteries of God, to prepare and strengthen the psychological faculties for growth in grace, to temper this growth to the differences in human makeup, to continue along the dark and difficult coasts of God's demands toward that transforming union... this entire process is one of slow and unnerving difficulty. Of all human endeavors, advancing to the depths of a life with

God is the most complex, difficult, and tremendous task. Prayer is not easy.

Grace offers a limitless array of possibilities, from zero to infinity. Not everyone is given the same capacity for development; not everyone is demanded to accomplish the same amount; it is to each one according to the measure of the gift. The difficulty is that no one is able to say, I have been given so much potential and I will be demanded such-and-such a result. God alone is the giver, He alone knows the measure. We are to be totally faithful, without arguing about how much we have been given and how much we ought to return.

Be that as it may, with only a little prayer, lacking perseverance or discipline, we cannot expect a powerful experience of God; nor can we expect transformed lives; nor, as a result, can we expect to see shining prophets.

Prayer is an art

Although prayer is primarily the work of grace, it is also an art; and like art, it must submit, on a psychological level, to the norms of all learning, just like any other human activity. Good prayer demands, then, method, order, and discipline. In a word, it demands technique.

I know that a simple peasant, without need of any technique, by way of graces and extraordinary gifts given by God, is able to discover God and the unfathomable panoramas of the mystery of His being and His love. But these graces are not merited, nor are they obtained by strength. They are "received," apart from any planning or logic, because they are absolutely freely given.

Technique without grace does not lead to results. But think of how many years, how much energy, how many methods, and how much schooling are needed for any human development: that of a painter, composer, professional, technician. If prayer is, among other things, an art, let us not dream that we can arrive at a high state of life with God without effort, order, and method.

It is true that here we are speaking of a different type of schooling that may disregard all methods, follow the most surprising paths, and override psychological and educational laws.

But normally, God is found in the evolutionary laws of life, the same as in the case of the mustard seed: it is an insignificant seed, almost invisible. It is planted. Days and weeks pass and, to all appearances, nothing happens. Nevertheless, at the end of a certain period of time, something begins to sprout that looks like a plant but that is barely visible. Months pass, and it grows and grows until it forms a thick shrub, puts out its branches, and the birds come and make their nests in it (Mk 4:30-33).

This slow and gradual process is true of all life. It is especially true for growth in prayer, and in community life, with the aim of incorporating the figure of Jesus Christ into our lives.

A bird's-eye view

If we take a bird's-eye view of the march along the path of life with God, from vocal prayer to more profound communication, we will have the following general outline. In the first stages, God leaves the initiative to the individual, who functions according to the norms of psychology. God's participation is rare. He leaves it to the individual to find the means and supports, as if the individual were the only carpenter in the house. And although it is true that, in these first stages, divine consolations may abound, prayer appears to be an edifice exclusively supported by human scaffolding.

As we advance toward higher levels, God slowly and gradually takes the initiative and directly intervenes, by means of special supports. We begin to feel that the psychological supports, which helped us so much before, are now useless crutches. God, with ever greater decisiveness, takes the initiative from us; He places us in submission and surrender, to the point where another subject, the Spirit, comes on the scene and remains as the only architect, to transform us into a "child" of God, a living image of His Son, our Lord Jesus Christ.

> The Spirit too comes to help us in our weakness, for, when we do not know how to pray properly, then the Spirit personally makes our petitions for us in groans that cannot be put into words; and he who can see into all hearts knows what the Spirit means because the prayers that the Spirit makes for God's holy people are always in accord with the mind of God. (Rom 8:26-28)

The first steps are complicated. All of us, like children learning to walk, need psychological supports, methods of concentration, ways of relaxing, and points of reflection.

But when God enters the scene, we, in such close proximity to Him, sense the contrast between our "face" and the "Face" of God, and we are then dragged along through successive purifications by means of a general detachment. Having gained purity, liberty, and peace, nothing stands in our way, and we speedily advance with open sails under God's direction toward a transforming union. In the meantime, we are completely sculpted into the figure of our Lord Jesus Christ, full of maturity, humility, grandeur, love, and service.

Writing about prayer in his book, *Quiero Ver a Dios,* Father Eugenio del Niño Jesus says that these interior transformations have an echo that reverberates in the psychological consciousness. Independent of any extraordinary favors which cause true shocks in the consciousness and leave a healthy scar upon it, grace grows in the individual, silently and slowly, through the passing joys, through violent suffering, and with these, to a region of peace: a refuge where sound or storm rarely come, an oasis of springs of strength and joy.

Patience

Many undertake the path of prayer. Some abandon it almost from the beginning, saying, I was not born for this. They also say, It is a waste of time; I do not see any results. Fatigued, others are stopped on the first slopes, stuck in mediocrity. They continue the activity of prayer, but on level ground. And there are those who advance, amid difficulties, to the unfathomable depths of God.

The primary enemy is inconstancy, which is born out of the feeling of frustration that some people suffer when they notice that results are not forthcoming or do not correspond to the effort they have given to it. So much effort and so few results, they say. So many years dedicated to prayer and so little progress.

We are accustomed to two very typical laws of our technological society: speed and efficiency. In any human activity, the dynamic cycle works something like this: from such a cause, such a result; from any action, a reaction; from so much effort, a corresponding result. The result seems to be a prize and stimulates us to new efforts. We continue the effort because we can see the results while, at the same time, the results promote greater and renewed efforts.

However, the same thing does not happen in the life of grace. We seem to be more like those fishermen who keep watch all night long with nets spread out, and in the morning, find them completely empty (Lk 5:5).

We need *patience* to accept the fact that with great effort there will be few results, or, at least, to accept the eventual disproportion between effort and result.

Some say that patience is the art of waiting. Others answer that it is the art of knowing. We could combine the two and say that it is the art of *knowing how to wait*. One waits because one knows. In other words, patience is an act of waiting because one knows and peacefully accepts reality as it is.

Which reality? In our case, there are two realities. The first, that God is essentially free and, as a result, that His "conduct" is essentially disturbing. And the second, that all of life advances slowly and gradually.

* * *

The most difficult thing, for those who have embarked on the march of faith, is to have patience with God. The "conduct" of the Lord, for those who have delivered themselves up to Him, is often confusing. There is no logic in His "reactions." Because of this, there is no proportion between our efforts to discover His blessed Face and the results of this effort; and many lose patience and, confused, abandon the whole thing.

God is the source from which everything is born and in which everything is consumed. He is the bottomless well of all life and grace. He disposes and dispenses everything according to His goodwill. In the general scheme of His economic policies, there exists only one rule: that of *giving*. No one may demand anything. No one may question Him, confronting Him with questions.

Relationships with Him are not the same as our human relationships. In our interrelationships, there are contracts of bargain and sale, work and salary, merit and reward. None of this exists in the relationship with God. There is only gift, grace. He is of another nature; we are in different orbits. Whoever decides to take God seriously needs to be conscious of this difference and accept it peacefully. That is what it means to be patient with God.

It is good to walk toward God by means of proven methods of prayer, but without losing sight of the thick curtain that is the mystery of grace. Patience means to be aware of and to accept peacefully the fact of our having to operate in this strange, disturbing, and imperceptible dynamic that often puts faith and patience in check.

Our God is disturbing. All of a sudden, unforeseen, like

a sneak attack, God descends upon us, overwhelming us with His powerful presence, confirming us forever in faith, and leaving us shaken for the rest of our lives. In view of such spectacular and spontaneous events, many ask themselves, Why not me? Questions cannot be asked of God. We must accept Him as He is.

Others are carried by the Lord to the sands of the desert, in an everlasting afternoon of aridity. To others, He gives a marked sensitivity for the divine as an innate predisposition of their personalities and, yet, He never grants them a special grace as such. There have been people throughout history who never worried about God, neither attacking Him nor defending Him; yet, this same God came to them in splendor and glory. There are those who sail on a sea of consolations for their whole life. There are others destined to make their pilgrimages during a perpetual night, and a starless night it is. There are those who walk upon uneven ground, beneath a brilliant sun or under thick clouds. For others, their life with God is always a gray day. Each person is a story, an absolutely unique and singular story.

Whoever wants to enlist in the army of God must begin to accept this primary reality: God is free, constantly new, and unforeseen.

No one may question God, saying, What is this, Lord? To the one who worked only one hour, You are paying the same salary as the one who worked all day? He will respond, What I gave was not a salary but a gift, and I may do with what is mine what I consider to be right.

In this kingdom, God continues, the verbs *to pay* and *to earn* do not exist. Nothing is paid here because nothing is earned. Everything is received. Everything is gift, grace. You must realize that we are in different orbits. My laws are not your laws. I have other criteria because My nature is *other*.

If we, who begin the climb to God, I repeat, do not begin to realize and accept the free and disturbing nature of God, we are going to sink often into complete confusion.

My observation of life has brought me to the conclusion that the common reason given for the abandonment of prayer is this: life with God, for many, often appears meaningless, illogical, out of proportion; they end up with the impression that it is all unreal, irrational... and they abandon it altogether.

There is more: just as there is no logic in God's activity, there is also no logic in the reactions of nature. And life with God takes place on the border between nature and grace.

Say, for example, that a person slept very well during the night and yet awoke in a bad mood, tense. The night before that, he could not sleep at all because of the noise and mosquitos, and yet he arose relaxed and refreshed. In the ups and downs of human life there are no straight lines. Because of this, our reactions are unpredictable.

In a single day, the same person may jump among the most varied and contradictory emotional states: now one feels sure; a little later, afraid; after that, happy; and in the evening, anxious. We are not talking about clinically unstable or disturbed personalities. An author or an artist can go to work and in twelve hours produce nothing, yet, all of a sudden, in sixty minutes, produce more than is normally accomplished in twelve hours. Who understands this? That is just the way we are.

Naturally, every phenomenon has its cause or series of causes. There are no accidents. But normally, the reasons for moods and emotions are not detectable. And when it is impossible to detect the cause of something, we say we are confronted with something *mysterious.*

In the life of the spirit, the same thing happens: in a single afternoon, a believer who goes to a quiet hermitage to pray passes through a prism of the most varied emotional situations, from moments of complete aridity to those of the greatest consolation, as well as moments of apathy. What does this mean? Is it a question of different biological states, psychological reactions, or responses to grace? It is impossible to say. Without a doubt, it has to do with a great complexity of causes, beginning with bio-chemical processes. Life, by its nature, is motion. And motion is versatile. And because of this, emotional states are constantly changing.

Without realizing it, we are already involved in a question that troubles many people: in a single spiritual phenomenon — for example, strong consolation — at what point can we say that it is something from God and at what point is it merely a product of one's physical nature? In other words, what is natural and what is grace?

I believe that no one knows the answer. It is useless to pretend to discern it because there are no instruments by which to measure and point out the boundaries. I also think that this preoccupation, more than being useless, is harm-ful, because it causes us to be self-centered.

Nevertheless, speaking in general terms, we could es-tablish an approximate criterion, the criterion of the fruits: anything that causes us to reach out and give of ourselves to others is something from God. Everything that produces a sense of calm and a state of peace is also from God. We might also venture further: we are going to suppose that any given emotion, at its roots, is a strictly biophysical product. Even in this case, if, in fact, the person is prompt-ed to reach out and give to others, we could consider it to be a gift from God.

Perseverance

Patience engenders perseverance.

In the general sphere of life, there are no leaps: neither in biology, nor in psychology, nor in the life of the spirit. The grain of wheat is planted in the afternoon, and we do not think to go out early the next morning to see if the wheat has grown. Many days and nights must first pass. After many weeks, the wheat begins timidly to appear, like a miniature plant. Then, during the months that follow, that little plant rises into the air until it is transformed into a beautiful stalk of wheat.

Patience means to know (and to accept) that there are no leaps, only steps. And patience leads to perseverance.

This is directed at those who are pushing themselves to obtain (or recover) a relationship with God. Both groups, especially the latter, are marked by a common denominator: the atrophy of spiritual energy and a real desire to get out of that situation.

These people determinedly begin the search for the Face of the Lord. And, taking the first steps, they realize, lamentably, that it is impossible for them to walk; they have forgotten how to walk with God; their feet do not obey their desires; they are not certain how to establish a running dialogue with God (the living God); their wings are too bruised for such a flight. Is God "dead"?

They speak to the Lord and have the feeling that there is no listener, that their words are swallowed up in a vacuum. This happens particularly to those who have lost their familiarity with the Lord and want to recover it. It is a night of the spirit.

These people seem to be overcome immediately by a deep hunger, and impatience appears in the disturbing words already alluded to: I am getting nothing.

What happens to those who say they "get nothing"? It is an everlasting drama, a fatal spiral. I will explain: they do not eat because they do not feel like eating; they do not feel like eating because they do not eat. And death comes, due to anemia. Where and how can we break this deadly cycle? By eating without feeling like it, so that the desire to eat may be regained.

Many believers, because they have not prayed for a long time, do not feel like praying. And because they do not feel like praying, they do not pray. And so they enter the cycle: the faculties become stiff, God is more and more strange and distant, and the deadly circle is closed, trapping them in its womb. How do they get out of this mess? By praying with perseverance and without feeling like it, in order that the desire to pray and the sense of God might blossom.

We must persevere in this personal relationship with God, even though we have the impression that we are wasting time. Supported by vocal prayer and spiritual reading, we establish a line of communication with the Lord; in pure faith, we repeat the words that will be the bridge between our attention and the person of the Lord; and we even persevere when we have the feeling that there is no one on the other end.

If we have lived on the "outskirts" for many years, it is insane to pretend that in one week we are going to travel into the Living and Unfathomable Mystery. We take steps, not leaps.

Perseverance is the high price we must pay for all conquests in this world.

* * *

All growth is mystery. A little plant, appearing timidly from the ground, extracts organic elements from the soil and transforms them into a living substance. It barely gives signs of growth, but it grows. Likewise, the growth of grace is not detectable at first glance, or even by means of instruments. How many people were aware of the divine power and nature in Jesus, the Son of God? Must we imagine that the Nazarenes venerated their kinswoman Mary as an exceptional being? How disturbing and unfathomable is the mystery of grace!

Some may answer me: growth is observable in its effects, when the individual advances in love, maturity, humility, and peace. It is true, but only up to a certain point. We know from our own experience how much effort we need to overcome natural faults; nevertheless, only God and we are witnesses to that effort; others do not even notice.

On the other hand, grace adapts itself to different

natures, operating in accordance with the one receiving the grace. Grace does not go against human nature: the extrovert is not made an introvert; a talkative person does not become reserved and quiet. Grace respects human limitations.

1. PEACE THROUGH SURRENDER

Upon entering, or wanting to enter, into a transforming relationship with the Lord, we begin to sense the existence of certain roadblocks within us, which interrupt the progress of our attention to God. It is then that we realize that it is impossible for us to "remain" with the Lord in faith and in peace. Why precisely then?

In our daily activities, we are normally alienated, that is to say, separated from ourselves. Consciously or unconsciously, we are fugitives from ourselves, avoiding confrontation of our own mystery.

But, upon entering the profundity of God, we also enter our deepest recesses and touch our own mystery, which is summed up in these three questions: Who am I? What is the fundamental purpose of my life? What is necessary to keep this plan going?

Then, confronted by the God of peace and illuminated by the Face of the Lord, we notice that within us there is an agitation, a disturbance as if an earthquake were present: we feel as if there were a great deal of aggression stored down below. And, as a result, we feel out of step, as if someone in this temple of peace were shouting: "War!"

We are aware that selfishness has unleashed a state of war in our interior. Tall, living flames of resentment burn throughout, resentment toward ourselves, toward others, toward the mystery of life and, indirectly (and subconsciously transferred), toward God. When our sensitive eyes are opened more and we begin to analyze these most hidden worlds, we discover, and not without surprise, a generally sorry state: depressing sadness, melancholy, emotional blocks, frustration, antipathy, insecurity, all kinds of aggression... We appear, deep within, to be like a threatened and threatening castle.

We know that, with so much turbulence within, it will be impossible to establish a current of peaceful and harmonious intimacy with the God of peace. As a result, we feel the real need for purification, and we see that such a purification is only possible by way of a total reconciliation. We feel the necessity and the desire to put out the flames, to cover the trenches, to silence the battles, to accept the negative aspects of our personality, to forgive others, to abandon all resistance. In short, the need for general reconciliation. And a fruit of this will be — peace.

The genesis of frustration

Without trying and without taking the initiative, we find ourselves already alive, in life, as consciousness. We suddenly awaken for the first time and find ourselves in a world we did not know before. We did not seek existence; we were pushed into it and find ourselves there.

Awakening to our own existence, we are aware of being *ourselves*. We look around and observe that there also exist other realities that are not part of ourselves. And, even without leaving the sphere of our consciousness, we encounter basic elements of our being such as shape, character, popularity, and so on.

It is in this moment that we begin to *relate* to the *rest*, to the *other*. In establishing relationships, what we follow and what comes into play is the primary motive of all human behavior: the pleasure principle. We meet realities (within or without) that we like: they cause a pleasant feeling. We also meet other realities that we do not like: they are disagreeable.

Against this background, we establish three types of relationships. In the first, with pleasurable realities, desire, attachment, or appropriation is spontaneously born, depending on the situation. In other words, whatever causes pleasure is thought to be *good*; we appropriate it emotionally and establish a possessive tie to it.

Second, when the *good* that we already possess, or intend to own, is threatened (by the danger of losing it), then fear is born, we are uneasy; that is, a substantial amount of defensive energy is released in order to retain the pleasurable reality that seems to be escaping our grasp.

Third, we resist other realities, on any level, that cause not pleasure but pain; that is to say, an emotional discharge is let loose and sets out to attack and destroy these realities.

Accordingly, we have three types of relationships: possessive attachment, resistance, and fear. The three are intimately conditioned relationships.

Our "enemies"

Everything that we resist becomes an "enemy," as does everything we fear, because fear is a certain form of resistance.

We fear and resist a variety of enemies; for example, sickness, failure, loss of prestige... and included in this are those persons who take part in these "enemies." As a consequence, we may find ourselves always gloomy, fearful, suspicious, aggressive... We feel surrounded by enemies because everything we resist has been labelled "enemy." Basically, this situation means that the individual is full of attachments and possessions. Now then, in order to enter deeply into God's presence, we have to be poor and pure.

Emotional resistance, by its very nature, has as its end the elimination of these "enemies," once the emotion has been acknowledged. There are realities that, when resisted strategically, are partially or totally neutralized; for example, sickness or ignorance.

Nevertheless, the majority of things that we do not like — and so resist — do not have a solution; by their nature, they are indestructible. It is what, in common language, we call an *impossibility*, or *fact of life*, against which we can do nothing.

If some evils have solutions and others do not, two paths lie before us: that of folly and that of wisdom.

It is foolish to mentally resist realities that, by their nature, are unalterable. With a clear head, we see that a great many of those things that disgust, sadden, or shame us have absolutely no solution whatsoever, or the solution is not within our reach. Why fight it? No one can do anything now so that what happened before might not have occurred at all.

Wisdom consists in discerning what one can change from what one cannot change, putting into action the steps necessary for changing whatever can be changed, and when confronted with insurmountable barriers, surrendering oneself, in faith and peace, into the hands of the Lord.

Experience of freely given love

The experience of God has various facets. One is the experience of the love of the Father. In this case, the person feels unexpectedly flooded by an unmistakable paternal, sweet, and tender Presence. It is a deeply liberating impression in which we sense an irresistible impulse to reach out and relate to others as the Father has related to us. It seems to me that this experience is always a gift, especially when it comes clothed in certain characteristics, such as surprise, disproportion, vigor, and liberating strength; that is, when it is not the result of a slow and ongoing acquisition, but the result of a surprising interruption.

There is the experience of contemplative intimacy, which also has specific characteristics and is frequently accompanied by great emotion.

There is also the experience of freely given love, which we are going to treat here. I say freely given, not emotional. No one likes to fail or fall from the pedestal of his popularity. No one likes the feeling of being forsaken, of being the subject of rumors or the victim of misunderstanding.

But these and other eventualities may be accepted with peace and a sense of unbounded love, like someone who surrenders into the hands of the Father as a painful yet pleasing sacrifice...

It is a pure love because there is no return of tangible satisfaction. Furthermore, it is a pure love because it is the product of blind faith. Beyond the visible signs of injustice, we look for the will of the Father, who allows this test.

The liberating purification we are proposing here is not, then, a psychic therapy but a religious experience of the highest caliber.

In the deepest regions of each person, the following occurs: confronted by any injustice or aggravation, many different flames are ignited — the desire for revenge, aversion, antipathy, not only for the thing itself but above all for the person who caused the particular situation.

There are also more painful situations in life, in which others are not to blame; for example, an accident, a physical deformity, a failure in one's own past... in general, all of the *facts of life*. The normal human reaction against such things, we repeat, is some form of violence: a feeling of powerlessness and fury at the same time; shame and rage against oneself; frustration; sadness... in a word, resistance.

Faced by such a negative thing, instead of violence, we can adopt an attitude of peace, if we opt for the way of offering. In the presence of a painful and inevitable situation, we feel at one with the Father, freely loved by Him; a feeling arises somewhere between thankfulness and admiration for that Father of love; interior violence is calmed; the child takes the painful situation in hand; we deliver it and ourselves to the will of the Father; and resistance is transformed into a desire of pure love, into an offering. This oblation does not produce emotion but peace. This is the experience of freely given love.

In a spirit of faith

Now, what do our sorrows have to do with the Father? Why involve the Lord in our pettiness or injustice? The attitude of surrender depends on whether or not the facts of life are seen in the perspective of faith. Peace depends on this. Let me explain.

God the Father organized life and the world around a system of normative laws. The development of the universe was based on the laws of space and He made human conduct subject to the law of freedom. Normally, the Father respects the cosmic and human structures as He designed them, and so they follow their natural course, surviving despite disaster and injustice.

Nevertheless, speaking in absolute terms, nothing is impossible for God. The Father, metaphysically speaking, *could* interfere in the laws of the world, scattering what He had previously gathered and interfering in human freedom so as to avoid this accident or that rumor. But, I repeat, the Father respects His own work — creation — and allows the misfortunes of His children, although He does not like it.

Now then, if God, being able to avoid all evil, does not avoid it, it is a sign that He allows it. And so, we can never say that a slander has been deliberately caused or desired by the Father; rather, we say that He allows it. When we speak of the will of God, we mean that we are involved in the orbit of faith in which things and facts are seen at their roots, beneath all appearances.

Yes, the last link of the chain is held by the Father's hand. The last thing that happened to me was the most bitter. So many sleepless nights! I know that resentment, by "profession," is bound to destroy me. The thing is that it almost finished me off. But ever since last night, everything has changed. I let go of the resentment, relaying my misfortune to my Father. He held the last link; He permitted it all. I remained. I remained silent. The flames were put out. I took the incident in my hands. I placed it with love in His blessed hands, saying, "Because You have permitted it, I agree to everything, my Father. Your will be done." An ineffable peace, like the peace at the dawn of the world, invaded my whole being. No one would have believed it. I felt like the happiest person in the world.

Hidden in the golden coffer of faith, we carry the magic wand of surrender. At its touch, failures cease to be failures, death ceases to be death, misunderstanding becomes understanding. Everything it touches, it transforms into peace.

Surrender

This process of purification is called *surrender*.

This word and its meaning are couched in ambiguities. Wherever this word is spoken, it unleashes a wide range of mistaken impressions among those who hear it: to some, it speaks of passivity; to others, it suggests resignation. Resignation was never Christian but Stoic; as a result, a resigned attitude is close to pagan fatalism. What is specifically evangelical is surrender.

In every act of surrender there is a *yes* and a *no. No* to that which I wanted or had wanted — revenge against those who had a part in this mess, shame for being myself, resentment because everything turns out badly for me, or because I wish it had never happened. *Yes* to that which You, in reality, wanted or permitted, O Father.

If we surrender into the Father's hands, peacefully accepting those realities we cannot alter, anxiety dies and the peacefulness of a calm afternoon is born.

Human wisdom is reduced to an extremely simple question: Can I change what I don't like? If there is anything left to do, why suffer? If the opposite is true, if there is nothing left to do, why worry? As the ancient proverb says, If you have a remedy, why complain? If you do not have a remedy, why complain?

Impossibility

Relentless laws surround our lives like rings of fire: the law of uncertainty, the law of transitoriness, the law of failure, the law of mediocrity, the law of solitude, the law of death.

Who has been given the opportunity to choose life? Was existence offered to me, or was it imposed on me? Who chooses his ancestors? Does everyone like his parents or the socioeconomic condition of the home in which he was born? Who, before embarking upon life, has chosen his sex, temperament, physique, moral tendencies, intellectual capabilities? Who arranged his own genetic code?

This is the source of much frustration, resentment and violence. What can we do in the face of such an absolute barrier, such a *limited situation*?

Ultimately, human beings are radically incapable of stopping or changing reality as it appears before their eyes. We are essentially limited. Dreams of omnipotence are shadows of stupidity and leftovers from childhood. Wisdom consists in having a proportionate and objective appreciation of the world within, and of the world outside: of *all* reality.

After measuring the world (within and without) exactly, we ought to accept it as it is, peacefully accepting the fact that we are limited, bounded on all sides by absolutes.

We ought to place ourselves in the realm of faith and peacefully accept the universal mystery of life; peacefully accept the fact that we are going to obtain few results from a great deal of effort; accept with surrender the fact that the ascent to God is slow and difficult; peacefully accept the fact of sin (that I do what I do not want to do, and I do not do what I would like to do); and accept with surrender the reality of human insignificance. We ought to surrender to the fact that our ideals are so high but reality is so small, surrender to the fact that we are so small and powerless. Our Father, into Your hands, I surrender myself.

Another source of frustration is the irreversibility of time. This is perhaps the most absolute of our boundaries. Everything that happened before this moment is irreversibly anchored in the web of time, transformed into something essentially immovable. These are *accomplished facts.*

There are those who are ashamed, perplexed, angered by thousands of memories from their past, and they spend day and night banging their heads against the wall.

There are those who constantly look back on their lives to try to remember all of their successes or the events that have caused them much shame and anger. Why cry over spilled milk? Why waste energy on accomplished successes or on things we cannot change even if we want to?

It is necessary to return, above all, to basics. It was the Father who permitted everything. Everything is possible for Him; He could have avoided everything; if certain things took place, it was because He allowed it. Why did He allow it? Why question that for which there is no answer? And, although it is an impossible hypothesis, if we could obtain a satisfactory answer to this question, I would rather give the homage of my silence to my God and Father.

I only know one thing: He knows everything and we know nothing. I also know that He loves me a great deal and that whatever He allows is in my best interest. So, I close my mouth and accept, silently and in peace, each and every incident that, at the time, caused me so much suffering. Your will be done. My Father, into Your hands I surrender myself.

We need to heal the wounds. We are the sowers of peace and hope in the world. If we do not heal the wounds one by one, very soon we will be breathing through them, and through the wounds, only resentment is breathed.

Anyone who relives painful memories is like the one who takes a burning coal in his hands. The person who feeds the resentment he feels toward another is like the one who stirs the flames of a fever. Who is burned? Who suffers more: the one who hates or the one who is hated? The one who envies or the one envied? Just like a boomerang, what I feel against another comes back and destroys me. How much wasted energy!

Life has been given to us to be happy and to make others happy. We will make others happy to the degree that we ourselves are happy. The Father has placed us in a garden. We are the ones who have changed that garden into a valley of tears through our lack of faith, love, and wisdom.

A way out

There are those who say, Don't bring God into any of these conflicts. He has nothing to do with them. They are physical laws following their natural development, a normal bridge between frustration and violence. They are sociopolitical "givens," irreversible biopsychological laws. There is no way out.

I will never tire of repeating: the only liberating and consoling way out that we will find in this world is faith. The only window of transcendence open to us, when all else is closed, is the window of faith. The only thing capable of consoling us, giving us peace, and alleviating our suffering when our mortality dawns on us is the vision of faith. This is the faith that tells us that, beyond all phenomena and appearances, there is the Hand that organizes, coordinates, allows, and orders everything that happens in the world.

Life seen from this perspective will never let blind fate dominate our destinies. I know that beyond all first-level explanations, misfortune has been willed or allowed by the Father. I then close my mouth; I kiss His hand; I remain silent; I accept everything with love; and a profound peace is mine.

What do we know

There are others who say, How can this be? If He is powerful and truly is a Father, how can He consent to His children being tossed about by the winds of misfortune?

Those who talk like this are ignorant. They are ignorant because they are superficial. They are superficial because they see, analyze, and play with facts and reality on a surface level. We do not know anything; that is why we open our mouths in protest or burst out with foolish words. We are myopic in that we stand with our noses to the wall without the least bit of perspective, and the wall is called time. We do not give ourselves enough experience or the perspective of time so that we may ponder reality in true perspective and in right proportion. By being ignorant, we are insolent.

Do we know what will happen to us in the next three days or in the next three years? What do we know of the deepest caverns of the world of faith: for example, of the transhistoric destiny that many follow, giving life to the body of the Church, beyond their own biological existence?

There are those marked by God for a messianic future, destined to participate in the redemption of Christ, to redeem others together with Him; they were born to suffer for others and to die in the place of many. Is life not full of enigmas that are deciphered only by the light of faith? We must always remember this: what is essential is invisible. And if we live looking only at the superficial and visible, we will know nothing of the essential.

Faced by an unknown world with so many contingencies, it is better to stop and remain silent, surrendered into the hands of the Father, accepting with gratitude our personal condition and the mystery of life. I have known many in whom sickness suddenly appeared and remained until death, which ended up being the greatest blessing of their lives.

I am sure of this: if we had the perspective of eternity

that the Father has, all of the adversities that we face every day would be considered as special kindnesses from the Father to us, His children, in order to free, heal, awaken, purify...

Faced with the future

Surrender lives in two tenses: the past and the future.

With respect to the *past*, surrender takes the form and name of reconciliation. Those who want to ascend to the highest reaches of God's interior need first to practice, often and for a long time, a general purification: putting away anxiety, softening the tensions, accepting everything within the closed boundaries of life. In order to facilitate this purification, I have put together some practical exercises below.

With respect to the *future*, surrender might take the name of *wisdom*, according to which — we repeat once more — everything that I am going to encounter from this moment until the end of my life can be summed up in the simplicity of the same questions: is there anything left to do? Does it depend on me? In that case, get to work! Is it all accomplished? Are all avenues closed to me? Then, into Your hands I surrender myself, my Father.

* * *

Here, we are going to imagine that there are possibilities open to us. The following reflections are made with this in mind.

In the course of my life from now until the grave, wisdom suggests that I discern between effort and results.

The stage called effort is what we do now: we organize the battlefront; we say that God does not take part in this affair; it is not the hour of surrender but one of action. We act as if everything depended on us; we do not overlook details and we do not waste energy...

And then, what happens? Although the effort depends on us, the *result* does not depend on us, but rather on a complex combination of causes, such as, our emotional state, insufficient preparation, unfavorable circumstances, overlooked details, and, above all, the reactions of others to my action.

But, in the light of faith, we know that everything, ultimately, depends on the Father, as has already been explained. Here, a practical conclusion neatly emerges: if effort depends on us and the result does not depend on us, then we are responsible for the effort and not for the result. In other words, when it is time for effort, we go to battle; and in the hour of the result, we surrender into the Father's hands.

In our plans, we try for the maximum result, one hundred percent. That is legitimate, and the way it should be. However, once the struggle is over, we find ourselves with very different and often discouraging results. Sometimes we attain seventy percent of what we attempted; other times, forty or fifty percent. From one hundred on down, the law of failure takes over. Better yet, the negative result becomes "failure" the more we resist it. The lower the result, the more we are ashamed of ourselves, and so it is transformed into a greater failure. This foolishness does not exist for those who practice surrender.

Once we have done everything possible and have finished the battle, we cannot go back. Wisdom tells us that it is insane to spend night after night ashamed of negative results. At the heart of the matter lies the fact that we are not wise: we do not open our eyes and we resist accepting ourselves as we are.

People often have an inflated image of themselves: they feel a burning desire to have the results of their actions correspond to the elevated image they hold of themselves. And, because this is not generally achieved, they end up frustrated and resentful. They are on the brink of insanity, within the mist of hallucination.

And so, a great deal of energy is uselessly spent. Complexes arise. People become insecure. If future projects are presented to them, they reject them because of their past "failure." Those who might give ninety percent in their life only give twenty. Because of this, they feel unfulfilled. Frustration turns to violence against themselves. So, (like a snake with a thousand rings), a chain of evils is stretched over their lives.

In whatever activity or profession — the education of children, formation of youth, profession, apostolic work — we ought to give our utmost. Now then, if the results do not correspond to the energy spent, we should not destroy the energy by humiliating ourselves; instead, we ought to wisely accept reality as it is and, in faith, place ourselves in the hands of the Father.

High-speed path

Let us summarize these ideas.

To surrender ourselves is to renounce ourselves, freeing ourselves in order to entrust everything, unreservedly, to the One who loves us.

Surrender is the surest road because it is extraordinarily simple. It is also universal in that all possible situations in life are included here. There is no danger of illusion because, with this vision, reality is contemplated purely and nakedly, with objectivity and wisdom. Where there is wisdom, there are no illusions.

Surrender causes pure faith and pure love to live in high gear. Pure faith because by crossing the forest of appearances one discovers a reality that is invisible, basic, and lasting. Pure love because one takes the painful and wounding blows peacefully.

Surrender causes one to live permanently in a spirit of prayer, because in every moment of our lives we are presented with little troubles, frustrations, deceptions, heat, cold, pain, impossible dreams... and all of this is referred to the loving Father by the child who is loved. There is no more effective aspirin for the pains of life than surrender.

On this path, we die with Jesus in order to live with the Father. Jesus died to "what I want" in Gethsemane to accept "what You want." The one who surrenders dies to his own will, which manifests itself in resistance. The one who surrenders quiets the living voices of resentment, is supported in the hands of the Father, remains in peace and lives there, free and happy. We become like the white host, so poor, so free, so obedient that, before the words of consecration, it lets itself be converted into the Body of Christ. We come to be like those drops of water that surrender without resistance, losing themselves in the wine of the chalice.

Surrender adds to life because complexes disappear, security is born, we struggle without anxiety, we are not worried about the results (which depend solely on the Father) and all human potential is exercised to the fullest. In the end, death is softened.

Those who surrender live in the arms of the Father. These arms can carry us anywhere, perhaps to the bottom of the abyss or to the middle of a rushing river. The rushing river might be called death. It does not matter. We cross this torrent too, carried in powerful and loving arms. Death may be the hardest blow of them all. This blow, too, will be cushioned, as if we were to fall into a sea of white linen.

Surrender is the fastest and surest road toward all liberation.

PRACTICAL EXERCISES OF SURRENDER

Acceptance of family

Generally, children demand too much of their parents, as if the parents had an obligation to be perfect. This idea (prejudice) is born in infancy, when the child is easily mystified by the parents.

The memory of certain events causes a feeling of aversion in some children toward their parents. Often these parents lack beauty, intelligence, economic success, a creative personality... All of this, at times, leads to a feeling, almost a complex, of shame in that the children are ashamed to have their friends meet their parents.

In other cases, the parents have personality defects leading to unbalanced behavior: all of which causes the child to harbor a secret indignation that makes it difficult to forgive those defects.

There are also those who feel resentment for the place in which they were born and grew up, a very poor home, very insignificant.

These resentments cause many people to carry, throughout their lives, an underground river, latent but very real, of general frustrations. Because of this, nothing makes them happy and they do not know why. This is the explanation: that hidden river comes to the surface, without their realizing it, in forms of dissatisfaction and in various types of violence.

Many of us, for our encounter with God, first need to reconcile ourselves with our roots.

* * *

Place yourself in the presence of God. Let yourself be penetrated by the Spirit of the Lord. Slowly let yourself become calm and peaceful.

Make your parents mentally present. Especially bring to mind those incidents or features of their personality that cause you embarrassment. If your parents have already died, bring them to mind as if they were alive.

Repeat the words of this prayer many times until you experience peace and a complete reconciliation:

My Father, I surrender myself to You! In this moment, I accept my parents with peace and love, with their defects and limitations. If I have felt a hidden embarrassment toward them, I wish now to be completely reconciled.

Holy Father, before You I want to accept them as they are. In Your presence and from Your hands, I now receive them, I embrace them, and I love them with gratitude and tenderness.

I accept them deeply and totally in the mystery of Your will, because You made them the source of my existence. Thank You for the gift of my parents. Your will be done. I surrender myself to You. Amen.

Acceptance of the body

Our enemies begin on the surface. There are those who make destruction into a profession in their lives. They have an excessive amount of energy, originating in the permanent rejection of themselves — beginning with their physical makeup — and they need to let go of this energy.

They feed an unspoken "animosity" toward their own color, height, eyes, hair, teeth, weight, and other aspects of their anatomy. They are ashamed of who they are. They experience an overall insecurity. They attribute the failure of their lives to the lack of certain physical characteristics.

This hatred toward themselves is ridiculous because it is artificial. They make themselves their own victims and executioners, which is a most insane attitude. We must awake from this craziness and remember the words of Jesus: Who, by worrying, can add an inch to his height?

This observation must be applied to the whole sphere of organic nature. In this sphere, we can change little or nothing at all. So, why resist it?

For a general reconciliation with ourselves, many of us need to make a profound and repeated act of acceptance of our body, with a sense of gratitude for it.

* * *

Place yourself in the presence of the Lord. Remain completely calm. Bring to mind and focus your attention on each aspect of your body to which you are an "enemy."

While saying the following prayer, *feel tenderness* for each rejected part of your body, one by one, slowly and carefully. *Feel* them as integral parts of your personal identity.

Repeat the prayer until you feel gratitude and joy for having the good fortune to be alive, thanks to that body.

My Father: I surrender myself to You! I have often felt shame for this body of mine. I fed an artificial resistance with my useless wars against it. It was crazy. After all, I rejected one of Your gifts. Forgive my insensitivity and ingratitude.

In this moment, I want to be reconciled to myself, to this body. From now on, I will never feel sorry for being the way I am.

I now accept, with thankfulness and love, this body which is part of my personality. One by one, I love and accept each part of my body... Your will be done. I surrender myself to You. Amen.

Acceptance of sickness, old age, and death

There are three black chargers that drag human beings down the path to the bottom of the abyss: sickness, old age, and death.

Just as the day becomes night, so everything that has a beginning is destined to have an end. Everything that is born dies, normally passing through the corridor of sickness or old age.

Once in the world, we lift our heads, open our eyes, and find ourselves against a backdrop that will never disappear: *death*. We are left with the feeling of being limited, and destined to die. This is where anxiety is born. The only way of overcoming this anxiety is to abandon all resistance, accepting this unbreakable boundary, delivering ourselves into the hands of the Father, who organized everything in this way.

We only live once. We would like to make this unique journey with a sense of well-being and perfect health. However, *sickness* lies in ambush for everyone, like shadows on every corner, waiting their turn: one disappears and another appears, this one goes away and another comes on the scene, in an unending cycle of suffering.

We might be called *biological parables*: we are born; we climb the blue sky up to its zenith; we begin to decline, descending lower and lower before disappearing completely.

Old age is the waiting room of death. In itself, death is empty and without substance. It is in old age that this emptiness is filled with fantasies and fears.

It is in old age that we slowly say good-bye to everything. Better yet, all riches are slowly denied to the aged: strength, beauty, health, various abilities, until they are transformed into useless beings, devoid of all richness.

Faced with such limitations, we ought frequently and deeply exercise the act of surrender, accepting the painful mystery of life with its biological curve. Accepted limitations launch us into the arms of the Infinite; accepted temporality launches us into the arms of the Eternal. Anxiety is exchanged for peace.

* * *

Take a reclining position. Practice some form of relaxation. Place yourself in the presence of the Lord in faith.

Center your attention on your actual illness, or on the ones that worry you or that you fear the most. Focus your attention on each one; accept each of the pains one by one, slowly, in the mystery of the will of the Father, until the fears disappear and you begin to experience complete peace.

Imagine the final days of your life, when you will be cast aside and useless. While praying the following prayer, try to experience sacrificial love in this sense: because the Father has organized life in this way, accept the inevitable, the painful mystery of the biological curve, the incapacity for anything, the hope of death – and rest in the love of the Father.

Do the same with death. Imagine that you are on the eve of your departure. Like Jesus, surrender yourself once again. Do not resist. Let yourself be carried. Accept the will of the Father who, in His wisdom, organized life in this way. Imagine that death is like a river that you cross, carried in the arms of your Father.

My Father, I surrender myself to You! These limitations make me sad and I feel like protesting. But, no. Because I love You, I close my mouth, I remain silent, I peacefully accept the painful mystery of life that is the mystery of Your will. My God, I will fight with every means to be healthy; but if the results are negative, I will resist no more. From now on, I surrender myself to You. I accept everything. I am ready for anything. One by one, I lovingly accept, my God, the pains that now afflict me.

I accept peacefully the days of my old age, the complete limitations and inabilities. I accept the fact that life is this way because You made it so. Your will be done.

My Father! What is written in Your book about my end? A slow agonizing death? Give me the strength not to resist, and to pronounce my "Your will be done." What is written? A sudden or violent death? I close my mouth to tell You with my silence: if that is written, if that is what will happen, fine! Your will be done. I accept. I am ready for anything.

Into Your hands I commend my life and my death. Amen.

Acceptance of our personality

Suddenly we awake in the world and find ourselves with everything, almost everything, predetermined. We have little to choose. We must enter the race with the mount we have been assigned. Some have been given a docile and speedy charger; others, a slow horse; others, a wild stallion. We must all ride into the ring on these.

The source of the most profound frustrations is our own personal conditioning. The greatest disgrace is to feel shame for who we are. The greatest sadness is to feel sad for being who we are without being able to change it.

Too many people suffer horribly and do not know why. And although an analyst may help them to discover the roots of their dilemma, they may get no further because they may still be left with the bright red wounds, without the benefit of healing therapy.

There are those who want to demonstrate a high intellectual ability; instead, they discover their limitations and must give up their dreams of success.

There are others who would like their conduct to correspond to their ideals; but, they realize that their impulses do not obey their desires.

Some people want to have happy temperaments and, often, deep depressions overpower them; nothing makes them happy, everything makes them sad. There are those who want to be well-balanced and, yet, frequently let themselves be carried away by neurotic excesses.

Others are envious and they suffer. Some are resentful. Some are shy and suffer from fear and the desire to escape.

Because we only live once, carrying such a heavy load on our shoulders is a sad thing. Just as we take off a suit and put on another, why can we not do the same with *this* apparel?

If we wish to arrive at close intimacy with the Lord, we need to exercise surrender to the point of a profound reconciliation with every aspect of our personality.

* * *

Take a comfortable position. Practice some exercises of relaxation. Let yourself be enveloped in the presence of the Lord.

With calm introspection, become conscious of those aspects of your personality that hurt you the most because they are contradictory or negative. One by one, accept the things that you do not like and those things you would like to change but cannot.

Imagine that you are carrying the cross of your personality. Imagine that in the "way of the cross" of your life, Jesus, like Simon, offers His shoulder to help you carry the cross of your personality.

Repeat the following prayer, applying it to each aspect of your temperament. Forgive yourself over and over again. Place all of the aspects of your personality, one by one, like an offering of love, into the hands of the Father, until you experience complete reconciliation.

My Father! I surrender myself to You! Into Your hands I place what little I am. I accept and love this small light of my intelligence. In Your will I accept and love the mystery of my limitations. I do not wish to feel any more sadness because of my insignificance. I give You thanks for having made me able to think what I think. Thank You for my memory.

Into Your hands I place what little I am. For many years

I stored up anger and frustration against who I am. I felt such melancholy and depression, such fright and pride! My God, I did not choose any of this. A heavy cross was placed on my shoulders. I do not like this way of living. But I cannot divest myself of this as if it were a piece of clothing. My God, I do not want any more interior battles; I want peace and reconciliation.

In Your love, I accept and love this strange and contradictory personality. Your will be done. In Your love, I accept and love these aspects of myself that I do not like, one by one, slowly... Jesus, I know that for me You are the good Cyrenean who helps me carry my cross. Thank You for the help. Thank You for my soul. Thank you for my eternal destiny. My Father, I surrender myself to You! Amen.

Acceptance of others

The same walls that separate one person from another are also walls that come between ourselves and God. It is foolish to dream of attaining deep intimacy with the Lord when we are at war with one another.

When God looks at the human race, the primary area in which we are challenged is that of community, with the surprising question: where is your brother or sister?

Communal harmony is woven with a pattern of demands, like respect, communication, dialogue, protection, acceptance... But there is a primary and necessary condition: to forgive. We need peace. Only in peace does the encounter with God take place. And only by means of forgiveness does peace come about.

When we speak of *accepting others,* we understand it exclusively in the sense of *forgiving.* To forgive is to let go of resentment toward another. With the act of surrender, resistance is placed in the hands of the Father — resistance to the other and resistance to myself — in a unique act of adoration, in which and by which we are *one.*

There is what is known as *intentional* forgiveness. It is a willful forgiveness because we *want* to forgive. We want to wrench from the heart all hostility and not feel any hard feelings. We sincerely forgive but this includes those who say: I forgive but I do not forget. This forgiveness is not enough to heal the wounds.

There is also *emotional* forgiveness. This does not depend on the will because the will does not have control over the emotions. Emotional forgiveness heals the wound.

There are three ways of granting emotional forgiveness. The first is given in a state of *prayer with Jesus*.

Take a prayerful position. Step by step, calm yourself. Center yourself. Evoke, through faith, the presence of Jesus. When you have entered into full intimacy with Him, bring to mind the memory of your "enemy" brother or sister. Slowly, trying to feel each word, say this prayer:

Jesus, come within me, to the deepest roots of my being. Jesus, take possession of me. Calm this sea of hostile emotions. Jesus, accept my heart with all of its hostilities. Take it and substitute Your own for mine.

Jesus, I want to feel now what You feel for that person. Forgive that individual within me. Forgive him in me, through me. Yes, Jesus, I want to "feel" the same sentiments You have for that person. I want to forgive, Jesus, as You forgive. Right now, I want to "be" You. I want to forgive that person as You would. I want to forgive...

Imagine how darkness disappears in the presence of any light. Now, *feel* the anger fade in the presence of Jesus. Feel the peace, like fresh air, entering and filling your soul. Imagine yourself, in this moment, approaching your "enemy" to embrace him or her.

When the wound is healed and does not open up again, it is a sign that emotional forgiveness has been a gift from the Spirit, an extraordinary and infused grace. Do not forget that every wound needs many treatments in order to be healed completely.

The second path of emotional forgiveness is *understanding*.

If we could understand, we could not fail to forgive.

Think of your "enemy." When your attention is focused on him or her, make the following reflections.

Except for extraordinary cases, no one in this world acts with evil intentions, no one is evil. If others offend me, who knows what is happening with them? Who knows but maybe they are going through a serious crisis? What seems to be pride may really be shyness. Their attitude toward me appears to be stubbornness, but it may be something else: the need for self-affirmation. Their behavior appears aggressive to me; in reality they shout empty threats in order to assure themselves.

If I suffer because of their behavior, they suffer even more. They would like to be at peace with the whole world, and yet they are always in conflict with it. They did not choose this way of life.

After all this, can our "enemy" be that much to blame? Does it make sense to be irritated by a behavior they did not choose? They do not deserve rejection but, rather, understanding. By all accounts, is it not I who am mistaken and unjust in my attitude, and not the other? Don't we always ask for the Father's mercy?

If we knew how to understand this, the sun of anger would set, and peace, like a blessed shade, would enter our innermost rooms.

* * *

The third way of forgiveness is *detachment*.

This is an act of mental effort to detach and divert our attention.

Ill feeling is a river that runs between my attention and

111

my "enemy." On my part, it is an intentional and emotional resistance launched against the other.

Forgiveness then, consists of interrupting or detaching this chain of aggressive attention, remaining intentionally detached from the other, in peace.

This manner of forgiveness can be practiced anywhere and anytime. Do not fail to be relaxed.

When you become aware that you are overpowered by the memory of some "enemy," make an act of mental control and detach your attention; simply cut this link of attention. Empty yourself inside, suspending for a moment all thought. Then begin to think about something else and mentally fly in some other direction.

Take every opportunity to practice this exercise of forgiveness. Soon you will feel that you are no longer bothered by the memory of that person.

Acceptance of our own past

The archives of life! We can only say that history is a battlefield covered with dead leaves.

Many people, nevertheless, live tormented lives because they are always looking back, focused precisely on their red, open wounds. The sad fact is that many people relive dead pages, reopen old scars that they never allow to heal completely. They live a sad life because they only remember sad events. Their own museum is the most abundant source of resentment.

As we have already explained, time does not go backwards, even for an instant. The past is comprised of accomplished facts that our tears and anger will never alter.

We need to practice this purification of memory often and deeply: to accept, once and for all, the painful history that the Father has allowed to take place.

Take a reclining position. Place yourself in the presence of the Lord and enter into a state of intimacy with the Father.

112

Slowly take inventory, diving into the pages of your own history. One by one, come to accept your painful memories in the love of the Father, with an "I surrender to You."

Begin with the time of your childhood. Climb through your life: through childhood, adolescence, adulthood... Those persons who so negatively influenced you. That adolescent crisis. That event, so small in itself, that has left its mark on you. The first declared enemy. The first failure. The first mistake, so regretted afterwards. That person who never understood you, or at least did not appreciate you.

That emotional crisis that shook the plans you had made for your life. This failure and that one. That miscalculation in the family budget. Those projects that fell through, and we know whose fault *that* was. The arbitrary and unjust attitude of that group.

That sinful situation, which even today does not leave you in peace. Those ideals that were not realized...

Take possession of all of it, in faith, and the peace of surrender will stretch over the battlefield.

Lord of history, Master of the future and of the past, I surrender to You. For You, nothing is impossible. You allowed everything to happen as it did. Your will be done. Because You love me and I love You, I extend my silent homage over the pages of my past.

Now I take possession, in the mystery of Your will, of all of the events whose memory disturbs me. One by one, like red roses of love, I want to place these painful events in Your hands, from childhood up to this present moment.

At Your feet I also leave the heavy load of my sins. Send your angel to carry them and bury them in the depths of the sea. May I never remember them.

I peacefully accept the fact of wanting to be humble and not being able. I accept the fact of not being as pure as I would like to be. I accept in peace the fact of wanting to please everyone and being incapable of it. I accept in peace the fact that the path to sanctity is slow and difficult.

Accept, O Father, the offering of my heart. Amen.

Prayer of Surrender

Father,
I put myself in Your hands.
Whatever may be,
I give You thanks.
    I am ready for anything,
    I accept everything,
    such that Your will be accomplished in me
    and in all Your creatures.
    I want nothing more, Father.
I commit to You my soul,
I give it to You
With all the love I have.
Because I love You
and need to give myself to You,
to place myself in Your hands,
without limitations,
without measure,
with infinite confidence,
because You are my Father.

(Charles de Foucauld)

2. INTERIOR SILENCE

Once we have met people in prayer, and as soon as we have made the introspective dive into our own interior waters, we will realize that the primary obstacle to submersion in the sea of God is superficiality: that is, nervousness, agitation, and general distraction.

To be true worshippers in spirit and truth, we need, as a necessary condition, control, calm, and interior silence.

On top of the Mount, Jesus said that to adore and worship the living God, loud voices or many words were not necessary but rather inner silence, withdrawing into the most secret corner, isolating ourselves from all noise, establishing "contact" with the Father, and then, simply, "being" with Him (Mt 6:6).

If prayer is an encounter, and that encounter is a meeting of two persons, for this meeting to take place — to truly be — it is indispensable that the two individuals first "reach out" and project themselves onto a point in a particular moment of time.

Nevertheless, the reaching out of an individual for his or her encounter with God is not an "exit" but, paradoxically, an entrance, an inward movement in order to reach out to the One that is "*interior intimo meo*," more interior than my own intimacy. Then and "there" will the encounter take place.

We must begin by calming the waves, silencing the noise, being master and not slave, being "lord" of our interior life, controlling all movement, without allowing memories and distractions to toss us from side to side. This is the "private room" we need to "enter" for the true encounter with the Lord to take place.

Jesus adds: "Shut yourself in" (Mt 6:6). To close doors and windows made of wood is easy, but here, we are dealing with windows that are much more subtle, over which we have no control.

We have no difficulty disengaging ourselves from the external world. We need only climb a hill, go into the woods, or enter a solitary chapel. The difficult thing, inescapable and necessary, is something else: to detach ourselves from (and by detaching ourselves, dominating) the compact and turbulent horde of memories, distractions, worries, and preoccupations that assail and destroy interior unity and silence.

The spiritual masters constantly tell us of the almost invincible difficulties that accompanied them for many years before achieving that "silent music," the indispensable climate for the "meal that is enjoyed and loved."

Scattered and distracted

The problem above all problems for those who wish to enter into intimacy with God is this: interior distraction. If we can cross this true Rubicon without drowning, we will find ourselves already within the sacred precincts of prayer.

What is *interior distraction*?

We go through life with an enormous burden of hopes and fears. We feel shackled by such a weight. Worries overpower us. Anxieties disturb us. Frustrations make us bitter. There are ambitious projects ahead that disturb our peace. We carry feelings and resentments that are literally rooted in the soul. Now, this great burden of life ends up by slowly destroying and disintegrating our inner unity.

We go to pray, and our head is a veritable insane asylum. God is suffocated in the midst of an infernal clamor of worries, anxieties, memories, and plans. We ought to be *one*, as God is One, so the encounter is a meeting of two *unities*. But, at the time, we see ourselves as an incoherent mass of "pieces" that pull us in one direction and then another: memories here, fears there, desires on this side, and plans on the other. All in all, we are totally divided and, as a consequence, dominated and conquered, unable to be our own *lords*.

Furthermore, each one of us is a complex web of motivations, impulses, and instincts that sink their roots into the irrational subconscious. The conscious is a small light in the darkness, a tiny island in the middle of the ocean.

In the complexity of our world, we (as free consciousness) are buffeted, tossed, and disturbed by an army of motives and emotional impulses that arise from the deepest regions of our personalities, without ever telling us why,

116

how, or from where they come. Saint Paul's description in the Letter to the Romans (7:14-25), exquisitely debated by theologians and psychologists, does not seem at all strange to me.

J.M. Dechanet expresses a similar thought in his book *Christian Yoga*:

> Prayer presupposes a pure thought, a dominion over the mind such that the one who prays tries to withdraw from exterior impressions as well as the surgings of the subconscious, in order to focus it on something, centered on a fixed point, where it establishes contact with the Lord of peace and silence.
>
> By definition, mental activity is something that bustles, that moves across the land of memory and knowledge in order to achieve the association of ideas from where spring induction and deduction. It is a pilgrim that is always on the road, wandering, straying, forgetting the goal, losing itself in the clutches of confused and disordered images. Even at the end of its investigations, the mind continues to be agitated. At the slightest invitation, it returns to the road of the wanderer.

* * *

Distraction has the same characteristics as dispersion, or scattering, and both words have an almost identical meaning.

The human mind, because of its dynamic nature, is in perpetual motion, while we sleep and, above all, while we are awake. The mind, riding on the associations of various images, jumps from memory to memory like a restless butterfly. At times, logic carries us along the links of a rational chain. Other times, no logic exists, either visible or latent; and suddenly we are surprised by the most foolish thoughts.

Other times, the mind goes off in apparently uncontrolled directions; however, a latent or subconscious logic is at work. In any event, the mind dances in perpetual motion, everywhere.

To pray means to retain attention, and to keep it centered and focused on a *Thou*.

The more we practice mental control, the more we directly strengthen the mind's ability to concentrate on God. Distractions, the eternal nightmare of those who pray, will disappear the more we practice, patiently and with perseverance, the exercises that will be discussed later.

"Yahweh is not in the hurricane" (1 Kgs 19:11). I would say, more exactly, God is not encountered in disorder. This disorder may or may not be external; that is not important. Anyone can have a powerful encounter with God in the bustle of an airport or in the noise of the street. But it is interior disorder that puts silence in check.

When we say interior silence, we mean the ability to achieve inner emptiness, with its resulting lordship, in such a way that we are subject and not object, capable of centering all efforts at concentration on the Object, which is God, in complete quiet. An interior disorder is that which impedes the silence.

This difficulty, sometimes an impossibility, of achieving unity and silence carries with it tragic consequences for those who have been called to a higher union with God. They have not been taught or have not had the patience for practicing mental control.

As a consequence, they do not achieve that "silent music" coming from the mystery. They have never arrived at the meeting and integration of the two mysteries, God's and their own. They have never come to experience "how good is the Lord" (Ps 34; 86; 100; 145). And within, they feel a strange frustration that they are not sure how to explain, nor do they want to. But the explanation is this: an insane interior distraction defeats and destroys every good intention and every effort, and they remain on the edge of a powerful experience of God.

And so, they choose different directions: some completely abandon a life with God, with serious repercussions for their emotional stability and for the basic problem of the *meaning* of their lives. Others silence not their consciences but their high aspirations, taking part in a little liturgical or community prayer (like giving a few crumbs to a hungry person). Others throw themselves into frantic activity, shouting to the four winds that "the apostolate is prayer."

I have met people who seem to be allergic to just the word *prayer*: they feel and express a real hatred for it. And they are always ready to throw poisoned darts at it: alienation, escape, sentimentalism, wasted time, childishness, and other such words... I understand them. They have attempted the encounter a thousand times and have always been shipwrecked by the rushing river of interior distraction. They associate the word *prayer* with a long and painful frustration.

EXERCISES FOR ACHIEVING INNER CALM

Here we are, then, trapped in the web of our imagination without being able to control it, concentrate, or pray. What are we to do?

The Christian mystics had high spiritual experiences that they have given to us in the form of theological reflections. But they do not tell us — nor do we know whether they practiced them — of the practical methods for overcoming distraction and obtaining that interior silence, the indispensable condition for realizing a transforming union with God.

They lived in a peaceful society of faith or, perhaps, in hermitages or lonely monasteries, far from the turbulence of the world. We, on the other hand, live in a society harassed by confusion, noise, and speed. If we do not take precautions, not only will our *call* to union with the Lord be frustrated, but we will fail in our most basic and fundamental destiny: to be unity, interiority, person.

I will never tire of repeating: those who feel that God is worth the trouble (and, in the end, *He alone* is worth the trouble and without Him, nothing has meaning), those who seriously desire to take the road that leads to a transforming experience with the Father, will frequently have to practice the following exercises. Furthermore, without these or similar practices, there will normally be no progress in prayer.

Remarks

1. All of the exercises ought to be done slowly and peacefully. I will not tire of repeating: when the fruit of the exercise is not received, it is normally due to a lack of serenity.

2. All of these exercises may be done with the eyes open or closed. If the exercise is done with the eyes open, it is better to have them focused (not rigidly, but in a relaxed fashion) on some fixed point in the distance or nearby. Wherever you look, the important thing is to "look" within.

3. Physical inactivity helps mental inactivity and concentration. It is very important that during every exercise, mental activity be reduced to the minimum.

4. If, in the course of a particular exercise, you begin to feel agitated, which often occurs at the beginning, stop for a moment. Calm yourself for an instant and begin again. If at any time the agitation is very powerful, get up and stop for the day. At all times, avoid interior violence.

5. Keep in mind that, in the beginning, the results will be few. Don't be discouraged. Remember that the first steps in any human activity are difficult. You need patience in order to accept the fact that progress will be slow, and you will need perseverance.

Results will probably be widely varied. There will be days in which you will easily obtain the desired results. Other times, everything will be hard for you. Accept this disparity with peace, and persevere.

6. Almost all of these exercises produce drowsiness when relaxation is achieved. It is best to practice them during the hours you are most awake.

For those who suffer from insomnia, it is best to do any of the first three exercises, especially the first one, upon going to bed. Ten minutes of this exercise will result in the most pleasant sleep.

7. After trying all of the exercises, you may choose to stay with the one or few that are best for you, depending on the benefit received. You may also introduce modifications to any of these, if you see that it will go better for you.

8. After a serious offense, a disturbing incident or a depressing hardship, go to your room. Fifteen minutes of exercise will leave you partly or totally relieved.

In order to forgive, to free yourself from obsessions or depression, use these exercises. In the beginning you will not get any results. Later, you will; above all, you must let yourself be wrapped in the presence of the Father.

9. Some of these exercises place the individual directly in the orbit of a quiet union with God. Others are preparatory exercises for prayer.

We cannot give any clues as to how to combine the preparatory exercises with the prayer itself, as long as the exercise proceeds from preparation to prayer. All of the exercises are experiences of life, and prayer is even more so. Now then, experience is lived in a unique way. Our advice is the following: try the different exercises; see which are most beneficial; see if certain combinations yield better results. Test everything and keep what is good.

Preparation

Every exercise should be preceded by preparation. Sit in a chair or on a couch. Assume a comfortable position. If possible, do not rest your back against anything. Cause the weight of your body to fall along the straightened spinal column. Put your hands on your knees, open, with the palms up and fingers relaxed.

Be calm. Be at peace. Feel at ease. Without taking too long, "become conscious" of the shoulders, neck, arms, hands, stomach, feet... and "feel" them relax.

"Observe" the movement of your lungs. Mentally accompany the rhythm of your breathing. Distinguish between inhaling and exhaling. Breathe deeply but without straining yourself.

Calm yourself. Let yourself go, little by little, from memories, interior impressions, noises and exterior voices. Take possession of yourself. Remain at peace.

This preparation should last about five minutes, and should never be omitted from the beginning of any exercise.

You may, if you want, do the following exercises seated on the floor, on a cushion, with your legs crossed (if this bothers you, keep the legs outstretched), lightly supporting your entire body (including your head) with the wall in such a way that you feel completely relaxed.

They may also be done lying down on the ground or on a carpet (this helps the back), or on a bed, face up, arms extended along the body, without cushion, if possible.

If some muscle or other part of your body bothers you during any one of these exercises, change your position until you find a comfortable one.

Some of these can also be done in a chapel, for instance, when you want to pray and cannot because you are distracted or agitated.

First exercise: interior emptiness

What is attempted in this exercise? Tension is a tightening of nerves, localized in different areas of the body. The mind (the brain) produces them. If we stop the motor (the mind), then those loads of energy disappear and we feel rested and at peace.

This exercise, then, results in two things: relaxation and mental control.

It may be practiced in any of these three ways:

1. Once the preparation has been done, then, very peacefully, stop all mental activity. "Feel" as if your head were empty; "experience" as if there were nothing (no thoughts, images, emotions...) in your entire being. It will help if you softly repeat: *nothing, nothing, nothing...*

Do this for about thirty seconds. Then rest a bit. Then repeat. Do it five times.

After some practice, you will feel that not only the head but your whole body is empty, without nervous currents, without tensions. You will feel relaxed and calm.

2. After the preparation, and the first time you do the exercise, close your eyes and imagine yourself before an immense white screen. Holding this image, keep your mind blank, without thoughts or images for thirty seconds or more. Open your eyes. Rest a bit.

The second time, close your eyes and imagine yourself before a dark screen. Remain at peace. Your mind will remain in darkness, without thinking or imagining anything, for thirty seconds or more. Open your eyes. Rest a while.

The third time, imagine being before a large stone. The stone "feels" heavy, senseless, dead. Mentally, make as if you were this rock; "feel" like it and stay there, without moving, for a half minute or more. Open your eyes. Rest.

The fourth time, imagine being like some great tree; "feel" like that tree, living but without feeling anything. Open your eyes. You will find yourself rested and relaxed.

3. The preparation done, take a clock in your hands. Remain still, gazing at it.

Very calmly, focus your eyes on the tip of the second hand. Follow, with your eyes, the revolutions of the second hand, for a minute, without thinking or imagining anything. Your mind is empty.

Repeat this five times.

If distractions interfere, don't be impatient. Eliminate them and calmly continue.

Calmly, say, Lord, Lord! Remain with your attention centered and focused on the Lord for fifteen seconds. Repeat this a number of times.

With great serenity, in a soft voice, say the word *peace*. And remain for some fifteen seconds in complete interior immobility. You will feel inundated by peace.

* * *

Direct control will escape you many times; your faculties will be intent on recovering their independence; and, through a series of free associations, images will try to disturb the quiet. Don't let this scare you, and don't be impatient.

In this task, in the preparation as in the prayer itself, the results will be highly varied and different. At times, without any effort, after only a few minutes, the soul will find itself in a quiet peace. At other times, a half hour will be spent in a fruitless struggle, without any results. We have to accept this variability with peace.

This first exercise, in any of its variations, has as its goal that the one who practices it comes to "feel" like a stone or piece of wood. This momentary state of the absence of any mental activity brings, as a result, the relaxation of nerves, the disappearance of anxieties, and the perception of inner tranquillity. All of that, I repeat, on condition that we practice the momentary stopping of the mind and break ourselves away from that mass of thoughts, images, and feelings.

Then we begin to experience the feeling of our *reality* within us. We call this *perception of interior unity,* in which the consciousness is made present to itself.

Although this state may not be attained perfectly, if we practice this *mental suspension*, we will sense that our house grows calm, that the relationship with the Lord becomes a far easier activity than had previously been thought. And, without realizing it, we will find ourselves introduced into a profound interrelationship of consciousness to Consciousness, in quiet and recollection.

Second exercise: relaxation

This exercise directly tries to relax and pacify our entire being. Indirectly, mental concentration and self-control are obtained.

We also gain — when it is done well — the elimination of neurological problems and the alleviation of organic pains.

How is it practiced? In the first place, do the preparatory exercises.

Close your eyes, place yourself (your complete attention) "in" the brain, identifying yourself with your cerebral mass. With attention and sensitivity, find the exact point that bothers you or is tense. With a great deal of peace and tenderness, while you are identified with that point, begin to say, mentally or speaking softly, *Calm down, be quiet, be at peace...* repeating these words many times, until what bothers you disappears.

Then, go (with your attention) to your throat, and do the same thing until you are relaxed.

Afterwards, go to your heart. Deliberately identify yourself with that noble muscle as if it were a different "person." It is necessary to treat it with tenderness, because we often mistreat it. Keep yourself immobile and, peacefully and tenderly, "pray" to your heart: *Calm down, beat slowly, quieter...* Repeat these words many times until your heartbeat becomes normal.

The greatest treasures in the world would be these two: control over the mind and the heart. How much unhappiness could be avoided! There would not be as many trips to the doctor, life would be prolonged, and we would live in peace. With patience and perseverance, these treasures can be had.

Next, go to the large area of the lungs and stomach. Remember where fear, anxiety, and anguish are felt: in the pit of the stomach. Remain motionless; find the tensions and bundles of nerves, and calm down with the same words as above.

If at this time you feel some bodily pain, go there and relieve that pain with the above words.

With peace and calm reigning within, take a walk around your body. "Feel" your head and neck, on the outside, and see that they are relaxed. "Feel" that your arms, hands, back, abdomen, legs, and feet are all completely relaxed.

In order to finish, experience deeply the following: *throughout my whole being, a complete calm reigns supreme.*

Third exercise: concentration

What is the purpose of this exercise? Two things: the facility for controlling and directing our attention and, second, unifying our interiority.

Do the preparatory exercises.

Quietly, calmly, with your mental activity reduced to a minimum, sense the rhythm of your breathing. Do not think, don't imagine, do not force the rhythm, simply sense the motion of your lungs for about two minutes. Observe yourself.

Afterwards, even more immobile and calm, remain attentive and sensitive to your whole body, and find your pulse in some part of your body. I repeat: in whatever part of your body. When you have found it (we are going to suppose that it is in the fingertips or somewhere else), stay "there," centered, attentive, motionless, for about two minutes, "listening."

Finally, we come to the highest moment of concentration: *the perception of your personal identity.* How is it accomplished? It is something simple and possessive. Without thinking, without analyzing, simply perceive yourself. You perceive and, simultaneously, are perceived. And you remain intimately with yourself, identified with yourself.

In order to arrive at this perception, which is the peak of concentration, it will help you to say softly, many times: So-and-So (mentally say your name), I am John Doe, I am Jane Doe, I am my consciousness.

Fourth exercise: hearing

What is this all about? Control and concentration.

How is it practiced? Do the preparatory exercises.

Remain motionless, looking at some fixed point; take a word and repeat it slowly, for about five minutes. And when everything has disappeared from your interior, only the word will remain, with its content.

The word could be one of these: *peace, calm, nothing...*

In order to help you in prayer, it could be the phrase: *my God and my All.*

Fifth exercise: seeing

What is the purpose of this exercise? Concentration and unification.

How is it practiced? Do the preparatory exercises.

First, take a picture (for example, of Christ, Mary, or some landscape). In short, some item that has great emotional power for you.

Place the picture in your hands, before your eyes. With great tranquillity and peace, let your gaze travel over the picture for a minute.

Second, for about three minutes, try to "discover" the feelings that the picture evokes in you: intimacy, tenderness, strength, calm...

Third, try to identify yourself with that image, and above all with the "feelings" you have discovered. End the exercise "impregnated" with those "feelings."

INTENSE MOMENTS

To solve the evil of this age — profound anxiety — and in order to insure a life with God, it is not enough to practice, methodically and in an orderly way, the various exercises of pacification. We need far-reaching remedies.

In my opinion, today more than ever before, it is absolutely necessary to alternate our professional or apostolic activity with a total retreat for a certain period of time. This means that we must organize our lives in such a way that there are intense periods of time available for an exclusive relationship with God.

After having given many sessions with various groups of religious men and women, I have come to believe that the *solution* for assuring an elevated life with God is these "intense moments."

At one time we said, "Let us make the Divine Office alive; let this be the food for our life of faith." With the best of intentions, the community tried to make it alive through every possible means available: everything was prepared with great care, there was great variety every day. After a couple of months, monotony returned and variety became routine.

The problem is bringing prayer alive. Vitality does not come from outside but from within. When the heart is empty, the words of the Psalms and the Mass are empty. When the heart is overflowing with God, the words are, too. When this is the case, even when the same psalm is repeated a hundred times, the last time may have more newness than the first.

For example, say, a person lives intimately with God by means of Psalm 30. Later, when this same Psalm is part of the Divine Office, the words are already filled with deep

128

meaning for that person, and prayer becomes a spiritual banquet for him. Intense moments are, in my opinion, the most valuable instrument for renewing ourselves, for transforming our faith, and for maintaining ourselves in fidelity.

However, intense moments are not something new. They go back to the time of Jesus and the prophets, when men of God retired in complete solitude, generally in the deserts or mountains, in order to train themselves intensely in the familiarity with God; they were healed from the wounds suffered in the battle of the spirit, and they returned to the fight, strong and healthy.

Intense moments are not only for growth in our relationship with God but also for recovering our emotional balance, given the fact that today our interior stability is imprisoned and attacked like never before.

Erich Fromm, the noted psychoanalyst, observes:

> Our culture leads to an unconcentrated and diffused mode of life, hardly paralleled anywhere else. You do many things at once; you read, listen to the radio, talk, smoke, eat, drink. You are the consumer with the open mouth, eager and ready to swallow everything — pictures, liquor, knowledge. This lack of concentration is clearly shown in our difficulty in being alone with ourselves. To sit still, without talking, smoking, reading, drinking, is impossible for most people. They become nervous and fidgety, and must do something with their mouths or their hands. (Smoking is one of the symptoms of this lack of concentration; it occupies hand, mouth, eye, and nose.)

It is necessary to retire every so often in complete solitude in order to recover our interior unity. If this is not practiced often, we will be swept away by the current of distraction and will be shipwrecked in our "call and election," as well as in our basic goal in life.

Throughout my life, I have met many people who have not appeared to be *persons*. To be a person means to be *lord* of oneself, and they were not. Thrown into an uncontrolled whirlpool of activity (that they always label "apostolic," even though it is not always so), they continue interiorly disintegrating themselves to the point of losing mastery over themselves, and at times, even losing the meaning of their lives. They are excitable people, nervous...

They are people who are incapable of stopping for a minute and asking themselves, Who am I? What is the primary goal of my life and what are the commitments that keep this goal alive? Because they do not want to face these questions, they are always avoiding the mystery of their being. They are fugitives from themselves, and their so-called apostolic activity is their island of refuge. All day long they jump from one activity to another, from group to group, just so they need not stop; for if they stopped, the questions about the mystery of their life would soon appear. It seems as if it is better to close their eyes, to continue so as not to face the challenging enigma of their mystery. Naturally, this type of person has no richness to give to the world, only empty words.

It is absolutely necessary to stop and retreat every so often, to recover our integrity and lordship over ourselves.

Intense moments — I repeat — are necessary in order to transform us into *people of God.* On the faces of people like these, others notice and see a special brilliance from afar: they are those who speak without speaking.

The prophets of God are forged on the anvil of solitude: there, on the burning coals, they endure the gaze of God without blinking, and when they descend to the plains, they transmit splendor, spirit, and life. In the silence of the desert, they "saw and heard" something, and once again among the people, no one can silence their voices. They perceived something, and there is no one in the world who can destroy their testimony, and invariably, they are transformed into trumpets of the Invisible that cannot be silenced. The masses know whom to distinguish between one who is sent and a meddler.

It is necessary to retreat to be people of God.

What if there is no time for these breaks? There *is* time for anything that we really want.

Time is not the trouble. The evil is something else. We seem to be like those who are sick and afraid, avoiding doctors and X-rays. Distraction and diversion feed us at first, but we do not want to become involved in anything that involves frustration and restlessness because then we feel alone. Furthermore, it costs a great deal to begin again our life with God. As an added note, God is a frightful challenger: it is much easier to live far from His fire.

"Desert"

What we call *intense moments* are those fragments of time, relatively prolonged and exclusively reserved for the encounter with God. For example, in the organization of our own lives, we might set aside twenty or thirty minutes each day for the Lord.

When, for example, we set aside one day a month to be dedicated to God alone, this is the time we call "desert."

Living or celebrating the "desert" has peculiar characteristics. It is very useful, almost necessary, to spend a "desert day" by leaving the daily turmoil in which we live and going to a solitary place, be it in the country, the mountains, or a retreat house.

For mutual support, it is useful that this going out to the "desert" be done in groups of three or four, for example; but once they have arrived at the place where they are going to spend the day, the group should scatter and spend the time in complete solitude. It is also useful to give the "desert" a penitential character in terms of food.

So that the "desert" does not become a frightening day (in which case it would not be repeated a second time) it is necessary that we have at hand some guidelines by which to spend a productive day. Know beforehand what ought to be taken along; certain psalms, biblical texts, exercises in concentration, a notebook for recording impressions, vocal prayers, spiritual reading, etc.

Here are some suggestions. Once you have arrived at the place where you are going to spend the day, it is good to begin praying with some psalms in order to tune the senses in faith and to create a suitable interior climate. In case you should find yourself in a state of distraction, you should practice some of the exercises for achieving calm, concentration, or self-control. The most important thing about this "desert day" is the personal dialogue with the Lord, a dialogue which is the sharing not of words but of interiorities. The greatest amount of time should be dedicated to establishing this current of dialogue between *I and Thou*, to be face to face with the Lord. During the day, there might be spiritual readings, reflections over one's own life, over pressing problems of the community or some other problem. On this day, we should accept those things that normally we reject with the exercises of surrender and forgiveness, healing ourselves of the wounds of life in the same way that the people of God come down from the mountain completely healed and strong.

We ought to realize that, throughout such a day or afternoon, we may pass through the most varied and even contradictory spiritual stages. Do not be afraid. And don't be too pleased with the consolations or depressed at the times of aridity. Impatience is the most subtle daughter of the ego. Where there is peace, there is God. Remember, if you have peace, even in complete aridity, God is with you.

Never let yourself be carried away by illusion. It has a face very similar to that of hope, but is quite the opposite. Yes, you have to learn to distinguish between violence and strength, between illusion and hope. Do not dream of obtaining powerful feelings. Because if you do not get them, you will become impatient; impatience will generate violence, and you will try to gain the desired feeling by force. Violence will generate fatigue, and fatigue degenerates into frustration. It would be a shame if we, instead of returning strengthened from the "desert" to life, returned frustrated.

Once again, the guardian angels of the "desert" are patience, perseverance and hope. Do not forget that Jesus made many "deserts"; organize your life and set aside certain days each year for God alone, and by doing so you will be demonstrating that God is important in your life.

* * *

What have been explained up to this point are valid means for taking the first steps. Further on, these same methods will be useless crutches. When prayer has become a habit and lives in our spirit, placing ourselves in the state of prayer and "remaining" with God will be the same thing, a soothing ointment in times of aridity and dryness.

As we advance, God is the one who takes the initiative. God's action surges from the depths of the soul and takes possession of the castle. The One unifies, and the Center centers everything.

At this point there is no need for mental gymnastics or psychological strategies. The castle is unconditionally "taken," and its armies surrender to the new Master. But all of this occurs only after a long period of purification.

3. POSTURES AND CIRCUMSTANCES

Once more, we must remember that each person experiences life in a unique and unrepeatable way. There are no sicknesses but only sick people, and the same prescription applied to different sick people produces different effects in each one.

We are going to give some specific suggestions, but each person must try each of the prescriptions; later on, a variety of combinations may be made from these and, finally, each individual should stay with the best one for him or her.

We are not angels. We often think in terms of dichotomies or dualistic concepts. We speak of grace and the soul. There is no such thing as the soul but only nature; that is, body *and* soul. Both are integrated into a unity so indivisible that there is no scalpel in the world that can separate the two.

To pray, we must take the body into consideration. A comfortable body posture can alleviate a state of dryness. Breathing, done slowly and deeply, may cast away anxiety. A proper posture can make distractions disappear. When, for whatever reason, it is impossible to pray, we can assume bodily positions of adoration; for example, prostrating ourselves on the ground, worshipping without any mental or vocal expression. This could be an excellent prayer on certain occasions.

When you find yourself in extreme pain or sick in bed, do not try to pray or say anything. Simply stretch out your arms like Jesus on the cross. Surrender yourself like a gift. It will be an offering of your painful body.

Any position that, as an external sign, indicates receptivity, openness or surrender helps the soul to have the same attitude.

Naturally, external postures are extrinsic to the prayer itself and, as a consequence, are of secondary importance. However, at certain times, they may be of great help in the encounter with God.

Many complain of their almost invincible difficulties and distractions in placing themselves in the presence of the Lord. Does this not happen, many times, because external factors are not taken into account? For example, with rapid and shallow breathing, it will be difficult for us to arrive at any profound encounter.

Positions for prayer

Standing. Let us not forget that the Jews — and so, Jesus — prayed while standing.

Stand up. Your feet may be more or less pointed outward; they need not be touching. However, the heels should touch in such a way that the weight of the body falls evenly along the spinal column, resulting in muscle relaxation and calmed nerves. The head should be held erect, but not rigid. This position regulates the breathing, aids the circulation, and avoids muscle fatigue.

The *arms* may be in any number of positions: *open and outstretched* forward in an attitude of receptivity; *open and raised upwards* to express an intense plea or any strong feeling, be it gratitude or exaltation; *open,* the elbows bent and the arms and hands raised upwards, palms up to express readiness and willingness; arms or hands *crossed* over the chest to express recognition or intimacy; *hands together* and fingers crossed on the chest, to show interiorization, gratitude, plea; arms completely *open* in the form of a cross, for the prayer of intercession lends a universal character to the prayer.

We should not forget how many times the psalms refer to the arms outstretched: "I call to you, Yahweh, all day, I stretch out my hands to you" (Ps 88; cf. Ps 63; 119).

The *eyes* may be completely closed. This in itself signifies intimacy. In fact, it helps a great deal in recollecting ourselves. Others, with their eyes closed, find themselves assaulted by every kind of image. The eyes may be turned and focused on the tips of the toes, the navel, or some other fixed point, such that they always look, somehow, "within." The eyes may be completely *open,* directed upward, forward, looking at a fixed point or toward infinity. The immobility of the eyes (and of the body in general) helps in achieving interior silence.

Depending on the person, one may look at a statue, crucifix, or something similar.

Sitting. If you are seated on a bench or a chair, your back should be supported by the back of the chair in such a way that the weight falls evenly, remembering the general rules for the arms, hands, eyes.

You might also sit in the "Carmelite" position: kneeling, sitting on the heels, with the tips of the toes close together and the heels a bit separated. The arms ought to fall freely with the hands (palms up or down) resting on the thighs.

For anyone not accustomed to this position, it may be somewhat uncomfortable at first. When the body becomes accustomed to it, it becomes a most restful and expressive position, indicating humility, readiness, admission. To avoid discomfort, many use pillows in the following manner: once on their knees, they place the pillow under their legs, near the tips of the feet, moving the heels and knees apart; they sit (slowly and completely) on the pillow. It is a very comfortable position.

There are many other ways of sitting while praying.

Lying down. Lying on the ground is the position of greatest humility, and it indicates and aids in the most profound worship. Saint Francis was caught by surprise many times by his companions while he was in this position, on Mount Alverna.

First way: slowly kneel down. Stay there for a few moments. Then, lean forward (again, slowly), curving the whole body until your forehead touches the ground. Your arms and hands are placed on the ground near your head. The weight of your body falls on four points: the feet, knees, forehead, and hands. Maintain this position, breathing deeply and regularly, until you feel completely comfortable. At the end of the prayer, return to a sitting or standing position, again, doing so very slowly.

Second way: first kneel down; then, slowly, completely lie down on the ground with your arms stretched cruciform or along the length of your body, or with your hands as support for your forehead.

In the beginning, these will have to be practiced gradually. The first few times you will not be able to stay in any one position for very long. You should avoid those positions that are forced or uncomfortable. If you feel comfortable, it is a sign that the position is right and that you have adequately relaxed the nerves and muscles.

Each individual has to experiment with the various positions, in all of their combinations, until he finds those that suit his particular nature.

Every attitude of the body should correspond to a certain interior attitude.

Where to pray?

There are those who find it easier to enter into communication with the Lord in a closed church or a darkened chapel.

There are those who pray better out on a balcony, in the garden, or in the country on a dark night, beneath the stars, when the voices of the world are silent.

Others feel more at one with God looking intently at a flower, or with a lost stare, or contemplating a beautiful panorama, or in the loneliness of a hill.

There are those who have never felt the presence of God as strongly as when they were visiting someone ill with a repulsive disease, or when they work among the poor.

There are those who cannot center themselves if they are in the middle of a group; others need the support of a group.

When to pray?

There are those who wake up in the morning refreshed and at peace. It is their best time for concentration and prayer.

On the other hand, there are those who have an intense subconscious life, and the following happens to them: while they are asleep, enjoying the absence of the guard called the conscious, the unconscious arises from unknown depths, assaulting and invading the individual's interior like a thief, acting out its every whim during the night. As a consequence of this nighttime invasion, these people wake up tired and in a bad mood, more tired than when they went to bed, as if they had spent the entire night fighting with some unknown enemy. Owing to this phenomenon, I have known those who feel a deep aversion for all prayer, beginning with its name. But they soon discover the unconscious association between their bad mood and drowsiness on the one hand, and prayer on the other; both things had come together every morning for so many years.

The evening, in general, is the best time to pray. Agitation has been calmed. The bright light has set. It seems that everything quiets down and rests. The battle ends. It is the hour of peace and intimacy.

There are those who prefer to pray at night. There are certainly those who, when night comes, are no good for anything; they can only sleep. But for others, the nighttime might be the best time for prayer; commitments are finished; silence fills everything; everything is sharing in the intimacy of the Lord. In biblical tradition, people looked forward to and used the night as the ideal time for communication with the Lord. That is what Jesus did.

Complete spontaneity?

We live in an age of spontaneity. Today there is an intolerance of anything that is imposed. There is an instinctive repugnance in the air for anything that smells of authority, superiority... From the time of Bonhoeffer, a myth has been running around that dominates our environment and that is accepted as an absolute truth: the notion that we have arrived at the full maturity of the human race and, likewise, the maturity of the individual. Two myths — in one — that do not stand up to careful analysis.

There are certain self-evident and common axioms: those who feel that they are adults do not advertise the fact. Those who shout to the four winds that they are adults can be sure that they are not. A mature individual never feels treated like a child. If we feel that way, it is a sign that we are really very childish.

Do you pray? And they respond in chorus: Always, and whenever I feel like it. This, which seems like maturity, contains a great deal of childishness. What if we took it to its logical conclusion? Work? When I feel like it. Study? When I feel like it. What would the world be like with such spontaneity? Childish anarchy, labelled as adult maturity.

In dialogues and conversations that I have had, there are many — almost a majority — who confess that when they do not participate in the prayer of the community, they never pray afterwards in private, and if they do not pray at a set time, they do not pray either in common or in private.

That which says that humanity has arrived at maturity is an empty myth. It is enough to take a little look within ourselves and another quick glance around us to see that there is an inability to keep commitments and that words are written in thin air.

I have met many people who, professionally, are the epitome of efficiency and organization: capable of efficiently handling colleges with thousands of students, or hospital complexes. In their work, they are true adults: there is order, punctuality, responsibility.

These same people, nevertheless, as they themselves confess, are completely irresponsible in terms of their religious commitments. Who can make sense of this contradiction?

I think that if they did not dedicate certain times to common prayer, set up by the community, they might easily abandon prayer altogether. It is necessary to establish priorities, to organize our life according to what is important to us, giving to God that which is God's, and that the community come to the aid of human frailty by establishing common times of prayer. This does not mean that each one, spontaneously, cannot set up his own *intense moments* for prayer.

We ought to remember, as I have already said, that prayer is not easy — it demands effort, and human instinct adheres to the law of least resistance. Because of this instinct, we prefer any other activity — because it is easier — to the interiorizing activity of prayer. Due to this instinct, we flee from prayer, and only then do we become convinced of its necessity.

Many look for psychological support in a community. Let me explain. There are persons who look for someone else to stimulate them in their life with God. Sharing their experiences, they are encouraged to continue their faithful following of the Lord. I know many such people. I know many who, because of this support, have maintained an intense spiritual life.

Do we relate to Jesus or to God the Father?

It is difficult for many people to place themselves in contact with the transcendent God. Nevertheless, these same people rapidly and easily enter into dialogue with the risen and present Jesus. This ease is all the more notable when they relate with Jesus in the Eucharist.

While at prayer, they sense Jesus as Someone concrete and very near, like a close friend. They adore Him, praise Him, ask Him for forgiveness, strength or consolation; with Him and in Him they place their commitments and hardships; they are forgiven and they forgive others, and so the wounds of life are healed. There is no way to classify this prayer or even define it: figment of the imagination? A simple vision of faith? Although the greatest freedom is granted each individual, it is advisable, for the first steps, to have this familiar relationship with Jesus, in the simplicity of faith.

On the other hand, there are those who, from the beginning, feel a dark and irresistible attraction to the Invisible, Eternal, and Omnipotent. No one knows whether this is a particular predisposition or a special grace.

Now then, when the soul ventures into the deeper contemplative areas, the spiritual masters point out that we tend to overcome the imaginary and corporal forms — of Jesus the Friend — and advance to the direct encounter with the simple and total God who penetrates us, envelops us, sustains us, and keeps us, in which silence is substituted for words, in pure faith.

Opposed to this teaching, generally agreed upon by the spiritual masters, Saint Teresa of Avila rises up with renewed energy, affirming that in every stage of the spiritual life we have to fix our gaze on the humanity of the risen Jesus.

Be that as it may, we, in this as in everything else, suggest that we let ourselves be carried by grace, in meekness and surrender, because there is a different path for each individual, and for the same person, different paths at different times.

4. FIRST STEPS

Because all grace is a filial movement toward the Father, it is important and necessary to cultivate that aspiration in a tangible way.

We always place ourselves in one of two groups. The first are those who are beginners in the things of God, and who want to reach, for the first time, intimacy with the Lord. The second group is made up of those who have lived this friendship for a long time. Later, they became careless: they threw so much dirt and sand on it that they extinguished the divine flame. Today, they feel the weight

141

of sadness and emptiness, and they want to recover, at whatever cost, that lost treasure.

Both groups — the ones who want to acquire it for the first time and those who want to recover what was lost — need to take beginners' steps. On the path of life, the first steps are always unsteady and unsure. It does not matter. We have to go through this and pay the price of patience and perseverance.

Vocal prayer

First steps are always taken with support. In our case, vocal prayer is that support.

As has already been explained, the human mind, by nature, is a restless butterfly, wandering like the wind. It needs to move, forever flying, jumping from the past to the future, from memories to ideas, from ideas to plans. True adoration, on the other hand, consists in mastering our attention and centering it on the Lord. How do we do that with such a crazy mind?

We need crutches in order to walk. The support is verbal prayer or, rather, written prayer. It is supposed that the prayer is written in dialogue form. How is it done?

We focus our eyes on the written prayer, and the words capture our attention and establish a tie between ourselves and God. If I read, for example, "You are my God," and try to make those words my own, identifying my thoughts with the content of that statement, my mind is already "with" God. The words are a bridge, a tie.

But the mind disengages its attention very rapidly from the center and scatters in a thousand directions. We again focus our eyes on the written prayer; and again the written word seizes and holds our attention. As our attention remains fixed, centered on the content of the written prayer — as if the content were God Himself — the mind "remains" with God. Given its nature, the mind again gets loose and flies away. Again, patiently, our eyes are directed to the written word and the word directs our mind. In other words, the printed word evokes and awakens God "for" us. That is, the word takes the human mind and deposits it in the goal that is God.

This is written prayer but it is, above all, *vocal prayer.* Why? Because we begin by reading the written word; reading it, it is vocalized; vocalizing it, it is "intellectualized"; and, in this way, we remain in prayer. This has nothing to do with prolonged prayer. That is, our attention remains with God for only a few intermittent instances. But those instances may stretch out to thirty minutes or so. In that case, we might say that we have had thirty minutes of *true* prayer.

Today there are valuable booklets with selections of the best prayers. There are also some with selected psalms. Furthermore, there are psalters within the reach of everyone. Take them in hand whenever you pray. Take them to the "desert."

How do we pray with them?

Take a prayer that you like. Put yourself in a praying attitude. Ask for the assistance of the Holy Spirit. Begin to read. After reading the words, make them "yours": try to identify yourself with their content. There will be expressions that fill you from the start. Repeat them again and again, until these words and their "content" completely flood your whole being.

Continue reading (praying) slowly, very slowly. Stop. Repeat them again from the beginning. Repeat them out loud — if the situation permits — loudly or softly according to the circumstances. You may want to take some particular posture that will help you, such as extending your arms. Let your interior, your feelings, and your decisions be impregnated with the Presence that emanates from those words.

If, at any given moment, you feel as if you could walk without "crutches," put the written prayer aside and allow the Holy Spirit to speak within you and to echo in your mouth with spontaneous expressions. Conclude the prayer experience with some resolution that will affect your life.

For many people, the following method of vocal prayer has excellent results: Take a praying position. Select one or two powerful expressions, for example, "You search me and You know me"; "from the beginning and forever, You are God"; "my God and my All"; "You are my Lord." Use one of these or some other one. Begin to repeat it softly and out loud. Say it very slowly, trying to enter fully into the "substance" of the expression with serenity, without violence. Say the words, each time with more of a pause between repetitions.

There may come a time when silence takes over for the words, and there only remains silence and Presence. In that case, remain silent *in* the Presence. Conclude with some resolution for your life.

To those who want to take God seriously, I would give this advice: learn some of the psalms, verses of psalms, different short prayers, by memory. While you are driving along or walking through the streets or doing household chores and you feel the desire to say something to God but nothing "comes out," uniting yourself to God by means of these memorized prayers can be an excellent spiritual benefit.

Psalms

In my opinion, there is no vehicle that carries us more rapidly to the heart of God than the praying of the Psalms.

The Psalms are carriers of a tremendous amount of experience with God. They have been enriched by the fervor of millions of men and women, for as long as three thousand years. With these same words, Jesus the child, the youth, the adult, the evangelizer, the crucified, communicated with His Father. They are, then, expressions that are saturated and charged with an enormous spiritual vitality accumulated over thirty centuries.

Among the Psalms, there are passages of superior quality; there are also those that say nothing to us. Others that scandalize us. In a single psalm, we may find beautiful verses as well as verses that ask for curses and revenge. We can skip over the latter and focus on the first verses.

How do we pray them? It must be pointed out that we are not talking about the praying of the Divine Office, but how to use the Psalms as training tools for acquiring the experience of God, for taking the first steps in the form of vocal prayer.

Take the Psalms or verses that most satisfy you. Repeat the expressions that "say" the most to you. While repeating these slowly, let yourself be touched by the profound strength that the psalmists, prophets, and Jesus felt. That is, try to experience what they experienced. Let yourself be invaded by the living presence of God, enveloped by the feelings of dread, exaltation, praise, contrition, intimacy, sweetness, or other feelings that fill these words.

If, in a given moment, you begin to feel a "visit" from God, stop there, repeat the words; and even though you may not do anything else for an hour but penetrate, experience, be frightened of the richness contained in that verse, remain and do not be worried about continuing. Always conclude with some resolve for your life.

It is true that there are psalms full of anathemas and curses. In these cases, if we allow ourselves to be freely carried by spontaneity, we will feel that the Spirit is teaching us to apply those anathemas to the "enemy" — singular and multiple — that is our selfishness with its countless offspring such as pride, vanity, anger, resentment, sensuality, exploitation, ambition, irritability...

I always advise everyone to make a *personal "study"* of the Psalms.

Since each one of us is a unique mystery, our manner of experiencing and knowing ourselves is singular and unique; so, what says a great deal to one may say nothing to someone else. What says a lot to another may say little to

145

me. Because of this, a personal study is needed. How do we go about this?

Begin with the first Psalm. On a certain day, relate to the Lord with the first Psalm, during a time set aside for prayer; that is, speak with God through those words. If in the Psalm there is a verse, maybe a complete strophe or a series of linked phrases, that "says" something to you, after repeating them several times, underline those words with a pencil.

If there is an expression that is particularly rich, you might underline it several times, according to the degree of richness you find there. Make a mark in the margin, a word, that characterizes that verse for you, such as *confidence, intimacy, praise, adoration...*

It may happen that the same Psalm will say little or nothing to you one day, and the next day it may say a great deal. It can happen that the same person may perceive the same thing in different ways on different occasions.

If the Psalm says nothing to you, leave it unmarked.

Another day, "study" the second Psalm in the same way. Do the same with all 150 Psalms. At the end of a year or two, you will have a "personal knowledge" of all of them. When you wish to praise God, you will already know which psalm will help you. When you wish to meditate on the precariousness of life, or you need consolation, or you wish to adore Him, when you are looking for assurance or confidence, or feel the "need" to enter into intimacy, you will already know which psalms will be of assistance.

In this way, little by little, you will learn by memory the verses laden with richness that will serve as nourishment in any circumstance. Conclude with some resolution for your life.

The following is a list of the psalms according to their corresponding themes. The italic numbers indicate that the given theme is more intense. Also, this enumeration follows the Catholic version of the Psalms.

Psalms that express *confidence, surrender, intimacy, nos-*

talgia, and desire for God: 3, 4, *15*, 16, 17, 22, 24, *26*, *30*, 35, 38, *41*, *50*, *55*, 61, *63*, 69, 70, *83*, 89, *90*, 102, *117*, 122, 125, 129, 130, *138*, 142.

Psalms that express *awe* before the contemplation of creation with a sense of personal *joy* and *glory* in God: 8, *18*, 28, *64*, 88, 91, *103*.

Psalms that express *praise, exaltation, thanksgiving*: *3, 66*, 91, 112, *134*, *135*, *144*, *146*, *148*, *149*, *150*.

Psalms that express the *shortness* of life in the face of the *eternity* of God: 38, *89*, *92*, *101*, 102, 134, 138.

Spiritual reading

Meditation is an activity in which the mind deals with concepts and images, moving from premises to conclusions, distinguishing, deducing, explaining, applying, combining different ideas about a previously selected topic, with a number of purposes: to clarify a truth, to get to know God better, to examine the life of Jesus and so be able to imitate Him, and finally, to make resolutions so as to transform our lives.

Meditation enriches the soul with the knowledge of divine life. But, in my opinion, it is too complicated for beginners in the relationship with the Lord God. It is like rowing, depending only on oars and one's own strength, and today we have a hard time arriving at the port that is God Himself because we live in intuitive times and not discursive ones; we are inclined more toward the emotional than the rational. Teresa of Avila herself felt very little sympathy for discursive meditation:

> Returning, then, to those who can make use of their reasoning powers, I advise them not to spend all their time doing so; their method of prayer is most meritorious, but... let them imagine themselves, as I have suggested, in the presence of Christ, and let them remain in converse with him, and delighting in him, without wearying their

minds or fatiguing themselves by composing speeches to him, but laying their needs before him...

Nevertheless, meditation is an absolutely necessary spiritual activity if we are to deepen ourselves in the mysteries of God and grow in divine life.

Now then, if meditation is as necessary as it is difficult, where do we find the solution? Primarily in spiritual reading. And, to a lesser degree, in group meditation.

I repeat again: we need support in order to take the first steps to acquire or receive the sense of God in our lives.

Many persons have a true desire to fly to the heights of God but they do not yet have sufficient consistency and strength to sail over such deep and unknown waters. They feel incapable of being alone at the feet of the Master for any length of time. They need crutches to walk. They would like to, but they are not sure how to speak, just like children. They do not find emotional currents to carry them, in a spiral, toward the Center. They need supports. And there is no support more helpful for them than spiritual reading.

Everything that I have said concerning vocal prayer must be applied here also: it is the written word that will master the mind and lead it along the path to an orderly and fruitful reflection.

Saint Teresa gives us this moving description in the *Way of Perfection*: "I myself spent over fourteen years without ever being able to meditate except while reading."

Spontaneously and without any inhibition whatsoever, Saint Teresa admits that if she had not just received Communion, she never dared enter into prayer unless accompanied by a book. And if she tried to pray without a book in her hand, she felt as if she were about to enter a fierce battle with a great army. If she had a book in her hand, it acted as a shield that received the blows of distraction, and she was left calmed and consoled. She confesses that dryness never caused her struggle. However, without her book, she would fall into complete powerlessness. Only when she opened the book would her thoughts become orderly, leading her directly to the Lord. Sometimes she read little, other times a great deal, depending upon how the Spirit moved her.

How is it practiced?

In the first place, the individual should have a well-chosen book that will facilitate both reflection and feeling at the same time, a book that places and maintains the soul in the presence of our Lord and God. However, the best book for spiritual reading is, naturally, the Bible.

I often advise that we make a personal "study" of the various topics found in the different books of the Bible. It is very useful for every one of us, after having done this "research," to have a notebook in which to record our findings in such a way that if we want to meditate, for example, on the life of God, hope, eternal life, consolation, faith, fidelity, etc., we will know exactly which book of the Bible to choose.

Second, the spiritual reading itself should be done as follows.

Take a comfortable position. Ask for the light of the Lord. Know exactly what subject you wish to meditate upon or, at least, on which part of the Bible you are going to focus your attention. Let us suppose that you have chosen one chapter of the Pauline letters. Begin to read. Read slowly, very slowly. After reading a bit, meditate. As much as you meditate, read.

Suppose some idea appears interesting to you. Stop; lift your eyes from the book. Explore the idea. Continue reading slowly. As you read, continue meditating. Suppose that you do not understand a passage. In that case, go back. Skim and examine the context of that idea, and from the context you will surely understand the meaning of the paragraph. Continue reading slowly.

Suppose that, suddenly, a thought arises that makes a

powerful impression on you. Lift your eyes and take all of the juice from that idea, applying it to life...

If you then feel like conversing with the Lord, adoring, standing in awe of Him, giving thanks, asking forgiveness, strength... do it calmly. If nothing special comes about, continue with the reading, calm, concentrating, relaxed. We have to remember that the ideal is that the reading "seize" us and place us affectionately in the arms of the Lord, in order, finally, to transform us into a living likeness of Jesus, His witness in the world.

If through this spiritual reading, a "visit" by the Lord occurs, do not even think of continuing to row. Put the oars aside and let yourself be carried by the wind of God, simply letting yourself be with the Lord.

It is very useful, even necessary, that each spiritual reading conclude with some concrete resolution for your life, depending on the flow of ideas during your meditation.

This method is not only helpful for beginners but also for those more advanced in the mysteries of God, above all during times of dryness, aridity, testing, and dark nights.

Group meditation

The second path, relatively easy and helpful for meditating, is group meditation.

This involves a small group of people who come together to reflect on different themes of Christian life.

It begins with a reading from the Bible, or from some book that deals with the topic upon which the group is going to meditate. In this way, the theme is given substance or illumination. It is also useful to pray in common, using some psalm or invocation of the Holy Spirit.

Then, each person offers a spontaneous reflection in front of the others, relating what occurs to him or her about the topic or its application to life, always dealing with the central theme. And so, likewise, spontaneously and each in turn, everyone takes part in the reflection.

So that group meditation may bear fruit, it is absolutely necessary that, within the group, there be peace, sincerity, and mutual trust. Otherwise, spontaneity is blocked and so is the action of the Spirit. It is also necessary to avoid *egotism* at all costs; that is, the eagerness to shine, to say something original, or to appear more brilliant than the others.

It is important that each member of the group, besides enriching himself mentally, deal with practical concerns, making decisions in common for the community or pastoral life together. In this way, group meditation is transformed into a school of life and love.

I have known many people who let the Gospel fall from their hands because it did not say anything to them. But, once a part of a meditating group, these people discovered unsuspected riches and — it is a strange thing — pulled by the community spirit, they have taken from their interiority and shared with the others a great *newness* about Jesus, discovering things that they had missed within themselves. If this process establishes an emotional current with the Lord on a personal and group level, then there will be beautiful community prayer.

Community prayer

By community prayer, I mean the act of a number of people coming together to pray spontaneously and out loud, one after another.

For community prayer to be authentic, it is necessary that those who participate have previously lived their faith and have been "trained" in the personal relationship with the Lord. Otherwise, they will give the impression that words, sometimes beautiful words, are "spoken" but, in the words of dramatist Eugène Ionesco, the words will be incapable of standing on their own because they lack content.

It is necessary also that there be no emotional short circuits among those who are praying. Although the individuals may be personally filled with fervor, a curious phenomenon occurs: the conflicting states of members of the group hardens the personal fervor and blocks the individual in his or her relationship with God; in short, the distance between individuals is converted into distance between the soul and God.

This need not be the case. There does not have to be a great deal of trust among the participants. There have been many cases of beautiful results among participants in community prayer who did not even know one another. The important thing is that there be no conflicts among them.

Some individuals, because of their shy nature, feel lost when faced with these situations. It is good to invite even these people to speak, but without doing violence to their reserved nature.

There also is a general law of psychology that states that intimacy requires reserve, and the greater the intimacy, the greater the reserve. Just as lovers in this world leave all human presence and sight, so also do the great contemplatives such as Moses, Elijah, and Jesus look for complete solitude for their encounters with God. Francis of Assisi not only went to the high mountains for his conversations with the Lord but, even there, he hid himself in dark and lonely caves.

In spite of all this, if true contact with God is made in a group at prayer, that group is transformed into a new cenacle, and that community prayer will embody the force and the richness of Pentecost. Yet, in order to place themselves before God and before one another, it is necessary that those who are praying come from the "desert," laden with faith and love.

Liturgical prayer

Liturgical prayer, in the present case in which we are looking for a direct means for acquiring or recovering the sense of God, follows the same line as vocal prayer. It certainly has a particular dignity and efficacy by virtue of its being the official prayer of the Church. On the other hand, its rites contain an exceptional beauty, offer the finest texts from the Word of God, and in every moment presents an elevated sense of community. All of which makes liturgical prayer the Great Prayer of the People of the Covenant.

However, that liturgical prayer, which is the nourishment for the masses and the solemn homage of a People to their God, is in need of personal interiority and devotion to become true worship "in spirit and truth" (Jn 4:24). Paraphrasing Ionesco, words are like coats: empty, they fall; what keeps them on their feet is what's in them.

This means that if we are "trained" in the relationship to God, "laden" with God, then liturgical prayer will be like a gourmet dish, a superb banquet that will not only nourish us but, because of community contact, will stimulate the masses, transforming them into a people of worshippers.

But if we come empty, or do not pay full attention to the ceremony, it can happen that liturgical prayer does not become an *encounter* with God or with others, fulfilling those words: "This people... honors me only with lip-service, while their hearts are far from me" (Is 29:13).

Charismatic prayer

In the last few years, a movement of prayer has arisen all over the world. It has been given different names: *charismatic prayer* (owing to the appearance of gifts [or charisms] of the Holy Spirit), *pentecostal prayer...* Their effects are like those of Pentecost morning: drunkenness without wine, glowing conversations, and an irresistible flooding by the Holy Spirit. Many books have appeared on the subject.

In my opinion, it is one of the more effective ways of giving life to faith, for experiencing the captivating closeness of God, and for leaving people marked, perhaps forever, by the living flame of God. Furthermore, there is the advantage that all of this takes place on a community level.

These prayer meetings come about with an admirable and risky spontaneity, without any preparation; no one worries about what they are to say or do, or who is going to speak. There is no agenda or schedule, no planning. All of this is left in the "hands" of the Holy Spirit.

Those who pray this way come with a happy spirit, fraternal and contagious. They begin with a song, with a reading or a shout of praise, depending on the "dictate" of the Spirit. Everyone prays out loud and at the same time; and the clamor of prayer rises and falls like waves on the sea.

The most complete spontaneity reigns supreme. The cries, praying, shouting all produce an indescribable happiness through a great opening up before God and in front of the others present, especially at the time of testimony. The shouts are of praise, supplication, joy, and spiritual exaltation. All of this prayer is generally directed toward Jesus.

At times, those praying do nothing but repeat over and over again a single exclamation. There are those who say nothing more than two or three sentences. Others, on the other hand, are captured by a wave of inspiration and give rise to expressions that cannot be humanly explained.

All of this becomes a real tumult, so many people talking (praying) at the same time. But, paradoxically, there appears to be real order or concert, in that the rumble of those praying rises and falls in an ebb and flow, like waves that come in and go out again. Time passes and yet no one feels tired.

Soon, someone gets up, speaks spontaneously under

the influence of the Holy Spirit, and the words are accompanied by the acclamations of the hearers with shouts of praise. Sometimes, people say things so sublime that even theologians do not understand what is said.

A radical sincerity dominates the scene, an honesty that opens all of the windows of the soul; individuals make public confessions with repentant humility, yet without feeling humiliated. They make promises, great plans for conversion.

The participants are left with the feeling of wanting to pray more, to go out into the streets and do good to others, treating them like brothers and sisters, to forgive, to serve, to love.

I know that not all is pure gold. In all of this there is some degree (Who could measure its extent?) of group dynamics. In some groups there is an exaggerated preoccupation with the *gift of tongues*, healing, baptism in the Holy Spirit...

In spite of the reservations, though, I consider this to be the ideal method for arriving, covering a lot of ground, at the experience of God. I consider it a providential movement for the Church, which was so ritualistic in the past, and has become so lacking in faith on the part of many people of our day. I have the impression that a great age of the Spirit is beginning for the Church of God.

5. DEVOTION AND CONSOLATION

Devotion

Devotion is easily confused with emotion or some other sensitive element. Devotion certainly does contain some emotional elements but, in essence, it is altogether something else.

It is a special gift of the Holy Spirit that enables and

readies us for good works. At times, it is the result of a "visit" by God that arises out of prayer and supports us.

Devotion makes us strong enough to overcome hardships, to heat what is lukewarm, filling us with generosity and courage, clearing the mind, maturing the enthusiasm for God, quieting the worldly passions, overcoming temptations with ease and happiness and, finally, placing readiness, decision, and joy in the heart.

The essence of devotion, then, is not sentiment but readiness. Jesus felt ill in Gethsemane; however, He had the filial devotion to fulfill the will of the Father.

Nevertheless, devotion does contain a certain amount of emotion that sometimes depends on our temperament; but this kind of emotion is not necessarily in proportion to authentic love, the exact thermometer of which is the willingness to comply with the will of God.

In her *Way of Perfection*, Teresa of Avila writes:

> The body experiences the greatest delight and the soul is conscious of a deep satisfaction. So glad is it merely to find itself near the fountain that, even before it has begun to drink, it has had its fill. There seems to be nothing left for it to desire. The faculties are stilled... It is the will that is in captivity now...
>
> This is a supernatural state, and, however hard we try, we cannot reach it for ourselves; for it is a state in which the soul enters into peace, or rather in which the Lord gives it peace through his presence... In this state all the faculties are stilled.
>
> The soul... realizes that it is now very close to God, and that, if it were but a little closer, it would become one with him through union...

By its own nature, love is always a burning force; and in the measure in which it grows in depth, it becomes more sensitive. This love is inevitably "felt" as much in the joy of union as in the painful emptiness of absence. In certain spiritualities, such as the Franciscan, the sensitive aspects stand out because of their intensity. All joyful devotion that leads to the overcoming of oneself through self-denial is good. However, it also contains subtle dangers of narcissism, spiritual gluttony, and alienating selfishness. We might search for God for the peace and comfort that His presence brings, and not for God Himself. We might search for the sweetness of God instead of the God of sweetness, retarding or definitively avoiding the transforming union.

However, the "visit" ("felt" presence of God) always produces "gentleness" and "delight" (Ps 34; 86; 100; 145). In the same way, eating and drinking bring a certain satisfaction and delight, for each faculty is designed for a certain objective and the achieving of the objective produces a sensation of fulfillment or satisfaction. Humanity was created in the image and likeness of God (like an arrow shot toward a divine target); it is inevitable that when we reach, to a certain degree, our Objective, we will feel an emotional joy (devotion).

Nevertheless, in order that we might avoid subtly looking for ourselves with this emotional devotion, God sometimes twists the natural rule: in spite of the fact that we have reached God on a fairly high level, God sometimes leaves us empty, anxious... This is the reason for the periods of dryness and purifying nights.

It should be understood that for us who come from the hard battle of life, the beating of God within us is refreshing; we need emotional devotion as much as we need to breathe. If there were no emotional joys for us, it would be like rowing with no oars.

Consolation

In sorrow, in illness, in mourning, in persecution, we are in need of consolation. Our relatives and friends try to console us when all others have abandoned us. But their words are only a slight relief. We remain alone in our pain. In any decisive moment, we are alone.

In the Bible, the typical case, the symbol of all desolation, is the total abandonment of Jerusalem, destroyed, sacked, burned, deported into exile, and forgotten by God: "Yahweh has abandoned me, the Lord has forgotten me" (Is 49:14). But both the prophet Jeremiah and the prophet Isaiah offer the "book of consolations." God is presented here as a loving Father who says, "I did forsake you for a brief moment, but in great compassion I shall take you back" (Is 54:7).

There are certain times when nothing or no one is capable of consoling us. Desolation reaches levels that are much too deep: friends, relatives, lovers are not able to reach that level. No one knows whether it is loneliness, frustration, nostalgia, emptiness, or everything put together. Only God can reach the bottom of that abyss.

There is no one who has not experienced, having found himself in such a state, suddenly and without knowing how, a profound comfort as if some soothing ointment had been poured on the wounds. God descends upon the wounded soul like a pure, sweet nursemaid.

Other times, we begin to feel like a helpless child: reproaches, a serious illness, a real failure, the closeness of death... The desolation is too serious, unable to be measured. Who is able to console us? Friend? Spouse? "As a mother comforts a child, so I shall comfort you" (Is 66:13). God's consolation is like cool ointment poured out until it reaches the wounds of desolation.

And if the desolation is due to the absence of God, then a "visit" from God is capable of changing the darkness to light; water will spring forth and the mountains will be laid low and the deserts changed into gardens (cf. Is 42:15-17).

All absence produces sadness. Jesus will be absent. His own will feel like orphans. In prayer, something similar happens: the sensation of darkness, the sense of distance, absence, or silence of God leaves us with a feeling like that of being orphaned, sad, or distraught. In both cases, Jesus says "Do not worry." I will send Someone who, by nature, is the Comforter. "In those days, the early Christian groups advanced in the love of God and continued to grow, encouraged by the Holy Spirit" (cf. Acts 9:31).

Saint Paul discovered that consolation springs from desolation. He had lived through a painful affliction, to the point of feeling the claws of death in his flesh; in that, it was proved that the God of all consolation comforts beyond all measure. His Second Letter to the Corinthians is the Magna Carta of biblical consolation. The introduction to the first chapter alternates between consolation and desolation. It gives the impression that both are meant to be "suffered" in a life-giving manner.

> Blessed be the God and Father of our Lord Jesus Christ, the merciful Father and the God who gives every possible encouragement; he supports us in every hardship, so that we are able to come to the support of others, in every hardship of theirs because of the encouragement we ourselves receive from God. For just as the sufferings of Christ overflow into our lives, so too does the encouragement we receive through Christ. So if we have hardships to undergo, this will contribute to your encouragement and your salvation; if we receive encouragement, this is to gain for you the encouragement which enables you to bear with perseverance the same sufferings as we do. So our hope for you is secure in the knowledge that you share the encouragement we receive, no less than the sufferings we bear. (2 Cor 1:3-7)

And in the seventh chapter, we see Paul crushed both inside and out, battered by struggles and fears. But, again, we see how from the wounds of affliction is born the flame of consolation.

> Even after we had come to Macedonia, there was no rest for this body of ours. Far from it; we were beset by hardship on all sides, there were quarrels all around us and misgivings within us. But God, who encourages all those who are distressed, encouraged us through the arrival of Titus; and not simply by his arrival only, but

also by means of the encouragement that you had given him, as he told us of your desire to see us, how sorry you were and how concerned for us; so that I was all the more joyful. (2 Cor 7:5-7)

6. TENDENCIES

If prayer is the concentration of the faculties, distraction is the scattering of the mind in a thousand directions, momentarily avoiding the control of the will and conscience. In speaking of *interior silence*, we have explained the nature of distraction and have pointed out ways of overcoming it.

Dryness

When distraction is not a temporary phenomenon but a total inability to center ourselves in the Lord, and this becomes habitual for a time, it is called *dryness*. Dryness is accompanied, at times, by a feeling of depressing helplessness and a certain unnerving of the senses. The pessimist tends to think that he or she was not born for prayer or that all has been lost.

Dryness, in some people, may produce sadness and even desolation because of a complete inability, though it may be only temporary, to relate with the Lord. In some cases, this dryness may come dangerously close to the borders of aridity.

Although they are different words, they are mutually conditioned in such a way that it is difficult to tell where the boundaries of dryness, distraction, and aridity begin and end.

The spiritual masters, describing their experiences, abound in extraordinarily vivid descriptions of the dryness through which they had to pass. Reading them, we are caught somewhere between fear and admiration. Saint

Teresa assures us that many times she went to the well and many times drew the bucket without obtaining a single drop of water.

It frequently happens — continues the saint — that the soul does not even have the strength to lift its arms to draw out the bucket; in those moments, the individual cannot form a single thought. Dryness demands a high price. Anyone who has gone through this knows that price. I remember many times, adds the saint, how happy I was to have obtained that single drop of water from that blessed well, considering it to be a special privilege from the Lord.

To remain firm in these periods of dryness, more courage is needed than for any other task in the world. For many years, Teresa confesses, I was more worried about the clock — in choir — than about prayer itself, counting how many minutes were left and wishing that prayer would end soon. And many times I have been ready to submit to any harsh penance before beginning to recollect myself for prayer. I do not know if it was the devil or my own nature, but the fact is that just thinking that I had to go to prayer filled me with laziness. And, entering the oratory, my soul fell to my feet and I was beset by a great sadness and I had to force myself to cheer up. Finally — concludes Teresa — those times were ended by the grace of God.

That is why thousands of people abandon almost all prayer. They made superhuman efforts and were not able to draw out a single drop of water from that blessed well. Later, they felt unnerved by the disproportion between their efforts and the results, and ended up thinking that it was not worth the trouble.

Nevertheless, they are ready to begin again because prayer is a matter of life or death in terms of the meaning of their lives.

The *causes* of dryness have various characteristics:

1. An uncontrolled activity that destroys inner unity.

2. The nature of the prayer itself: the silence of God, the darkness of faith, the tendency of the human mind toward

variety and diversification, the influence of the senses over the interior faculties.

3. Pathological tendencies of all types that escape diagnosis; bodily characteristics; strained and uncomfortable positions. Without having an actual illness, we can feel bad, in a bad mood, moments of depression, powerful instability, melancholy or something else. Certain hereditary defects appear that, in the normal course of life, pass unnoticed, especially in terms of dryness and versatility.

4. Well-done prayer is a complex activity, one in which there is intellectual work but, moreover, one in which there is emotional labor that affects emotional energy. A basic emotional balance is needed.

5. Periods of dryness may be tests sent expressly by the Lord. In the Bible there is a definite rule that the faith of one to whom it has been given is put to the test.

As Teresa of Avila said in her *Autobiography*:

> I believe myself that often in the early stages, and again later, it is the Lord's will to give us these tortures, and many other torments which present themselves, in order to test his lovers and discover if they can drink of the chalice and help him to bear the cross before he trusts them with his great treasures.

What are we to do?

When times of dryness occur, the temptation for beginners is to exert powerful efforts to overcome the dryness. A vain attempt. Dryness is not conquered with arms and oars. "The more we try to force it at times like these, the worse it gets and the longer the trouble lasts," says St. Teresa.

I have known persons who have been left exhausted and weakened by a great outpouring of energy in this regard. Afterwards, anxiety and anguish overpower them.

All of this, instead of solving the trouble, worsens the dryness. Stuck in this spiral, there are many who, in practice, opt for abandoning prayer as if they had failed miserably.

Once again, three angels will accompany us through the desert, that we might not be thrown and conquered by the night of discouragement; they are patience, perseverance, and hope.

Patience peacefully accepts a disposition which limits us and takes the desire to continue away from us. Nothing is gained by resisting, burning a great deal of energy in order to end this dryness. We are not to raise up an army in order to conquer this enemy, but, paradoxically, we are to conquer it by submitting, surrendering ourselves to it. In other words, by accepting it.

Counselling the Carmelite sisters, Teresa of Avila gives this advice:

> She must not worry, for that only makes matters worse, nor must she weary herself by trying to put sense into something — namely, her mind which for the moment is without any. She should pray as best she can: indeed, she need not pray at all, but may try to rest her spirit as though she were ill and busy herself with some other virtuous action.
>
> ... The poor soul must not be stifled... They must endure this exile as well as they can, for a soul which loves God has often the exceeding ill-fortune to realize that, it lives in this state of misery...

Hope tells us that everything is passing, that nothing is forever. Hope lets us know that the primary laws of the universe are not those of permanence and stability. Everything is in perpetual motion. Nothing is static. If everything is passing and nothing remains the same, tomorrow will be better, the dryness will pass, better times lie ahead. We ought to be conscious of this, and this alone will be enough for abandoning resistance, accepting dryness and, in accepting it, conquering it.

In the crossing of this open plain, perseverance accompanies us as a special help, daughter of hope.

We must realize that all of the great conquests of history have been gained with a tenacious perseverance. And this perseverance is put to the test precisely in difficult times. To continue when results appear to be worthless; to remain standing when the winds blow and darkness surrounds us; to advance when fog makes it impossible to see two feet ahead: this is what we do when we persevere.

To continue in search of the light when we find ourselves in the midst of a dark night; to shine endlessly like the eternal stars while others ask, Why do they shine?; to continue fishing with nets set out when not a single fish falls into them; to drop a bucket in the well in spite of not drawing out a single drop of water... that is to persevere.

The grain of wheat scattered on the ground perseveres, confronted by life, defending itself against frost and heat. The child who learns to walk falls and gets up; falls again and again, gets up with stubborn perseverance until, after a long time, it remains standing, runs, and jumps. In the same way inventors, scientists, the wise, artists persevere; all that is great on earth has been gained with ardent perseverance.

Our generation has special difficulty in persevering in that we are accustomed to speed, productivity, and efficiency — characteristics of a technological society. We want tangible results; we almost automatically demand them. The life of prayer, on the other hand, presents totally opposite characteristics: results are always imperceptible; growth is not always at the same pace; God's activity is disturbing because it is free, and our response is variable, like our nature. And so, depression immediately appears.

The result? Perseverance is much more difficult in this area. The important thing for us is not to abandon the enterprise, but to continue.

Faith and hope ignite the flame of perseverance; and

perseverance is the guarantee of eventual and final success. In order to obtain strength from laziness and to get hope from perseverance, we need to be supported by faith, which consists not in *feeling* but in *knowing*: knowing that, in spite of the fact that progress is not perceived, grace is moving; we move because grace is life and life is movement. I do not feel the movement of my liver, kidneys, intestines... Nevertheless I *know*, I have the certainty, that all of these are in perpetual motion. It is the certainty of faith.

Faith takes us and carries us to surrender: surrender into the hands of dryness, darkness, inability to pray; not resisting anything, allowing ourselves to be carried peacefully by the current of nonsense and apathy. Better days will come.

Spiritual atrophy

The spiritual masters have only spoken of three tendencies: distraction, dryness, and aridity. However, observation of life has brought me to "discover" another tendency, possibly worse than the already mentioned ones, found very often in our day: spiritual atrophy.

The following happens to the muscles: when they are not used, they lose their tenor and elasticity. They do not die but they lose their vitality. They are no longer able to develop strength, lift weights, run. They become atrophied. It is not death, but rather death's front porch.

Immobility is a sign of death and causes it. If life stops being motion, it ceases to be life: the tendons harden and are overcome with rigidity. A plant, if not watered or fertilized, dries out, loses strength, and slowly falls, due to its impending death.

The same thing happens to many people. For years, they did not make any orderly, methodical, patient, and persevering efforts to enter into frequent and profound communication with the Lord. For a long time, they made sporadic and superficial attempts at prayer. They invented a thousand rationalizations to justify this situation: the one who works is already praying; God is to be found among the people. ... In this way, they appeased their consciences, at least to a certain degree. They substituted reflection for prayer, and shared conversation for meditation. Little by little, they were losing the sense of God and the desire for prayer. Within, this is what happened: those energies which the mystics call potentials or faculties, not being used, were slowly losing elasticity. Losing their strength, they were used less and less. Not being used, they were entering a counter-productive course leading to extinction.

These persons, at least, are restless, and they have the desire to begin again and to use the methods. But there are others who have parked themselves in spiritual mediocrity and have no desire to leave that spot. They do not suffer by being in that state. They are satisfied with their success. The apostolate and other professional activities give them ample compensation. They feel complete and do nothing more. Life with God is no concern of theirs. It is enough for them to have a well-formed personality to balance the ups and downs of life. And their life is arranged as if God did not exist.

There is no discernible solution for such as these. Their own self-satisfaction is the fatal danger. However, there *is* "salvation" for the others, for the restless. What are they to do?

The orientations that I have offered in various parts of this book on patience, perseverance, and hope will have to be taken into consideration, as well as those on the nature of the life of grace and its growth. They will have to take the first steps, like someone relearning to walk. They will have to support themselves with vocal prayer, the psalms, spiritual reading, etc. And, with infinite patience and stubborn fidelity, they will have to continue climbing and climbing. The practical outlines I present here on dryness and aridity will also be of great help to them.

Aridity

Aridity is a time of helplessness and disinterest in applying ourselves to the relationship with God, a thing that at other times caused such joy and devotion. Generally, it befalls those who have begun their ascent to God.

In my opinion, aridity, as we are going to describe it here, is comparable to the "nights of the soul" of John of the Cross.

It has to do with true desolation. People found in this state speak like this: I feel nothing. Everything bores me to the point of making me ill. Just like Jesus in Gethsemane, "I am disgusted." It is a torment to pray. There were such happy times with God in the past... I have been in this state of aridity for two months and I feel like a stone. God is distant, absent, I do not even know if He exists. If I knew that, after a year of this aridity, the Face of God would shine again... But who knows if the Lord will ever "return"?

No night can compare with this darkness. The individual comes to the point of saying, I wish that I had never "met" God! In these moments that person could repeat the words of Jesus: "I am dying of sadness."

John of the Cross describes this as follows:

> The first purgation or night is bitter and terrible to the senses. But nothing can be compared to the second, for it is horrible and frightful to the spirit.

These tests are given to advanced people, and if they did not have the memory of joyful encounters with God in the past, they would turn their backs forever on the life with God. And if they have vividly experienced this relationship with God, the test of aridity might appear to be hell itself.

In the words of John of the Cross,

> These are the ones who go down into hell alive since their purgation on earth is similar to that of purgatory. For

this purgation is that which would have to be undergone there.

To my understanding, because dryness and distraction are phenomena that occur in the first stages and are generally explicable in terms of psychosomatic principles, aridity is a trial sent expressly by God; it is profoundly purifying and is given only to those accustomed to great familiarity with the Lord. There are many persons, superficially involved in prayer, who abandon prayer once and for all when dryness comes on the scene; included among these are people who, if beset by a crisis in this time of weakness, abandon the religious or priestly institution. On the contrary, anyone involved in the torment of aridity, although he suffers for a frightfully long period of time, does not abandon prayer.

Aridity is fundamentally a feeling of absence. If a person does not know or is indifferent to another, and this other is absent, the first remains unaffected. But if he or she loves the other intensely, the absence of the other leaves the first sad and desolated. And the greater the love, the greater the desolation.

The *Spiritual Canticle* of John of the Cross records these verses:

Extinguish these miseries,
Since no one else can stamp them out;
And may my eyes behold You
Because You are their light,
And I would open them to You alone.
    Reveal Your presence,
    And may the vision of Your beauty be my death;
    For the sickness of love
    Is not cured
    Except by Your very presence and image.

The tragic thing about aridity is that we suffer such interior disorder that we do not understand that the absence of God is the cause of it all. Better yet, we have the impression that everything is a lie, or that everything is happening because of irrational fate, or that God is nothing. Psychologically speaking, the sensation of aridity is probably comparable to what the Fathers called the "tedium of life," although much more intense.

Generally, these purifying torments are accompanied by social misunderstanding, slander, unjust accusations, desertion by friends, all wrapped in darkness and mystery. God brings together different causes in order to untie us from the thousands of fetters that keep us on the ground. No one is free from these purifying trials.

In her *Interior Castle*, Teresa of Avila advises her community:

> "So do not suppose, sisters, if you ever find yourselves in this condition, that people are wealthy, or free to do as they like, have any better remedy for such times. No, no; to offer them earthly consolations would be like telling criminals condemned to death about all the joys that there are in the world; not only would this fail to comfort them — it would increase their torment; comfort must come to them from above, for earthly things are of no value to them anymore."

It is true that in the area of psychology there can be phenomena similar to that of aridity, such as loathing and the death-wish. For those advanced in the mystery of God, a temperament of this kind could cause aridity to grow to the point of exasperation. It is impossible to discern precisely where God is influencing and where the personality of the individual is the influence. But let us not forget that such shining personalities as Francis of Assisi and Saint Teresa of Avila have acutely suffered the beastliness of aridity and darkness.

So then, without ignoring the possible influence of the personality — aridity is a trial of God to purify, liberate, heal, burn away, transform, and unite. The mystery operates very deeply, underneath all appearances, and psychoanalysis is not able to come close to the bottom of this mystery in any way.

In order to comfort those who have passed through or who may pass through similar situations, I offer this beautiful paragraph by Saint Teresa from *The Interior Castle*:

> Now what will a poor creature like that do if such a thing goes on for a very long time? If she prays, she might as well not be doing so at all — I mean for all the comfort it will bring her, for interiorly she is incapable of receiving any comfort, nor, even when her prayer is vocal, can she understand what she is saying; while mental power at such a time is certainly impossible –her faculties are not capable of it. Solitude is still worse for her, though it is also a torture for her to be in anyone's company or to be spoken to; and so, despite all her efforts to conceal the fact, she becomes outwardly upset and despondent, to a very noticeable extent. Is it credible that she will be able to say what is the matter with her? The thing is inexpressible, for this distress and oppression are spiritual troubles and cannot be given a name.

Aridity is the continuation of the drama of Gethsemane. In the Garden of Olives, on a clear night in the month of Nisan, a dark night overpowered Jesus. His soul was touched to the depths by aridity. Those who have experienced it in "high gear" use expressions very similar to those of Jesus on that night (Mt 26:30-46; Lk 22:39-45; Mk 14:25-43). All who have participated in the combat of the arid night also participate in that acute depression of Jesus.

What are we to do?

Remain standing, keep watch next to Jesus, with Jesus, despite the fact that our soul is ashamed and humbled. Faith and hope must illuminate, like a small candle, the night in the Garden of Olives, that faith and hope which tell us that beyond the night is a dawn. Yes, tomorrow the sun will rise.

What then? Do not let yourself be overcome by discouragement. Hope against all hope. Resist the darkness by accepting it. Overcome the confusion with humble surrender. Do not collapse if the night should continue. Keep watch, without sleeping, throughout the night next to Jesus, accompanying Him with love, with hope, with tenderness.

A "queen" of the "nights"

Our attention is drawn to the subtle descriptions made by John of the Cross regarding these purifying nights. We have seen the feminine concreteness with which Saint Teresa describes them.

But, without a doubt, the model and queen of the arid nights is the little saint of Lisieux, Thérèse of the Child Jesus, not only because of the clarity with which she expresses herself or because of the simple and dramatic force of her descriptions, but above all because of the wholeness with which she lived them — with an attitude of surrender. Because there are so many people in this purgatory of aridity (they probably imagine themselves to be in "hell" due to the atrocity of the absence of their Beloved), for their comfort I am going to share some of the moving testimonies of Thérèse.

Before taking the habit, having just left the world, she writes to a nun in January 1889:

Dryness and drowsiness — such is the state of my soul...

Calling herself "little lamb," she conveys the tragic silence of God with a childlike language in another letter of the same year:

Your little *lamb* — as you love to call me... I cannot speak to Our Lord, and he is silent too.

In the same year, amid fine ironies and symbolism, uniting simplicity of expression with pathetic grandeur, she says:

> The lamb fools herself believing that Jesus' toy is not in darkness; she is sunk in it... Even so, the lamb is right, this darkness is luminous, but nevertheless it is darkness...

Eighteen months have passed. She is going to promise herself to God with the covenant of profession. She prepares herself for the taking of the vows with the fervor we have all experienced in these moments, but she feels like a dried-up fountain in the middle of the desert. "Do you think" — she writes to a sister — "that I do not think of anything. In a word, I am in a dark underground passage."

None of her spiritual directors is capable of exorcising her aridity. God is, for her, "the Silent One," but she continues in peace, absolutely surrendering; and although she sees nothing, feels nothing, beneath all appearances shines the presence of her Beloved who inspires and edifies:

> My Beloved instructs my soul, he speaks to it in the middle of the silence, in the darkness.

She is still in her youth, having just reached nineteen years of age, yet we see in her a maturity disproportionate to her age. She is a fragile woman but she demonstrates a mature wisdom. There is in her life a mystery that is disturbing: she possesses a privileged intelligence and yet does not understand what she reads:

"Do not think" — she writes to a sister — "that I swim in the midst of consolations. Oh, no! My consolation is not to have it on earth. Without showing himself, without making me hear his voice interiorly, Jesus teaches me in secret; not by means of books, because I do not understand what I read."

She is a woman of unique strength. There are no

extraordinary events in her life. The only extraordinary thing is the density and the persistence of the silence of God throughout her life. But she lives peacefully. She feels the trust and poverty of a child. She lets herself be carried. She would not even complain of the darkness nor of the aridity. She accepts them almost with joy. With head-spinning speed she covered the distance to sanctity; with simple surrender she burns stage after stage. In the volume by Reverend Thomas Taylor, imagining herself to be a fiancée, she describes her path this way:

> Before starting, my Beloved asked me in what land I wished to travel, and what route I wished to take. I told him that I had only one desire, that of reaching the summit of the mountain of love. Thereupon, roads innumerable spread before my gaze...
>
> And Our Lord took me by the hand, and led me through an underground passage where it is neither hot nor cold, where the sun does not shine and where neither wind nor rain can enter — a place where I see nothing but a half-veiled light, the light that gleams from the downcast eyes of the Face of Jesus... I cannot see that we are advancing towards our journey's goal, since we travel underground; and yet, without knowing how, it seems to me that we are nearing the summit of the mountain.

This is the model and the conduct for continuing despite aridity: Not to let ourselves be dominated by depression. To believe and to hope against all appearances. We walk underground, yet we are scaling the peak. How? I do not know; but He knows. God is silent. But I know that, without anyone perceiving Him, the Lord instructs my soul in the middle of the silence. Consolations? Perhaps there will be none until the day of eternity. The consolation is hope. To surrender, to hope, and to watch with Jesus during the long night of aridity, that is the attitude we need.

Chapter 4

ADORE AND CONTEMPLATE

The tranquil night
At the time of the rising dawn
Silent music,
Sounding solitude,
The supper that refreshes, and deepens love.

John of the Cross

One burning afternoon, Jesus, covered with heat and dust, crossed the province of Samaria by way of the wide pass that lies between Mount Ebal and Mount Garizim. On top of the latter, the schismatics of Israel, the Samaritans, had erected a relatively modest temple, a faithful replica of the Temple in Jerusalem. And here on this mountain, the religious life of the Samaritan people developed. The rivalry between the Jews and the Samaritans had been going on since the days of the return from Babylonian captivity.

Coming out of the pass, Jesus entered the valley between Mount Ebal and Mount Garizim. At the entrance to the valley stood the city of Sychar, a city bound up in legends from the days of Jacob. Near the city was a well about thirty meters deep. Tired, Jesus sat down next to the well.

And a strange thing happened. With a bucket on her head, a woman came from the city, a woman of many years and much history. Jesus asked her for some water to relieve

His thirst. She found this to be a strange request. Very soon, however, the two entered into a highflying conversation. And, at a certain point in the discussion, in this unique experience, a word with the weight of eternity sounded: *adore.*

"I see you are a prophet, sir," said the woman. "Our fathers worshipped on this mountain, though you say that Jerusalem is the place where one ought to worship." Jesus said, "Believe me, woman, the hour is coming when you will worship the Father neither on this mountain nor in Jerusalem... But the hour is coming — indeed is already here — when true worshippers will worship the Father in spirit and truth: that is the kind of worshipper the Father seeks. God is spirit, and those who worship must worship in spirit and truth." (Jn 4:19-24)

Toward the interior

There is an oriental poem which says:

I said to the almond tree:
— Brother, speak to me of God.
And the almond tree blossomed.

However, the Face of God will not blossom that easily. That blessed Face is covered by dense clouds, always distant, beyond the sea of time. We need to place ourselves on watch and row amid the hostile waves of distraction, dryness, advancing ever further into silence with the help of psychological methods in order to reach the Center that concentrates and quiets all of the fears of the heart.

Glimpses of creation, common reflection and vocal prayers can make us present to the Lord, but in a scattered and indirect way. The deep and living fountain is far away. We may quench our thirst in the running waters of a rushing stream, but the source of that water is high above, in a glacier of eternal snow.

The more we experience God, the more we long for the Fountain itself, for the Glacier itself. As John of the Cross wrote in his *Spiritual Canticle,*

> Do not send me
> Any more messengers,
> They cannot tell me what I must hear.
> Since she is conscious that nothing can cure her grief other than her Beloved's presence and the sight of him, she asks him in this stanza, distrusting any other remedy, to surrender his presence that she may possess him.

Beyond glimpses, gifts and graces, we search, testing not only the water but the Fountain itself. We search for that quiet, identifiable, and ineffable relationship of the I-Thou. We search — how can we say it? — for that profound communication of presence to Presence, that interaction and interrelation of consciousness to Consciousness.

But once again, through the shadows, God begins to manifest Himself to us, but in a way similar to that of the sun which pours out its sunlight through a mass of trees in a dense forest. It is the sun but not the sun: it is bits of sunlight through the density. John of the Cross describes it thus:

> O spring-like crystal!
> If only, on your silvered-over face,
> You would suddenly form
> The eyes I have desired,
> Which I bear sketched deep within my heart.

We must understand that this presence is always obscure, but by remaining obscure it becomes more alive. I mean that when faith and love intensify, then the features of God are not perceived more clearly, but rather are more alive. The clarity does not refer to the form because God has no form except in the density and sureness of His presence. I can be, on some dark night, "with" another person; although we do not see each other, although we do not touch each other and we are completely silent, looking at the stars, I can vividly "sense" the other's presence, I "know" that the other is there.

When we try to enter into communication with the Lord, the first thing that we have to do is to give life to the presence of the Lord, after controlling and centering the faculties.

We have to be very sure that God is objectively present in our entire being, such that He communicates and sustains His existence and consistency within us.

We have to remember that God sustains us. It is not the case of a mother who carries her offspring in her womb but, rather, in our case, that God penetrates, envelops, and sustains us.

He is further and closer than time and space; He is around me and within me; and with His active presence, He is in the most distant and deepest areas of my interiority. God is the soul of my soul, the life of my life; He is the all and all-encompassing reality within which we are submerged; with His life-giving strength He penetrates all we have and all we are.

In spite of such intimacy, there is no identification or mixture but an active presence, creative and life-giving. This ultimate reality of humanity is expressed by the psalmist with an incomparably poetic expression: "All find their home in you" (Ps 87). The slow recitation of some of the psalms at the beginning of prayer can serve to make us "present" to the Lord.

* * *

It is necessary to venture into the interior because only our interior perceives God. Speaking of the Dark Night of the Soul, John of the Cross tells us:

The wisdom of this contemplation is the language of God to the soul, of Pure Spirit to the spirit alone... This wisdom is secret to the senses; they have neither the knowledge nor ability to speak of it, nor do they even desire to do so because it is beyond words.

People who move in the world of the senses and are dominated by them will not be capable of religious experience, at least while they are under that domination.

The Mystical Doctor speaks of an edge of the soul, which he imagines to be like the noisy suburbs; it would be the senses and fantasy, a world with its busy-ness that impedes the vision of the more interior passages. And, venturing further within, the saint points out the region of the spirit that is a "deep and vast wilderness... an immense, unbounded desert."

This is what we call the *soul*, a bounded region between us and God, simultaneously human reality and a theater of divine activity, a very real universe, like the wall we touch, but whose general perception escapes us because we live on the outskirts; those in touch with their interior distinguish it and perceive it although they too are unable to translate it into words. In his *Living Flame of Love*, John of the Cross describes this situation in these words:

> The soul's center is God. When it has reached God with all the capacity of its being and the strength of its operation and inclination, it will have attained its final and deepest center in God, it will know, love and enjoy God with all its might.

How the soul is the bordered region between God and us is explained by the Saint in the following way: it amounts to saying that the depth of the soul is proportional to the depth of love. Love is the weight that tips the balance toward God because love unites the soul with God, and the greater the amount of love, the more deeply is the soul centered in God. For the soul to be at its center (which is God) it is enough that it have an amount of love. And the greater the amounts of love we have, in this same proportion, will we continue to center and concentrate ourselves in God. And if we arrive at the ultimate level of divine love, we will have opened ourselves to the ultimate and most profound center of the soul.

It may happen, then, that successive levels of the soul are penetrated. And at each level, the Face of God shines more, His presence is more patent, the transforming seal deeper, and the joy more intense. Understand this well: I must necessarily speak in metaphors. When I speak of penetrating new levels, I mean *perceiving, distinguishing.* The soul (as well as God) is unalterable. In the way that faith, love, and interiority go on living, they point out new areas.

Saint Teresa symbolizes this grandiose reality by the mansions of a castle, each of them deeper within the castle.

Because of this, Jesus says: "Anyone who loves me will keep my word, and my Father will love him, and we shall come to him and make a home in him" (Jn 14:23). And the greater the love, the more interior and intimate the home. In those profound regions within each one of us, we experience the active and transforming presence of God.

1. THE ENCOUNTER

Intercessory prayer, as well as that of praise, is populated with persons: we pray for the sick, the missionaries, for the Holy Father... In adoration, the whole world disappears and we are left alone: He and I. And if we do not get to the point of being alone, just He and I, then there is no true encounter. I could be at a prayer meeting, amid five thousand people, where everyone is praying and talking. If I, in my own place and time, do not remain alone with my God, as if no one else breathed in the world, there is no real encounter with the Lord.

We began by saying that, before all else, every encounter is intimacy, and all intimacy is a closed room. Everything that is vitally important is solitary. The biggest decisions are made alone; we die alone, we suffer alone; the weight of responsibility is the weight of solitude. The encounter with the Lord happens alone, even in communal prayer.

The encounter, then, is the meeting of two "solitudes."

This is the great problem for achieving the encounter of adoration: how do I arrive, through silence, at my own *solitude* and the "solitude" of God. And, achieving this, how do I quiet (isolate, untie myself from) the outside clamor, nervousness, tension, as well as internal turbulence, so that I perceive, in complete silence, my own mystery? And, second, how do I overcome the forest of images, ideas, and conceptions of God and remain with God Himself, with the Mystery, in the total purity of faith?

Beyond the senses

On a late afternoon, I hear beautiful music. The melody, in this moment of faith, carries me to the living God. But if I, focusing all of my attention, try to "remain" with the Lord *Himself*, the music fades away, although it can still be heard. The Lord God is beyond the senses. Better yet, uniting myself with the One who is Sensed, the sensation disappears. How do I unite myself with the pure "solitude" of my God?

In the morning, we immerse ourselves in the heart of nature. This mixture of color, shapes and sounds, this inebriating variety of harmony and life, awakens in me the living and loving presence of my God and Father. But if, in pure faith and concentrating all of my energy, I establish an intentional link with my God, remaining alone with Him, the mountains, flowers, and rivers disappear, although the sun continues to shine. God is "beyond," which does not mean that He is distant, but that He is something different from the image we have of Him. The One who is Sensed appears, and the sensation disappears.

On this serene night, we go out in the country. We

181

contemplate the sky for a long time in silence, and we say: That starry firmament, light-years beyond and farther than measurable distance, evokes in me the pulsing mystery of my God, eternal and infinite. But if, in pure faith, I enter into a current of personal communication with that same Eternal, the stars fade away as if by magic. Here is the problem: How to arrive at the "solitude" of God and remain with Him alone, in simple and total presence? How to establish the relationship of mystery to Mystery?

Owing to His transcendent nature and our cognitive processes, we dress God with conceptual images and forms. But He, I repeat, is distinct from our representations of Him. To adore Him in spirit and truth, we have to divest the Lord of all that clothing which, if not totally false, is at least imperfect or ambiguous. We have to "silence" God.

It may be good to support ourselves with nature in order to pray, and for some it might be most effective for adoration. It is also good to attend theological classes, where the mystery of God is presented conceptually. But the prophets came from the deserts, there where the Lord emerges in the boundless expanse of monotony, in His "aloneness," in His inescapable Essence, as Himself. In a garden or in the country, a thousand reflections are distracting, and the soul resigns itself to glimpses of God among the creatures; but in the desert, in pure faith and naked nature, God shines forth in pure light.

We do not mean by this that, to adore, we should look for the burning sands of a desert. We are speaking figuratively. We need, yes, certain elements of what is meant by "desert": the nudity of faith, silence, and solitude. And this, if not every day, at least for the encounters of intense moments.

God *is* "alone," we *are* "alone." We advance toward the meeting of these two "alonenesses."

Our inner sanctum

To feel lonely is to feel alone. It is something negative. But to *perceive* myself as alone is to become conscious that, as myself, there is no, nor will there be, any other in the world: *only me and only once,* my mystery! Something ineffable, singular, new. By silencing the outer noise and, above all, the inner clamoring, we arrive at the perception of our own *solitude* (interiority, identity). What impedes, then, the perception (possession) of our identity is the interior scattering by which we are split by memories, sensations, plans, and preoccupations that disintegrate us in such a way that we end up feeling like a bunch of pieces of ourselves. If we are not (do not feel ourselves to be) unity, we cannot "possess" our mystery. In this case, the encounter with God, which is always one of unity with Unity, is impossible.

* * *

Human beings are not completed beings, but rather beings "in process," by the use of their freedom (*Gaudium et Spes,* 17).

A stone or a tree is a completely realized being within the boundaries or limits of its essence. I mean to say that it cannot give more than it gives, it cannot be more perfect than it is. The same for a cat or dog. They are bounded beings, finished, "perfect" within their possibilities.

We are not. We, essentially, are "able-to-be." We are the only beings in creation who can feel unfulfilled, unsatisfied, frustrated. And because of this, among created beings, we are the only ones who have the ability to overcome the barriers of our limitations. On the other hand, we are also the only ones capable of introspection, transcendence, and freedom. In a word, we are open beings, capable of a personal encounter with God, of a dialogue with our Creator.

The Second Vatican Council presents us as magnificent beings, "center and crown of all things" (*Gaudium et Spes*, 12), who carry within ourselves the image of God; carriers of countless seeds for improvement and, above all, "with the capacity to know and love our Creator." We are particularly distinct from other beings in that we have an interior zone of solitude, which is the site of the encounter with the transcendent and absolute.

> For by his *interiority* he outstrips the whole sum of mere things. He attains to these inward depths whenever he enters into his own heart. God, who probes the heart, awaits him there. There he discerns his proper destiny beneath the eyes of God. (*Gaudium et Spes*, 14)

This deals, then, with a secret and interior area to which we ought to descend if we want the face-to-face encounter with God; a place, on the other hand, where no one else may enter: "... the most secret core and sanctuary of a man. There, he is alone with God, whose voice echoes in his depths" (*Gaudium et Spes*, 16).

With this, the Council appears to be pointing out that, if that zone of solitude is not inhabited by God, we will feel uninhabited and empty. And it is then that the word *solitude* acquires a tragic meaning and becomes the number-one enemy of all humanity.

It is in this space of "aloneness" where God awaits us for the dialogue, in order to become part of our life and to fulfill and channel the high energies of His creatures.

This also means — always according to the Council — that the greatest value within our psychic makeup is the God who invites us to dialogue. Our life forces lean toward this greatest value when we look for the silence necessary for contemplation (*Gaudium et Spes*, 8). All of this leads us to wisdom, which is the final result of the filling of His "space of aloneness": "Steeped in wisdom, man passes through visible realities to those which are unseen" (*Gaudium et Spes*, 15), that is to say, to the Absolute.

* * *

I am going to perfect these ideas with other words. When we get hold of ourselves experientially, we realize that we "are" various deep or interior levels, as if the different levels were the various floors of a highrise building.

Among those levels and beyond them, we realize that within us there is an *inner sanctum* which no one can enter save he who is not affected by space, precisely because that room is not a place but, rather, *something*. When scholastic theology was being developed and everyone was looking for a definition of person, Duns Scotus (1270-1308) said that a person is the *ultimate solitude of being*.

In our most important moments, we see ourselves as *solitary beings*; our own unique identity emerges, for example, in suffering. At that time, we may be surrounded, for example, by our closest loved ones who, with their presence, words, and affection, try to "be with" us, accompanying us in this decisive time. The tenderness and words do not get beyond our skin or ears. In our "inner sanctum," there where we are *ourselves* and different from all else, where we are completely alone, and where there are no words, affection, or presence that can reach "there," everything remains on the surface. Others may be next to us. However, in our ultimate and definitive personhood, no one can even come close to us.

There is, then, in the constitution of each person, something that makes that person unique, different from others, and which, like a blanket of light, crosses and occupies the whole of his personality, granting him ownership, uniqueness, and identification. This solitude (being oneself) is perceived, we repeat, when our whole being is silenced: our mental, physical, and emotional world. This occurs in such a way that, experiencing it, two expressions — solitude and silence — are confused and identified with each other. The perception of oneself (solitude) is the result of complete silencing.

185

The possessive perception of our mystery is the "place" of worship. It is in this "temple" where we worship in spirit and truth, as Jesus asked, and where we arrive at the meeting of two mysteries.

Enter and close the door

On the Mount, Jesus, raised on a rock in front of a waiting crowd, had proclaimed the plan of the kingdom. He was saying that in order to worship, many words and long litanies were not necessary; nor were silver trumpets. It is enough to enter one's own room, close the door, meet the Father who is in secret, and remain with Him (cf. Mt 6:6).

I want to put these words in another language, broadening their meaning. After all, they have nothing to do with the meeting of persons of flesh and blood, who shake hands to greet one another and who sit in armchairs to talk. It is easy to close doors made of wood and to shut glass windows. But in our case, we are dealing with something much less palpable. That interior room is another "room," those doors are other "doors," and that entering is another "entering."

I will never tire of repeating: for God to "appear," for His presence in faith to be made real, open and pure attention, purified of all surrounding desires, is necessary. The more creatures and images are silenced, the more available we are, the purer and deeper the encounter will be.

According to my understanding, the majority of us remain outside of the powerful experiences of God because we have not done this difficult and essential work prior to the encounter. I understand that for us poor mortals, wearing ourselves out in the storm of life, it is not easy to make each day a profound encounter with the Lord God, but it is possible to do it during the *intense moments*. The more frequent these intense times are, the easier it will be to live in the permanent presence of God.

* * *

The task has two sides to it: *silencing* and *the perception of our own mystery*. We ought to busy ourselves first with the silencing. We have already put together, in the previous chapter, a series of exercises for silencing everything. Notwithstanding, I am going to add here some other practical advice.

We have to silence three very different areas.

The exterior world. A group of exterior phenomena, events, and things are, or become, different stimuli that, according to the sensitivity of each individual, disturb that quiet, excite and disintegrate us, and make us lose our sense of unity. To save ourselves from these destructive waves, we must *alienate, absent, detach* (three words and one meaning) ourselves from everything in such a way that our surroundings do not rob us of peace nor disturb our concentration.

The bodily world. This has to do with tension or nervousness that causes muscle cramps in various parts of the body. This uselessly wastes excessive amounts of energy and causes depressive fatigue, as well as a general state of restlessness. In this case, silencing is called *relaxing*.

The mental world. This is a mass of mental activity in which it is impossible to distinguish between what is thought and what is emotion. Everything is intermixed: memories, images, plans, perceptions, feelings, resentments, thoughts, criteria, desires, obsessions, anxieties. ... All of this has to be covered with the cloak of silence. Silencing is called, here, disinterest or detachment.

We are dealing with total purification. When the dust settles, peace is all that remains and my mystery appears in all its purity. And, putting ourselves in the orbit of faith, the mystery emerges "here and now," and the encounter of mystery with Mystery is consummated, achieving the encounter in spirit and truth.

We must begin by *silencing the exterior world.* We must realize that the birds will continue to sing, motors hum, and people shout; but we must detach our attention from all of that in such a way that we hear everything but listen to nothing. To silence means, in this case, to take attention away from all that bustles so that we remain absent or alienated from everything, as if it did not exist.

Do it very calmly. To suspend attention, the easiest thing is to suspend mental activity or to create interior emptiness, as was taught in the preceding chapter.

Seated in a comfortable position, breathing deeply and peacefully, practice detachment. Do not let confusion hook you; do not allow external influences, which normally assault the senses, disturb you or have any impact on you. Take advantage of every circumstance to practice this process of liberation.

Second, *relax all tensions.* The key idea is to *let go.* Let go of that which ties, or that which you have grabbed or that which has grabbed you. To let go of the muscles and nerves is to relax, and to relax is to silence.

Sit down comfortably, with the body erect. Breathe deeply and calmly. Like the master who goes about checking the grounds of the estate, go over your whole body, imposing tranquility upon it.

Quiet, concentrating and at peace, begin by loosening the muscles of your forehead (by muscles, we mean the nerves that control the muscles), until the forehead is relaxed and smooth.

Loosen the muscles of the head, those that surround the skull.

Loosen the muscles (and nerves) of the face, jaw...

Loosen the muscles of the shoulders and neck until they feel relaxed.

Loosen the arms, forearms, hands.

Loosen the muscles of the chest and stomach, legs and feet.

And now, as a whole, experience how your body is calm and relaxed.

Immediately, you should begin to let go or loosen the interior nerves and muscles. Do it first with the brain. Then with the throat. Continue with the heart and lungs and stomach, especially with the solar plexus. Finish with the digestive organs, the intestines, and the like. Upon completion of the exercise, you should vividly experience a profound and simultaneous sensation: in the whole of your physical being, complete silence reigns.

Finally, we have to *silence the mental world.* It is the most difficult and most important task. Once again we have to use the word *let go* or *loosen.* You will notice that memories or desires have a hold on you, tie you down. Let go of them and let them disappear into the land of the forgotten. Do it like someone erasing a blackboard in an instant. Seated, assume a comfortable position. Breathe deeply. Begin with your past life.

With a single stroke, put out of your mind all memories: those that bring joy, those that bring sorrow, those to which you are indifferent. Retain nothing from your past: persons, conflicts... Leave everything empty, like someone who turns out a light in a room, leaving everything in darkness. Cover the whole boiling cauldron of the unconscious with the mantle of oblivion, this living cemetery of all the remembrances of a lifetime. If memories come to mind, let them go one by one.

Let go of everything: plans, hopes, fears, ideals, desires...

There is nothing outside of this moment. Let go of all problems, real and imagined.

There is nothing outside of this place. Let go of absent persons, your place of work, your family...

Everything silenced, only the *present* remains:

   a consciousness of myself,
    here and now.
  I am myself: a perception of myself
  as subject and object of my experience.
  I am the one who perceives; I am the one perceived.
   To think what I think. To know what I know.
   I am one and unique,
   different from others.
  I am alone and only once,
   unity, "aloneness," *myself,*
    mystery.

We have said that worship is the meeting of two *presents* that come together as only one *presence.*

  Two presences mutually open and accepting,
  in dynamic quiet,
  in quiet movement.
  Two presents moving mutually toward one another,
  moving inward toward intersubjectivity.

This living the *present* does not mean disinterest in the rest. It is not camouflaged self-centeredness. On the contrary, this *present* encircles a great explosive charge of radiation; it dynamically extends itself from one horizon of life to the other: the past is made present, the future is made present, here and now, and, like the nucleus of an atom, in this present are included all of the possibilities for transformation and love.

It might be said, Prayer is a complicated thing. We know well that all prayer is a gift from God, and more so is the gift of contemplation. I know very well that the Lord God, without any preparation, is able to occupy every room of a soul. But it usually does not happen that way.

On the contrary, there are many who, because of a lack of systematic preparation, are left stuck in mediocrity. Those who live on the surface of prayer do so because they do not prepare themselves, and they do not prepare themselves due to a lack of interest. We cannot cross our arms, lift our eyes, and wait for the rain. Using the means at our disposal, we are showing our willingness and we demonstrate that, in truth, we are seeking the face of the Lord. We prepare the ground; the Lord will send the rain and growth.

Remaining with the Father

I arrived at and entered the deepest solitude of my being. I turned on the light of faith and, lo and behold! That solitude was occupied by an Inhabitant, the Father.

If the Father and I find ourselves in a closed room, what do we do now? What do we say? Jesus gives the answer: be careful with many words! Now that the Father is there in the most secret place, *remain with Him* (Mt 6:6).

Remaining with the Father means establishing an attentive and affective current with Him, a mental opening up in faith and love. My mental energies (what *I am* as consciousness, as a person) leave me, are projected onto Him, and remain with Him. My whole being remains quiet, concentrated, penetrated, paralyzed in Him, with Him.

But this does not only deal with my going out to Him, with my opening up. At the same time, it is pleasant because there is another reaching out — in love — by Him towards me. If He reaches out for me and I toward Him, if He accepts my reaching out and I accept His, the encounter becomes a crossing and crystallization of two reachings-out and two acceptances. In this way, a profound and transforming union is produced, in which the stronger assumes and assimilates the weaker, without either of the two losing his identity.

And so, from the start, the transforming process begins. The deeper the encounter, the more the presence begins to make itself present, to make an impact, to illumine and to inspire us in our deepest realities, because they are the vital center: the unconscious, the impulses, the reflexes, thoughts, criteria... The more alive and profound the encounter is, I repeat, in this same proportion will the Presence touch, penetrate, and bring to light our most intimate and most important threads.

We begin to walk in the Presence of the Lord (the Presence is lit up in the consciousness). The impulses and reflexes, reaching out, reach out according to God. And so, our general behavior (our lifestyle) appears to the world to be the "figure" of God. His being is made visible through my being and we are transformed into a reflection of God Himself. In this way, the Lord continues to advance in the conquest of new lands, and like ever-widening concentric circles, the divinization of humanity continues. But, everything begins with the nucleus of intimacy. There, all possibilities are contained.

* * *

This *remaining with the Father* is the same as *speaking with God.*

To talk with God is different than to think about Him. Whenever we think about someone, that person is absent. To think about someone is to make present (re-present) that someone who is absent by means of a combination of memories and images which I have of him or her.

But if that someone is suddenly present before me, I no longer think about him or her, but rather a dialogue is established with the person, though not necessarily one of words but one of intimacy.

When two known and loved presences are together, nothing more than a stream of giving and receiving, of loving and being loved, is established.

It is a living cycle of dynamic motion which, however, takes place in utmost quiet. In this type of dialogue, words need not cross (neither vocal nor mental ones) but rather consciousnesses cross in an intersubjective exchange, in a projection never identifying yet always unifying.

All of what has been said can be summed up in these words: *You are with me.*

Darkness does not hide You, distances do not separate You. There is no interference in the world that can keep me from You. You are with me. I go out on the street and You walk with me. I go to work and You are at my side. While I sleep, You watch over my dreams. You are not a detective who spies; You are a Father who takes care of me. At times I feel like shouting: I am a child lost in the forest, I am alone, no one loves me. Soon I hear Your response: I am with you, be not afraid.

In You, my roots are fed. I wrap myself in Your arms. You are with me. With the palm of Your right hand You cover my head. With the light of Your eyes You penetrate my depths. I am a child who is cold and You warm me with Your breath. You know perfectly well when I am at rest and when I begin to walk. My wanderings and path are more familiar to You than they are to me. I almost cannot believe it, but, wherever I go, You are with me.

Relationship of friendship

Saint Teresa has left us a famous definition of prayer: "It is nothing else... but to relate as a friend, often being alone with the One we know loves us."

To relate, in this context, presupposes, means, and contains within it an interior state — always interpersonal — affectionate, in a reciprocal movement, swinging back and forth between giving and receiving.

It is on the verb *to relate* that we must place the emphasis. Wherever there is relationship with God, there is prayer; for there to be prayer, there must be friendship, and this, in whatever type of prayer, from the recitation of a prayer learned by memory to the highest peaks of contemplation.

Following Teresa of Avila, we will say that the encounter is a communication — once again, intercommunication —

something like a business transaction in which the merchandise is love: that which God offers to us and which we also give back in return. It means an affectionate interchange in which we know that He loves us and that we love Him. "To be," to relate, to look, to feel reciprocally present, would be some of the words that might come close to expressing the essence of prayer. We could also speak of an interchange of gazes. Saint Teresa is much more emotional than she is discursive.

God is Love, He has created us out of love, has revealed Himself to us through love, and the final goal of all His interventions can be nothing but to transform us in love. Love is dynamic action; God, who is Love, is always in action, inviting us, soliciting us, offering Himself to us, and giving "movement" to the interior faculties. The "movement" is the *I-Thou* relationship: a projection and interaction of the *I* in the *Thou*, and the *Thou* in the *I*.

In the *encounter*, most of all when it is on the road toward the deepening of contemplative prayer, intersubjective intimacy takes the whole person, without excluding the physical strengths and weaknesses, up to a certain point. In a somewhat profound encounter, the relationship of friendship is a joining of the total person, totally in God. It will be better to invert the idea: God totally invades us and the more freedom we grant to God in our territory, the more areas God embraces, the more regions He conquers.

With French clarity and her feminine concreteness, Thérèse of Lisieux describes the encounter for us in these words:

> For me, prayer is an uplifting of the heart, a glance toward heaven, a cry of gratitude and of love in times of sorrow as well as of joy. It is something noble, something supernatural, which expands the soul and unites it to God.

Intimacy

The most significant human word for making us understand the sensation of the encounter is *intimacy*. Intimacy is at the root and at the same time the result of the crossing of two interiorities.

Each one of us, each "I," is always a closed circle by nature. Interiority is the result of organizing ourselves and living within, in a perpetual inclination and meeting at our center. Interiority has nothing to do with selfishness or egotism, although they are similar in some respects.

Now then, two interiorities that reach out and mutually project themselves result in a third zone which we call intimacy, a reality psychologically perceptible but inexplicable: another area distinct from the two interiorities, from the two persons, something like a third "person" born out of the two interiorities.

It is the fruitfulness of transcendence. To transcend is to reach out of oneself. To transcend is to love. Love is always fruitful, it always engenders.

Now then, two centered interiorities that have reached out and have mutually projected themselves, "engender" that encounter, intimacy. With psychological concepts, we can conclude that if prayer is an encounter and the encounter is an intimacy, then prayer is an *intimacy with God*.

Far from remaining in His essence, God overflows His interiority and opens Himself to us in many different ways.

God *is* "in Himself" and "through Himself"; nevertheless, He "went beyond" those borders and poured Himself out on His creatures. The universe is, then, an "overflow" of God.

Furthermore, in an admirable reaction of love, He discovered Himself for us, "declared" Himself to us, and freely "offered" Himself to us, in order to form a community of life and love with us. God wants to form a family, a society in that one region where the joining of God and the person takes place, the region of the spirit.

If we respond affirmatively to God's invitation, then we are already forming a community of life, as companions in life. The encounter presupposes a homelike atmosphere. The Scriptures explain this atmosphere with expressions such as "lived among us" (Jn 1:14), and "we shall make a home in him" (Jn 14:23) — very homey expressions which evoke certain feelings of warmth, joy, confidence, tenderness, something similar to what one feels in a true home.

In this atmosphere, intersubjectivity is born and grows; that is to say, the projection of a subject toward another in a mutual interaction.

In a word: the encounter is a living and unending deepening of interpersonal relations, in an intimate and affectionate climate, a turning of the "I" to the "Thou," between God and us.

Diversity

Owing to the fact that each of us is distinct in our own beings, in our feelings, and in our considerations, the "relationship of friendship" continues to acquire nuances and unique shades depending on the moods, difference of age, rhythm of growth, psychosomatic dispositions, etc., in each individual.

The *encounter with God,* as an integral part of life, will continue to adapt itself to the changing dispositions of the person. Worries, sickness, depression, euphoria, simple fatigue may make a certain type of encounter with God difficult or impossible, or may even favor it.

Just as to *relate* to someone is to live, and to live is to adapt oneself, the *relationship of friendship* with God will continue to adapt itself with vitality and flexibility to each person and their circumstances, alternately utilizing helps or obstacles, enthusiasm or aridity, intelligence or imagination, devotion or dry faith, giving rise to new or unexpected forms in each one of us.

PRACTICAL EXERCISES

Reaching out and projection exercises

Clarifications

1. In this first exercise, in its three versions, there is a reaching out and a projection. My attention, which is the integrated unity of all my spiritual energies, in other words, my soul, reaches out, supported by a word. That word is like a vehicle that carries my attention and places it in God. Said another way, identifying myself with the content or substance of the word (making the word *mine*) *I myself* am left in *God Himself*, identified and penetrated by Him.

2. This is, then, an exercise of quiet and immobility. As we said, my attention goes out of myself, is directed toward another, is concentrated and focused on Him, and is simply left "there". It is a static adoration. There is a simple *Thou. I* am not even there because, in this exercise, the *I* disappears, leaving only the *Thou.*

3. Contemplating God from the perspective of each word, we should not worry about analyzing it; we do not have to understand the statement. That would be meditation. Now we are adoring. So then, my attention is centered on God, not analytically but contemplatively, as John of the Cross would say, *lovingly.*

4. An object, depending on the perspective from which it is viewed, appears differently, but it is always the same object. In these exercises, God appears as Eternity, as Immensity, as Strength, as Rest... We should not worry, we insist, about understanding *how* God is eternal, immense, but only gaze at Him and passively admire Him, first as eternal, next as immense, later as strength... Gaze at Him

and admire Him from the infinite number of perspectives that the Lord has.

5. If, with any of these following expressions, you should feel that you are completely at rest (how does one say it?), that the statement evokes deep realities, awakens unsuspected riches and fills you entirely, remain there without going on to the following one. If the possession is total, let go of it and continue to worship in silence. However, if you feel the desire to say something, give a free rein to the spontaneity of the Spirit.

6. Each exercise variation ought to last forty minutes, and can be extended as long as is desired.

How to practice the exercises

Before each exercise, do the following preparation, without forgetting the various ways of silencing found in the previous chapter.

Take a prayerful position.
Nothing in your past: let go of memories, etc...
Nothing in your future: untie yourself from
  worries, plans...
Nothing outside of yourself: let go of noises,
  people, voices...
Nothing outside of this moment.
  Everything is left in silence.
  There only remains a *present*.
  I am present to *myself*, here, now.
I am left poor, empty, stripped, free, pure consciousness.

Now, in faith, present yourself to Him in whom we exist, move, and are, to Him who penetrates and sustains all things.

Begin to say the words softly, trying to *live* the content of each statement (which is God Himself): try to feel what the statement says until your attention is impregnated by its Essence.

After saying the words, remain in silence for fifteen seconds or more, passive, mute, like someone who hears a sound that paralyzes him, penetrated, identified "with" *Him.*

The same statement may be repeated many times or continuously. If a certain statement says little to you, go on to the next one.

Golden rule: no violence; always calm and serenity.

It is useful to end each exercise with a decision for the future.

First variation

Generally, this variation does not produce a loving current. It is the contemplation (adoration) of *Being-in-Itself,* the Absolute, the Transcendent. Given its nature, gazing and admiring are its components. There is awe, like someone awed by a world of unexpected grandeur.

You are my God.
You are God forever, from the beginning.
Lord my God, you are pure essence.
You *are* without contours, without measure,
 without boundaries.

You are the grounding Ground of all reality.
My God, You are all and all-encompassing reality.
You *are*, profoundly and invincibly.
Lord, You are immutable eternity.
My God, You are infinite immensity.

O Presence, always dark and always clear.
O eternity and immensity of my God.
O unfathomable abyss of Being and Love.
O my God, You simply *are.*

Second variation

This variation is composed of *contrasts.* We must be conscious that, in the three versions of reaching out and projection, the *I* is absent (it does not appear as a center of attention); only the *Thou* remains constantly present. We should allow ourselves to be carried away by the *Thou.* In this second variation, however, there are three expressions in which the I appears. But this happens in order to emphasize, by contrast, the *Thou.*

In practicing this variation, there is the danger of mental activity, owing to the conceptual contrasts which the mind tends to submit to analytical activity. But this should not happen. On the contrary, we ought to have the contemplative attitude of one who looks at a landscape and sees the lights and shadows but does not focus first upon the lights and then on the shadows but, rather, takes it all in at once. We ought to do the same thing as someone who admires a contrasting skyline (rainbow, threatening clouds, patches of blue) in an all-encompassing gaze.

Prepare yourself by doing the aforementioned exercises, always ending with a decision for the future.

You are present without past.
My Lord, You are the dawn without sunset.
You are the beginning and end of all things,
without beginning or end.

My God, You are closeness and distance.
You are quiet and activity,
You are immanence and transcendence.
You are in the distant stars,
You are the center of my being.

My God, You are my All,
I am Your nothing.
Lord, You are pure essence,
without form or dimension.

O my God, You are hidden Presence.
You "are" my I,
more "I" than myself.

O depth of the essence and presence of my God.
Who are You and who am I?

Third variation

In this variation, we continue with the sustained presence of a *Thou*, within the same boundaries: reaching out and projection. Here, however, God is not so much *in-himself* but much more *for-me*. There is, then, a greater closeness and, as a consequence, the relationship (adoration) is much more *loving*. Nevertheless, the attention must be focused on the *Thou*.

It may happen that, as we do this variation, we seem to be wasting time. We must be aware of practicing truly transforming exercises. I will explain: all of the fears, anxieties, and bitterness are born in us supported by and tied to the "I." Thinking that we are gaining security, insecurity is the result. The immediate and real effect in adoration is that the "I" is assumed by the *Thou* and, as a result, the feeling of security is born.

Prepare yourself as previously indicated.

Lord, You probe me and You know me.
You penetrate me, You envelop me, You love me.
You are my God.

Lord, my God, You are my complete rest.
My God, only in You do I feel at peace.
Lord, only in You does my soul rest.

My God, You are my strength.
Lord, You are my patience.
Lord, You are my security.
Lord, my God, You are my joy.

Lord, You are beauty.
You are gentleness.
My Father, You are my sweetness and tenderness.
You are our life eternal, great and admirable Lord.

Transforming exercises

In this exercise, there is a great deal of mental activity. Attention is divided in two directions: *You and I.* There is also, in this exercise, imaginative activity.

We will use the verb "to feel," within quotation marks, as a synonym for concentrating: I "feel" that I have a fly on my forehead; I "feel" that the floor is cold; I "feel" that my fingers are together; I "feel" the heartbeats in my chest... In each act of *feeling,* my attention is centered. To feel is different from to think; it is similar to imagining. It is exactly the same thing as focusing our attention on something.

First variation

To practice this exercise, we must not forget to do the preparatory exercises already outlined. Then, in each statement, we must *feel* how God is entering our mind, our insides; *feel* how God is taking on our most secret desires, the mass of thoughts, putting out the flames of dislikes; *feel* how He wipes out the stains, washes the impurities... And in the end, we must let go of the oars, letting ourselves be carried by the current: What does the Lord want of me? Do everything slowly.

My Lord and God, come inside me.
Enter and occupy the very roots of my being.

Lord, take me completely.
Take me with all that I am,
   all that I have,

all that I think,
all that I do.
Accept my most secret desires.
Take me in the intimacy of my heart.
Transform me in You completely.

Free me from resentments,
   oppressions,
   bitterness.
Rid me of all this, carry it away.
Wash me completely.
Erase everything, put out the flames.
Leave me with a pure heart.

What do You want of me?
Do with me what You wish.
I surrender myself to You.

Second variation

We are going to imagine that we are spending an
"intense moment" of a few hours. Let us suppose that we
have problems in our family, in the community, at work:
conflicts with others, situations we do not like, events we
resist. We need to forgive; we need to accept, and it is
necessary to do this *in God*.

Together in a spirit of faith, and once we have entered
into communication with the Lord, we ought to go back
down into our life with our God "at our right hand,"
making ourselves mentally present in the home, in the
community... facing that person, forgiving, understanding,
loving him or her, in the presence of the Lord; taking on
that situation with a "what do You want of me?"; accepting
some limitation with an "I surrender to You." Pray in this
manner, intensely and with liberating results until you feel
healthy, strong, fearless, and full of peace.

To practice this, the expressions of the preceding exercise may be helpful. You may also let yourself be carried

away by inspiration, inventing other ones. Always end with some decision for the future.

Visual exercise

Take some expressive picture, if possible, one with an image of Jesus, an image that evokes powerful feelings: strength, intimacy, patience...

Take a prayerful position. Place the picture in your hands. Do the aforementioned exercises of relaxation and silencing.

Simply look at the picture for a brief time.

Then, for some four minutes or so, calmly and with concentration, without trying to analyze it, try intuitively to capture the impressions that the picture suggests to you.

Third, nonviolently and with utmost calm, make yourself be that image, as if you were it or were within it. And, reverently and quietly, try to make your own the impressions which the picture evokes within you. That is, identifying with that picture, remain impregnated with the feelings of Jesus that the image expresses. Stay with this for a long time.

With this interior state, mentally move yourself to your family, to your job, or to any difficult situation. Mentally imbue that situation with that attitude of Jesus.

Hearing exercise

Find a place alone.

Take a comfortable position and a prayerful attitude.

Build silence; let go of memories of the past; let go of worries about the future. Untie yourself from the noises and voices you hear around you. Remain in the simple present; alone with yourself. Slowly enter into the world of faith.

Choose a short expression, one word if possible; for example *Lord!*, or *Jesus!*, or *Father!*, or some other.

Begin to say it slowly, every ten or fifteen seconds. While saying it, make the expression *yours*, that is, the *content* of the expression, until all of your energies of concentration are identified and impregnated with its Presence or Substance. Do this with utmost tranquillity and calm. Begin to feel how your whole being is filled with that Presence, beginning with the brain, the lungs, the heart... If you feel good, repeat the expression less often, leaving more space for the silence.

Make a decision for the future and return to your life, full of God.

Exercises of imagination

There are many people for whom the following ways of praying prove to be very effective.

First variation

Let us suppose that you had, in the past, a very powerful experience of God in some concrete place, very far from where you are now.

Go back with your imagination to that place, with greater reality if possible. Bring that place back to life, be it a chapel, a hill, a mountain, or a river, reliving all of the details: hearing the wind, the rustle of the trees, feeling the warmth or cold of the air, that brightness, shadow, or darkness...

In this way, in faith, now try to relive that experience of God that you had before. The memory of profound experiences feeds the prayer life of many people for many years, especially in times of aridity. How it comforts them to return to those moments of happiness while they lived with the Lord! End with a decision for the future.

Second variation

After the proper preparation, we should form an interior attitude of deep faith and recollection.

Imagine Jesus in adoration on a mountain, at night, beneath the stars. With utmost reverence, imagine yourself in the interior of Jesus, living what Jesus *lived*. What feelings of admiration and oneness did Jesus experience with the Father! What would that mixture of devotion, veneration, and offering be that Jesus felt for the Father! Those desires of pleasing Him, of being faithful, of making His life an offering to Him! That attitude of surrender before the will of the Father!

Try to make all of this *yours*, in faith. Take on the heart of Jesus with all of its emotions.

Return to life and be a bearer and beacon of the feelings of Jesus, and renew the face of the Earth.

Third variation

With the movement of your lungs, each time you exhale, say the name of Jesus, with the following various attitudes or feelings.

For example, every five minutes, repeat the formula of faith: *Jesus, I believe in You*. Do it in such a way that your whole being, including the body, joins in this attitude. Then, for another five minutes, (upon exhaling): *Jesus, I surrender to You*. Continue to repeat the expressions that indicate adoration, surrender... for some four minutes.

Slowly let your soul, head, heart, lungs... be filled with the presence of Jesus, with which you will return to life. End with a decision for the future.

Fourth variation

To create feelings of gratitude, relive some concrete event that in the past caused you great happiness, feeling now, if possible, something of that same happiness. Try to put yourself in "harmony" with Jesus when He said, Thank you, Father, for having heard me. And, with Jesus, thank and acclaim the Father.

Go back to a disagreeable event in your recent past. Relive that experience without fear. Then, imagine Jesus before Pilate or Herod, ridiculed, beaten. Observe His posture and admire His serenity. Interiorly, try to reproduce (in light of the memory of that disagreeable event) the same attitude, and, with Jesus and like Him, take on that event with the same dignity and peace.

2. PROFOUND ENCOUNTER

We have said that the encounter is a "relationship of friendship" with God. But we keep asking, what "happens" there? For suddenly, there is a realization, a knowledge. But it is not analytical knowledge, it is rather intuitive and possessive.

In that encounter, when it really is authentic contemplation, the *relationship* (knowledge? reflected consciousness? state of consciousness and emotion?) does not distract but centers.

This is something very difficult to explain: the encounter (when it is gradually more contemplative) tends to be simpler, more profound, and more possessive each time.

Reflection is left behind. The mind, working with the multiplicity and variety of facts, cannot "reach" that Total Reality (God) who is beyond the comings and goings, the ups and downs of life. When the mind begins to meditate, it finds itself subject to the multiplicity, the instability and the disquiet that divide and disturb it. Because of This, in the measure in which the encounter with God is more advanced and more contemplative, reflection tends to disappear and the encounter comes to be a much more simple and total act.

The instrument of the experience of God is not the

intellect but the total person. Language is abandoned and communication takes place between being and Being; vehicles or intermediaries such as words or dialogue are not necessary in order for us to unite ourselves with God. Because of this, I say that the intellect has little or nothing to do, because the mystery of the union is consummated between entire Being and entire being.

And it may happen that, in this contemplative experience, mysterious energies of "adherence" are attained, strange powers of "knowledge" (profound strengths that are normally atrophied in our subconscious because we generally live on the surface). They are supernormal forces, natural by nature, awakened by grace and interior vitality.

We can say of true contemplatives that they have overcome the rational and intellectual mind. When contemplatives enter the profound area of communication with God, the varied and pluralistic activity of the consciousness ceases; and, in this simple and total act, contemplatives sense themselves in God, within Him and He within them (Acts 17:28).

So, then, what does this mean? It means a type of intuition, dense and penetrating at the same time, and above all, very alive, without images, without determined thoughts; there is no representation of God. It is not necessary to represent Him because God is "here," He is "with" me; it is a real consciousness of the Great Reality that overflows me completely. But, it is not an abstract reality, it is rather a friendly, familiar, loving, concrete Someone.

In a word, we are dealing with super-knowledge; better yet, ultra-knowledge. It is the Wisdom of which John of the Cross speaks. It is an *immediate living* of God.

How could we describe the profound encounter? We can only speak in metaphors.

It is a starry night. Faith, that blessed theological virtue, surprises the child and the arms of the Father are opened. The child places himself in the heart of the Son and from that vantage point, contemplates the Father. The Father is a limitless panorama, without doors or walls, day and night illuminated by tenderness; it is an infinite forest of warm arms inviting an embrace, free of bitterness, full of sweetness.

Suddenly, everything comes to a halt. There is no movement in the world so quiet, or silence so dynamic. *Love.* There is no other word. Perhaps this other word: *Presence.* Putting the two words together we come close to what "this" is: *loving Presence.* Maybe this other expression comes even closer: *enveloping Love.* It is the Father. He is ten thousand worlds, He is ten thousand arms that surround and embrace the loved child. He is an unavoidable tide, like a huge tidal wave that violently floods the beach, a tide of enveloping Love (How can we put it?), an unexpected increase of water that floods the land. In this way the beloved child is surprisingly flooded by the Loving Presence which is definitely freely given.

The stars? They stubbornly continue to shine but there are no stars. The night? The night has been drowned, everything is light, although it is still night. The beloved child says nothing — what is there to say? The Loving Father says nothing either. Everything is consumed. It is an eternity.

Is there a loss of identity? Personal identity remains more clearly than before. The consciousness of the difference between God and ourselves, in some contemplatives, takes on boundaries as sharp as that between light and darkness. So we have the "nights of the spirit" of John of the Cross and the continual exclamation of Francis of Assisi: "Who are You and who am I?"

Alienation? The empty consciousness of the empirical "I" concentrated in the One, is irresistibly attracted to and taken by the Object, made totally one with Him. We, as contemplatives, are taken outside of ourselves, all differences disappear.

When we arrive at this state, everything will be the work of grace; psychological crutches, supports or human strategies do not exist nor do they work. It is God, in His infinite power and mercy, who unfolds Himself over the thousand worlds of our interiority.

Does the duality continue? Duality almost disappears, without losing the distinct consciousness between the individual and God. Up to a certain point we can say that there is only one reality, because this type of encounter engenders love, and love is unifying and identifying.

Because God created us in His image and likeness, the final goal of the Covenant is to become *one* with Him without losing our identity (the tendency of love, its intrinsic strength, is to unite those who love each other); and I would almost dare to say that the final end and perfection of the *encounter* lies in the disappearance of all duality between God and ourselves, and in the arrival at total unity. To quote *The Ascent of Mount Carmel* by John of the Cross:

> When God grants this supernatural favor to the soul, so great a union is caused that all the things both of God and the soul become one in participant transformation, and the soul appears to be God more than a soul. Indeed, it is God by participation.

Fusion? Thérèse of Lisieux says, "That day there was not even a look, but a fusion. We were no longer two. Teresa had disappeared like a drop of water which is lost in the depths of the ocean. Jesus alone remained, as owner, as king." Nevertheless, this expression is a way of speaking; not only is there no fusion but the more one advances in the sea of God, we repeat, the more the brightness that distinguishes and divides becomes painful and burning when we taste the sweetness of God in the face of the misery of our soul.

Transfiguration

The profound and contemplative encounter is eminently transforming. God assumes and consumes the "I." And we enter the rushing stream of love.

God visits the soul and does nothing more than awaken us from this obsession, and places us on the firm ground of wisdom, objectivity, and peace.

The Father cleanses us entirely with His enveloping Love. With this, we find that everything we admired up until then is artificial, that the illusions that adorn the "I" are vain. With His presence, the Father purifies us, strips us, and liberates us, destroying the castles in the air, burning the paper dolls and, as a result, true reality emerges, in naked purity. We have entered the abode of wisdom.

Who are You and who am I? You are my All, I am Your nothing. In my nothing, however, as a beloved child, I have everything in Your freely given love. Before the Splendor of Your Face, the figure of the "I" is reduced to nothing, like the stars that fade in the brightness of the sun.

When we are speaking here of the *I*, we do not mean our personal reality, much less our personal identity. We are speaking of the image of our personal reality, a shadow of reality. We transform this effigy into an object of our attention and devotion. Many people spend half their life erecting a statue and the other half in fear that the statue may fall.

A powerful experience of God begins in the center of the nucleus of the I. The Presence envelops and assumes the "I," better, the adherence to an image vanishes. When the beloved child is assumed by the Father, the "I" ceases to be the center. So, we let go of all appropriations and adherences, and are left free. The transformation has begun. God comes, rips off the masks, strips the "I" of its artificial clothing and, suddenly, we feel pure, free, empty, transparent, breathing in peace, seeing everything clearly.

The consciousness of the I is completely attracted by the other, as if taken off its hinges by the force of admiration and gratitude. As a result of this, attention and intention, free from attachment, are irresistibly seized by a new center of gravity. In this way, a new situation is established: the *difference* between the I and Thou disappears. Love takes on flesh and bones. There are no abstractions but only concrete reality.

Loving Presence awakens, inspires, and transforms our potentials in the interrelationship of brothers and sisters, and we, purified by the stripping, begin to experience love (coming from love) with full depth and purity. In this way, our life, for those of us who have been "visited," enters into an irreversible process of transparency, acquiring a new meaning and a new strength.

Poverty takes us by the hand and leads us to security. Things, the world, brothers and sisters begin to be pure for us: they are no longer distorted by our vision, disturbed by interest and appropriation; they — the things — begin to be *themselves* in the original purity in which God envisioned and created them, enveloped, too, in love and wisdom. In this way, our own reality is made real for us and is accepted in peace. Anguish disappears forever. Peace dawns.

Beyond space and time

Contemplatives tend to rise above the multiplicity of things and events; somehow they tend to place themselves above time and space and in certain respects, above the law of contingency, at least beyond the contingency of situations and emergencies, because they are anchored, by participation, in the absolute and immutable essence of God.

Certainly, the contemplatives do not escape time or the laws of space. But, because of that profound unity with God, they are able to catch a glimpse of the Unity that coordinates the successive instants which form time, and that glimpse makes them participate to a certain degree in the timelessness of the Eternal.

In this way, contemplatives begin to overcome the anxiety that is the result of the limitations of space and time. Surrendered to God, they have no fear of old age or death but rather participate in God's eternal youth.

God is Presence; there is no here, there, near, or far. He is *with me* and *in me.* He fills everything. Before Him, everything is relative and loses its individual profile. There only exists the immensity, better yet, there only exists the Immense. If *He is* with me and I *am* with Him, then I, too, am "immense," or, better, *child of the immensity.*

Yesterday, tomorrow, before, after, centuries, millennia do not mean a thing. Who defined time as the *movement of things?* In the profound encounter, movement does not exist. There exists Quiet, Eternity. The Lord my God is Being, quiet and eternal, but in His depths He carries a dynamism that in the splendors of eternity, like an expanding universe, put into motion and gave birth to this colossal fabric of the universe which our eyes contemplate. What are our concepts of difference, relativity, and distance worth? In light of the Absolute, everything is relative: time does not exist. I would not say that He "is in" time but rather that time has been consumed by eternity. The Lord is Eternity and I am a *child of Eternity.*

Brighter and brighter

At the risk of repeating advice that has already been given here and there, I am going to present some practical rules, following the suggestions of the spiritual masters.

When meditating on some topic of reflection, we should not stay with that material if we find no profit or devotion in it. If, at times, we feel warmth, brightness, or love, we ought to stop for the time being. The first rule is: let the Spirit carry you, rather than follow some preset plan.

The most important goal is the experience of God to transform life, rather than that any one particular experience.

We often display a great deal of enthusiasm for gaining or feeling devotion. But this can easily become an agitated enthusiasm, which is counter-productive because of its excessive force. We do not reach devotion with open arms. On the contrary, this forcing of the desire for something causes the heart to dry up and makes it incapable of the Lord's visits.

Perseverance, yes; force, no. A vehement desire for climbing ahead can toss all plans aside; what we experience instead is mental breakdown, nervous fatigue, frustration, and hunger.

The difficult and necessary thing is to obtain, at the beginning of prayer, an interior temperament in which two contrasting elements are integrated: a state of enthusiasm and a state of serenity. It is necessary to sustain a certain emotional balance at the closeness of our Loved One, and especially because that relationship of I-Thou is energy, movement of the faculties. But that balance can be fatal if it is not at the same time accompanied by a state of calm, peace, and gentleness.

Do not be discouraged if the feeling that comes is not the devotion that you desired. Patience and perseverance, we repeat, are the absolutely indispensable condition for anyone who desires to enter the castle of the experience of God.

If we have gained nothing, we are in the vicinity of the most dangerous reef, which is disenchantment. If we have spent the whole time and have felt nothing, we should not punish ourselves. In such a case, it would be good to take a book and try prayer by reading; doing this makes us always ready for the Spirit, which blows where it will.

Contemplation ought to flow out of meditation, like the final climb to the peak. As Saint Peter of Alcantara says: he who meditates is like one who strikes a flint in order to get a spark. Having achieved quiet, concentration, or feeling, there is nothing left but to rest and be silent with God; without arguments, concepts, or speculations but with a simple gaze.

Meditation is the road; contemplation is the goal. Reaching the end, there is no need of the means. Reaching port, sailing ceases. Ending the pilgrimage, faith and hope cease, which are like the wind that carries the ship to the harbor. Once we have arrived at the "sabbath rest," by means of meditation, we should abandon the oars and let ourselves be carried by the waves of wonder, amazement, jubilation, praise, adoration.

3. SILENCE AND PRESENCE

What we have described up until now is, in some way, *contemplation.* In my opinion, every true encounter (worship) is contemplation, and even more so, the *profound encounter.*

Life is coherent and one. We cannot take the easy road of saying: Up to here is the realm of meditation; here is the dividing line between discursive prayer and contemplation. In life, there are no chemically pure elements; everything is intermixed and combined. In all meditation, there may be a good dose of contemplation and vice versa. I, however, want to speak here (although there is the danger of repeating myself) of contemplation as such, of *acquired contemplation.*

In terms of *infused contemplation,* the Lord grants it when, how, and to whom He pleases. To have it, we cannot do anything: we do not deserve this gift, we cannot demand it, we cannot ask for it — it seems to me. It is absolutely and extraordinarily freely given.

We have already stated that normally, in the beginning, God lets us look for our own methods and supports, because there are no adequate methods for measuring when a spiritual state is the result of grace or when it is the work of nature. Later, the Lord Himself begins to intervene, making human techniques worthless, taking the initiative in submitting us to a passive state, taking complete possession of the castle where He is made Host and the castle is transformed into the greatest mansion.

Everything is the work of grace and, with these methods, we do not want to ignore or devalue the action of this free gift. With these aids that we are offering, we are simply preparing a receptacle (a cradle?) for the mystery; we are giving an affirmative response to grace, and we are *truly* seeking the face of the Lord.

In silence and solitude

For endless ages, God *was* silent. But in the womb of this silence, a more intimate and fruitful communication was developing. Within this interiority, the trinitarian relationships were going on, as in a closed and circular orbit, mutual relationships of attraction, knowledge (familiarity), and sympathy, of the Father for the Son in the Holy Spirit.

There is no dialogue more communicative than that in which there are no words, or that in which words have been replaced by silence. The contemplatives admirably underscore that fact. As we rise and deepen our relationship with God, first the exterior words disappear, then the interior words. Finally, all dialogue disappears. And there is no dialogue so intense as in this moment in which nothing is said.

The universe also was silent for many centuries. There was no above or below, there were no limits or boundaries. Everything was silence.

In the midst of this cosmic silence, the Word echoed, and the universe issued forth. The Word, then, was fruitful. But the silence was also fruitful.

Every artist, scientist, or thinker needs to have a grand interior silence in order to be able to generate perceptions, ideas, or intuitions.

Life grows silently in the dark womb of the Earth, and

in the silent womb of the mother. Spring is an immense explosion, but a silent one.

Spring has come.
No one knows how.

The most profound and dynamic people of history are those, like Elijah (1 Kgs 17:1-8), Jesus of Nazareth (Mt 4:1-12), and Paul of Tarsus (Gal 1:17), who have been able to sustain the combat with silence and solitude face to face, without falling apart. In my opinion, the "evil of the century" is *boredom,* which originates in our inability to be alone with ourselves. We of the technological age cannot stand silence and solitude. And to combat these, we grab a cigarette, a radio, or television.

To avoid silence, we blindly grasp diversion, distraction. As an effect of all this, disintegration is produced within us. This ends up by giving birth to the feeling of aloneness, alienation, sadness, and anxiety. That is the tragedy of the people of our day.

Without a doubt, the periodic cultivation of silence, solitude, and contemplation is more necessary, religiously and psychologically, than ever before.

Our interiority is assaulted and battered by speed, noise, and frenzy; we are, at the same time, our own victim and executioner; and we end up feeling insecure and unhappy.

There does exist a sterile silence. It is when we retreat into ourselves to escape communication with others, communication that is not always pleasant. This is the silence of the dead.

We have spoken of a zone of silence and solitude that radiates in our own constitution. But the dynamism of this silence does not impel us to hide from but to open ourselves to the dialogue with God. And just as this dialogue is love, and love is expansive, it opens us up to dialogue with our brothers and sisters. If this reaching out and these

217

results are not produced, we would be in an alienating silence. Paul VI wrote:

> For faith, hope and a love of God ready to receive the gifts of the Holy Spirit, not to mention a fraternal love open to the mystery of other persons, require as a kind of postulate, the necessity of silence.

The Word is always wrapped in silence. Silence is its natural receptacle in order to be fruitful. Only in silence can we listen to God.

> On the other hand, the disposition for an intimate union with God implies the need for a silence affecting one's whole being, whether those concerned are to find God in the midst of noise and confusion, or those who are dedicated to contemplation.

The moments of the advancement of the kingdom, just as in the great revelations throughout salvation history, have been given in the midst of silence. It is a given law of Scripture:

> When peaceful silence lay over all, and the night had run the half of her swift course, down from the heavens, from the royal throne, leapt your all-powerful Word like a pitiless warrior into the heart of a land doomed. (Wis 18:14-16)

Contemplation and combat

The Bible presents Moses as an extraordinary contemplative. His relationship with God is developed in a climate of immediacy, hand in hand and face to face with the Lord, notwithstanding a certain dramatic suspense which the nearness of God always produces.

The Book of Exodus sums up all of the human and prophetic greatness of Moses: "God spoke to Moses face to face, as a man speaks to his friend" (Ex 33:11). Moses had been cast in the mold of God, in the long days and nights within the cloud, enveloped by the silence and solitude, face to face with God, on the top of the mountain. Moses was God's own work of art. He is burning like fire and as gentle as the breeze ("extraordinarily mild": Num 12:3).

He was a military man, a politician, and a contemplative. Looking at his human breadth, we come to the conclusion that all contemplatives, when they let themselves be "taken" by the captivating closeness of God, will be transformed into a carved image of strength, purity, and fire.

The servant of God harmonized the tenor of a strategy of liberation with the demands of a hidden life with God. He alternated battles with God on the mountain peak with the battles with the people on the plains below.

These rules of silence and solitude for the encounters with God reach extraordinary heights in the case of Moses.

Whenever God wanted to speak with the contemplative Moses, He called him to the mountaintop (Ex 19:3; 19:20; 24:1).

There are times when the expression "to climb to God" and "to climb the mountain" are synonymous, as in the book of Exodus.

And, even when Moses was on the mountaintop, God demanded absolute silence. And so, on the first slopes of the mountain, He demanded that Moses meticulously draw a boundary across which no one must trespass, to the extent that "Anyone who touches the mountain will be put to death" (Ex 19:12).

It is a silent solitude so demanding that, even when Moses is accompanied by Aaron and the elders, they nevertheless have to stay behind while Moses enters into dialogue with God (Ex 24:2).

Sinai is itself a shining sign of the solitude of silence: 2,285 meters high, a burning sun, sand, rock, wind, solitude and, like a living symbol, eagles...

But here there is a tremendous mystery: God takes the form of a cloud, and the cloud is the symbol of silence.

Here, then, there appears to be an identical relationship between God-cloud-silence.

> Moses then went up the mountain. The cloud covered the mountain. ... To watching Israelites, the glory of Yahweh looked like a devouring fire on the mountaintop. Moses went right into the cloud and he went on up the mountain. Moses stayed on the mountain for forty days and forty nights. (Ex 24:15-18)

What happened during the forty days and forty nights in the interior of the cloud, on the mountaintop? We only know that, when Moses left there and descended to the plain, the Hebrews could not stand the shining light that lit the face of Moses. And he had to wear a veil so that the Hebrews could look at him and listen to him. And when he entered the cloud to speak with God, he took off the veil. "The Israelites would see Moses' face radiant. Then Moses would put the veil back over his face until he went in to speak to Him next time" (Ex 34:35).

Undoubtedly, all of this symbolism is filled with deep meaning, of which we can only uncover a little, but most of which escapes us. But in the midst of so much imagery, symbolism and theophany, a sensational lesson can be detected: Moses, the most "committed" of all the prophets, the Great Liberator and great revolutionary, was a man who, unlike many, cultivated silence and solitude.

Flame of fire

Another of the men who alternated the frenzy of battle with solitude in God is the prophet Elijah. He is not a writer-prophet but a prophet of action, and this draws more attention to his long periods of solitude. Elijah rises by surprise, "like a flame," on the scene of the history of Israel. God separates him from his surroundings and leads him to a dried stream in order to transform him into a "man of God."

> The word of Yahweh came to him, "Go away from here, go east and hide by the torrent of Cherith, east of the Jordan. You can drink from the stream, and I have ordered the ravens to bring you food there... The ravens brought him bread in the morning and meat in the evening, and he quenched his thirst at the stream." (1 Kgs 17:2-6)

And for the rest of his life, God keeps him apart from society, for his consecration. He does not have a home. He wanders like the wind, pushed and guided by God himself. His home is silence.

The prophet surrenders himself more and more to the will of God. This surrender is accomplished by the gradual interiorization of the most secret and profound intimacy with God. He makes a pilgrimage of forty days and forty nights to the top of Mount Horeb. Up there, within the cave, and afterwards outside of it, God displays, before the shaded eyes of the prophet, all of His glory and splendor (1 Kgs 19:8-19). The mystery of this theophany will always remain hidden and inaccessible to us. In Zarephath, when he restores the child to life, we sense that he is full of tenderness, intimacy and confidence in God.

> "Yahweh my God, do you mean to bring grief even to the widow who is looking after me by killing her son?" He stretched himself on the child three times and cried out to Yahweh, "Yahweh my God, may the soul of this child, I beg you, come into him again!"... And the woman replied, "Now I know you are a man of God and the word of Yahweh in your mouth is truth itself." (1 Kgs 17:20-24)

When he appears in public, Elijah is a man surrounded by flames. He is always attentive to the voice of God, according to his battle cry: "By the life of Yahweh, God of Israel, whom I serve!" (1 Kgs 17:1). The only things that mattered to him were the desires and glory of God. For this reason the power of God shone forth in his actions and his words.

He appears as a lookout, waiting for orders, and when God comes to him with the usual "Get up!", Elijah goes in all haste to complete his risky mission, to announce punishment to the king, to gather the people on the peak of Carmel, to bring down fire from heaven on the troops of Ahaziah, to unmask the powerful or to turn his back on the worshippers of Baal.

Solitude had tempered him for the more audacious undertakings. It is a two-sided life: he hides himself in God and shines forth before men.

The odyssey of the word

The "path" of Jesus through the world is the odyssey, the grand "tour" of silence, in its most profound and emotional sense.

In its first stage, the Incarnation is the great plunge into the waters of human experience. That is the meaning of the untranslatable *ekenosen* (Phil 2:7): he humbled himself, descended to the furthest depths of anonymity, humility, silence, to the utmost limits of humanity.

He descended into the humble womb of a silent virgin.

In the peace of a "silent night," he made his entrance into history, escorted by shepherds, on the throne of a manger. During that night in Bethlehem, silence climbed its highest summit.

During Jesus' lifetime, the Word of God was retained and trapped in the folds of silence. While he lived, how many knew that he was the Son of God?

The silence of the real presence of Jesus in the Eucharist is also impressive. There is no sign of life, no sign of presence; no one is heard, nothing is felt, nothing is seen; contrary to all evidence, there only remains the irreducible silence. Only faith frees us from the perplexity.

Silence covered, with a reverent veil, the totality of

Jesus' mystery during those many years in Nazareth. The new name for silence is Nazareth.

Jesus would have a rising career, from baptism to the cross. But before, in those unending years of silence, what calm hope! What long immobility! We see Jesus impatient: "I have come to bring fire to the earth, and how I wish it were blazing already!" (Lk 12:49). But, in those long years that preceded his preaching — what patience! What silence!

Meditation and contemplation

Contemplation is not a theological discourse in which a brilliant combination of ideas about God is woven, playing with premises and coming to conclusions. Neither does it deal with an exegetical reflection by which we arrive at an exact meaning of what the sacred author wanted to say, but it is rather, a penetration into what that author lived.

Some comparisons will shed light on the subject.

A botanist takes a flower. He takes a scalpel, divides the flower into various parts, places it on the laboratory table, takes the microscope, and studies the flower. In summary, he understands the flower by dividing it, with an instrument (*he himself* is far from the flower). He understands analytically.

A poet, on the contrary, does not pick the flower: he *is taken* by the flower. He "understands" the flower, going out of himself, marvelling, thankful, almost identifying with the flower, not partially but wholly. He understands possessively.

Contemplatives are, above all, not spectators but admirers. In their understanding (active verb), there are passive elements: admiration, gratitude, emotion. As a result, contemplation is in the same "harmony" as admiration. It deals with that suspense full of awe that Paul experienced when he said, "How deep and rich are the wisdom and knowledge of God! We cannot reach to the roots of his decisions or his ways!" (Rom 11:33).

223

I would dare to say that, in a certain sense, the contemplative capacity in a person is proportional to the capacity for wonder. Because of this, the contemplative is never with himself or turned inward. We are always in *exodus,* in a movement of reaching out and projection toward the Other, completely "ex-stasied" and taken by the Other.

As we know, the capacity for awe and narcissism are in inverse proportions. Narcissism and childishness are the same thing, just like maturity and narcissism are on opposite poles. In ourselves, the inordinate adherence to ourselves causes reactions of euphoria or depression, unbalancing our emotional stability.

In contemplation, there is no reference point in the self: the things that refer to the self are not important to the contemplative. The only things that have an impact are the things that refer to the Other. They are not elated by successes nor thrown by failures. Because of this, the great contemplatives are full of maturity and grandeur, with an unchanging joy, with the characteristic serenity of those who are in an orbit of peace above the ups and downs, storms, and troubles of daily living.

Those who meditate are expressive and eloquent. The activity of a beehive bustles within them, a perpetual coming and going, an endless jumping to conclusions, from inductions to deductions. Their heads are full of concepts which they analyze and decipher, distinguish and divide, explain and apply.

Contemplatives, however, are submerged in silence. In their interior there is no dialogue but only a warm and pulsing current of communication. It is a silence full of awe and presence which the psalmist felt when he said, "Yahweh, our Lord, how majestic is your name throughout the world" (Ps 8).

They affirm nothing. Nor is anything explained. The contemplatives do not understand nor try to understand. Arriving at the port, letting go of the oars, they enter the *sabbath rest.* This is the overwhelming possession in which all desires and all words are silenced forever. The union of being with Being is consummated (expression is not needed as an intermediary), of interior with Interior, of mystery with Mystery.

For the contemplative, it is enough *to be* "at the feet" of the Other without knowing or wanting to know; only looking and knowing that one is looked at, like a warm afternoon that completely surpasses all expectations, where everything appears to be quiet and eternal. We could say that the contemplative is mute, drunk, identified, enveloped, and penetrated by the presence, as John of the Cross says:

> I left myself and forgot myself,
> my face bowed before my Beloved,
> everything ceased, and I left myself,
> leaving my cares,
> forgotten among the lilies.

Contemplatives may be able to understand even better than theologians the profound mystery of God, of Jesus, of Eternal Life; yet, they cannot express those experiences and, it is possible, they might not have the direct consciousness of what they "understand." And this, because their living is too full, too profound, and there is no room for conceptualizing it.

In summary, meditation is analytical, conceptual, impersonal, inductive, differential, selective, and schematic. Contemplation, however, is intuitive, integrating, subjective, synthetic, totalizing, affective and unifying. Notwithstanding, as we said above, all of this is intermixed in daily life.

Adherence

The Council affirms that each person has been born so as to continue living beyond death. It adds that the final destiny of every Christian is the eternal contemplation of the endless mystery of God. And the Council concludes by giving us this splendid definition of contemplation:

> God has called and still calls man so that he might be joined to him with his entire being in an endless sharing of a divine life beyond all corruption. (*Gaudium et Spes*, 18)

It could not be said better. It is interesting to point out that when the Council refers to contemplation, it almost always does so using the word *join* (adhere), a word in which knowledge, love, admiration, commitment, surrender, and life are all wrapped up and intertwined.

As we have already said, the instrument of contemplation is not the discursive intellect alone. It is the whole being, integrated, that participates in unifying contemplation, "with the fullness of one's being."

Contemplation, as we are explaining it here, comes close to the word *know* in the Bible, to go beyond human knowing and to express an existential relationship. To know something is to have a concrete experience of it. This is how suffering is known (Is 53:3), as good and evil (Gn 2:9), it is a real commitment with profound consequences.

To know someone is to enter into a personal relationship with that person. These relationships may take on different forms and vary in the degree of relationship. In all respects, in the Bible, to know (just as to contemplate) is to enter a great current of life which overflows from the heart of God and flows back to it.

One notices the insistence with which Paul VI speaks of contemplation in his discourse at the closing of the Council. In the discourse, he speaks primarily of the "direct relationship with the living God," a precious and exact definition of contemplation. Then he asks if we "have looked for his knowledge and love," another very appropriate way of referring to the act and attitude of contemplation! Later, the Holy Father asks if we have advanced in the mystery of God during the conciliar sessions and then, finally, raising tone and emotion, he again summarizes the goal of the Council, proclaiming before the whole world:

> ... that God exists, that he is real, that he is living, that he is personal, that he is providential, that he is infinitely good, our Creator, our truth, our happiness; in such a way that the strength to center our sight and our heart on him, which we call contemplation, becomes the highest and fullest act of the spirit, an act which today can and should place in order the pyramid of human activity.

The object of contemplation is not an idea, not even a truth, but rather a Someone; a Someone who is, at the same time, original source and final goal of our destiny and our lives.

To lift all human efforts and join them to God is the most sublime act of the human spirit. And that action recapitulates and puts in order of priority all human values and activities.

Abounding in the same concepts, the Council makes another serious attempt to decipher the nature of contemplation, in its dynamic form. Speaking of how they ought to integrate prayer and action, it says that "it is necessary that religious combine action to contemplation by which they are adhered to God with the mind and the heart..." (*Perfectæ Caritatis*, 5).

General, confusing, and loving notice

As we climb the ladder of contemplation, the God who is the Object of that contemplation evaporates little by little. God begins to lose, step by step, forms, images, and models until He vanishes and is reduced to pure Essence. Never, however, is this God so much concreteness, transformation, strength, universality, and action as in this moment in which He is reduced to *essential purity*, in faith.

Yes. For pure contemplation, God has to be silenced,

stripped of the various clothing which our imagination places on Him. That is, God has to become poor. The contemplative is not interested in the "dressing" of God; what interests us is God Himself, in Himself, not the form but the substance, not God-word but God-silence — although the Lord is never so much Word, so much *Substance* as in this moment of silence.

When two silences are crossed until they blend, they crash with a great explosion. The words carry concepts and the concepts carry "little parts" of God. But only the silence can encompass *who He is*, and this is beyond concepts and words.

To know that we have entered that land of contemplation, John of the Cross offers us the following signs:

1) – enjoying being alone with the loving attention of God
   – being alone with loving and calm watchfulness
2) – allowing the soul to be calm and quiet although it may appear to be a waste of time
   – in peace, quietude, and rest
3) – leaving the soul free, unhindered, and rested from all mental discourse, without worrying about thinking or meditating
   – without any particular consideration, without acts and exercises of power, at least discursive power, which is a coming and going from one place to another
4) – avoiding methods and preoccupations that disturb and distract the soul from its calm tranquillity
   – only general notice and attention, yet very loving, without understanding about what

All of these characteristics are summed up by John of the Cross in these three terms: general, confusing, and loving notice.

He says *general* because it deals with an extensive or wide attention. That is, the attention is not centered on some specific aspect, but is stretched or diffused over the general object: God.

When we contemplate a landscape, our vision is not centered on the top of a hill or a tree-lined peak, but rather the eyes broadly scan the whole of the horizon. It is called "the infinite gaze." In an analogous way, the contemplative gaze is diffuse, extensive, or general.

He says *confusing* in opposition to analytical. Everything analytical is clear because in analysis there is division, and where there is division there is clarity. If we want to "conquer" a truth, we have to begin by dividing it: divide and conquer. The contemplative gaze, then, is confusing because it is not analytical.

It is also confusing because contemplative activity is not intellectual but living, and life is identified with my own person that lacks the distance and perspective to measure and ponder what is lived; because of this we cannot conceptualize, because the experience is, in itself, dense and complete and it is too near.

Nevertheless, although it is confusing, there is not a human gaze that infuses such certainty and that projects such clarity as the contemplative gaze.

The contemplative flies above the peaks of theology and exegetical clarity; and the more we are submerged in the depths, the more lost and found we are; the more dense the darkness, the brighter the light, the mind paralyzed and still, not understanding but possessing the Science and Divine Essence; wiser, more mute, climbing and soaring in the highest heights of all science. How well does John of the Cross express it:

> I entered into unknowing
> For I remained in unknowing
> Transcending all knowledge.
> I was so whelmed,
> So absorbed and withdrawn,
> That my senses were left
> Deprived of all their sensing.

And my spirit was given
An understanding while not understanding
Transcending all knowledge.

He says *loving*, that is, emotional. The closeness of the loved individual always produces suspense and emotion. The encounter of the contemplative is a person-to-person one. Because of this there is a touch of possessiveness, and the heart is ignited, and there is established a circular and reciprocal stream of giving and receiving, opening and acceptance.

Once again, John of the Cross:

O Lamps of fire!
In whose splendors
The deep caverns of feeling
Once obscure and blind,
Now give forth, so rarely, so exquisitely,
Both warmth and light to their Beloved.

In total fullness

God has predestined us for joining ourselves to Him with our entire being (*Gaudium et Spes*, 18). Fullness is the experience of interior integration. When attention (consciousness) penetrates every apartment of the human building, we can say that the person is integrated. Whatever is disintegrated is never whole. When we pray (or try to do so) in a scattered state, the prayer will always end with a feeling of frustration, only because we cannot pray in this state.

The same enemy always goes along with us: distraction. It originates in a state of conflict: criteria against impulses, behavior against value judgments. Where there is conflict, there is no peace; where there is no peace, God "is not."

How do we become integrated? On the one hand, there

is no integrating force like God Himself. Next to Him, none of the integrating exercises are worth anything. The profound mystery of the Lord, our God, fans out in every area of our life, crossing and purifying the different aspects, and in God we feel whole, solid and indestructible. But, on the other hand, before joining ourselves to God completely, we need to have an elementary degree of integration. How do we get it?

We perceive our unity when our consciousness is made present in every part of our being. But it may happen that the consciousness cannot be, *at the same time,* in different places. So, what do we do?

We have to get to the point where the consciousness is made completely present to itself. And, at this time, with our entire being in silence, we notice that the depth of our consciousness is extended over the entire landscape of our person, integrating everything with its presence. When the consciousness is "within" itself, it is also "within" all of its component parts. If the mind retains absolute control over itself, all of its parts are left integrated.

Exercise of silence and presence

It is possible that at first we may have the impression that we are wasting time with this exercise. Do not be impatient. Believe that it is the most helpful exercise for attaining the *spirit of prayer* and for "walking in the presence of God," a totally grand spiritual walking.

Adequate surroundings: choose a place where you can be alone, a chapel, a room, a forest, a hill.

Time: for this exercise, allow yourself an *intense moment* in which you are not pressed by hurry or preoccupation.

Position: comfortable and prayerful, in complete quiet.

Do the silencing exercises as described previously. Create interior emptiness, suspending the activity of the senses and emotions, putting out the memories of the past, untying yourself from worries about the future, *isolating* yourself or *distancing* yourself from the commotion outside of you and outside of this moment. Do not think of anything; better yet, think nothing.

Remove yourself more and more from the senses, beyond all movement, beyond action, without "looking" at anything outside or inside yourself, not holding on to anything, without letting anything hold you, without focusing on anything...

Nothing outside of you.

Nothing outside of this moment.

Complete presence of yourself "to" yourself, a pure and naked attention.

Once you have gained this silence, placing yourself upon the platform of faith, open yourself to the Presence.

Simply remain open, attentive to the Other, like someone staring without thinking, like someone loving and feeling loved.

In this moment in which you have placed yourself in the orbit of faith, you should avoid forming an image of God. Every image, every representation of God must vanish. "Silence" God, stripping Him of everything that signifies *location.* He *is not* near or far, above or below, before or after. He is Being. He is Presence, Pure and Loving and Enveloping and Penetrating and Omnipresent. *He is.*

Forget that you exist. Never look at yourself. Contemplation is fundamentally ex-stasis or going out. Do not worry about whether "this" is God. Do not disturb yourself with whether this is natural or comes from grace.

Do not try to understand or analyze what you are living. There only exists a *Thou* for whom you are, in this moment, an open, loving, and calm attention.

Practice the hearing exercises described previously. Without noticing, silence will replace the words until, in the moment in which the spirit is *mature,* the word, itself, will "fall." Do not say anything with your lips. Do not say anything with your mind.

Look, and you are "looked at." Love and you are loved.

Pure Presence, in pure silence and pure faith, will fulfill the eternal covenant.

It is nothing. It is Everything.

You are the receptacle. God is the content. Let yourself be filled.

You are the beach. He is the sea. Let yourself be flooded.

You are the land. The Presence is the Sun. Let yourself come to life.

Remain like this for a long time. Then "return" to life, full of God.

I also know people who practice *imaginative* contemplation. They go into a chapel in a complete silence. They look, in faith, at Jesus; they feel themselves looked at by him. They say nothing. They hear nothing. In complete quiet, they limit themselves to simply "being."

Chapter 5

PRAYER AND LIFE

He that has united himself to God acquires three great privileges: Omnipotence without power, drunkenness without wine, and life without end. (Kazantzakis)

I recognize that prayer can become, without our realizing it, a selfish and alienating escape. There are people who have made prayer a sterile activity, not because they were caught in the test of aridity, but because, living a devotion of the senses, they sought enjoyment, peace, and consolation in themselves.

Everything we are trying to promote in this book can sink us like a stone if we do not apply an honest and constant critique of life and prayer. Life has to be faithful to prayer and prayer has to question life.

Today, some young people judge and condemn their elders because they never stopped praying and yet, remained — according to the younger ones — selfish and immature for their whole life.

Young people (some of them) say that they do not care about praying because... Why? To be "immature" and "discontent," like those they know who *do* pray? Young people can easily understand that if some of the older ones are like "that," it will not be because they pray. It could be that they prayed poorly, or they did not pray well. However, we may ask, If they are like that and they pray, what would

235

they be like if they had not prayed? Might not those who criticize simply be rationalizing their own behavior?

Be that as it may, this phenomenon (the inconsistency between life and prayer) that some young people point out and criticize has always disturbed me. It certainly cannot be universalized. It does not happen to everyone. We know countless cases (without discounting the particular histories involved) in which individuals have made continual and superhuman efforts to overcome, *in God,* natural faults and negative aspects of their personalities. We cannot so easily say that "they pray and do not change." We do not know of their silent efforts. Change is always gradual and utterly slow. All in all, we have to deal with the frequent dichotomy between prayer and life, and set up an honest criticism between the two.

There are many people who dedicate countless hours to God. However, they carry their natural faults with them until their final days: always fighting, suspicious, aggressive, and immature. To all appearances, they did not *grow;* on the contrary, they seem way behind.

How is this possible? How does one explain those persons who dedicate so many hours to God, essentially a liberating God, who is not able to free them? For so many years they gave of themselves, with a lot of devotion, to the Lord God; how come this God was not able to put them in motion toward a world of maturity, humility, and love? How come they did not even grow a little? Where is the explanation for this contradiction?

Perhaps, instead of adoring God, they worshipped themselves. In their lives there was a subtle phenomenon, as unconscious as it was tragic, of *transference*: without realizing it, these people replaced their "I" for what they called "God."

That God, whom they treated with so much devotion, was not the true God. He was a projection of their fears, desires, and ambitions. They sought themselves in God. They served themselves instead of serving God. That God was never the *Other*. Their center of interest and attention was never the Other but themselves. They never reached out. They seemed to worship God, but they worshipped (in God) themselves.

They seemed to love God, but they loved (in God) only themselves. That God was a false god, an idol, a "god" made according to their desires, interests, and fears. Praying, they were always centered in themselves. Throughout their lives, they remained within a selfish circle. This is the reason why they did not grow in maturity, and carried their childishness, aggressiveness, and natural faults to the grave.

They never looked beyond themselves. If there is no going out, there is no freedom. If there is no liberation, there is no love. If there is no love, there is no maturity.

1. LIBERATION

The God of the Bible is a God-Liberator. He is the One who always intervenes, unsettles, and challenges. He does not answer, but questions. He does not solve problems, but creates conflicts. He does not make things easy, but difficult. He does not explain, but confuses. He does not foster children, but adults.

We have converted Him into the "God-explanation" for all that we know, the "God-power" who covers our weakness, the "God-refuge" for our limitations, failures, and discouragements. He is the projection of our fears and insecurities. But this is not the true God of the Bible.

Some famous people of our century have affirmed that religion fosters alienation and childishness. According to their psychoanalytic explanations, that "god" who explains and solves everything was the great "mother's womb" that freed (alienated) humans from the risks and difficulties of life, and let them avoid the open struggle on the battlefield of liberation and independence. In this sense, Nietzsche was right in affirming that the presence above of this "god" has impeded humanity here below from reaching adulthood, and so they have remained like children up to the present day. But this is not the God of the Bible.

That "god" had to die. In this sense, we may speak correctly of the "death of God." It was the lie of God, the false face of God invented by our imagination, used and abused by our pride, ambition, ignorance, and laziness.

The true God, always liberating, takes us out of our insecurities, ignorance, and injustices, not by avoiding them but by confronting them and overcoming them. The true God, according to the prophet Ezekiel, leads people to the desert where he enters into judgment with them face to face (Ez 20:35-37). He is the One who leaves His son alone in agony, faced with death. He is the God of adults.

He is the same One who, after creating us, does not keep us in our mother's arms to save us from the risks of life, but who quickly cuts the umbilical cord and says, Now be adults, push the universe forward and be lords over the earth (Gn 1:26). The true God is not one who alienates but one who liberates, forming older, more mature, and freer individuals and peoples.

Saved to the roots

In the Bible, there is not only or primarily the *salvation of my soul*. The salvation brought by Jesus, whose plan is announced to us in the Sermon on the Mount, seizes and takes hold of the entire individual. The plan of salvation goes to the roots of the individual, sinks to the repressed subconscious, illuminates the dark recesses of impulses and motives with a penetrating and revealing brilliance, awakens the reflective consciousness from its dreams of omnipotence and its delusions of grandeur, placing its feet on the ground, the ground of objectivity, causing us to enter the land of wisdom, of maturity, of humility, and of love.

In a word, it is the salvation of the whole. The God of

prayer ought to be a disturbing and questioning God. That is to say, a liberating God.

* * *

The drama of our humanity is this: from that fatal afternoon in Paradise, when we succumbed to the temptation "You will be like gods" (Gn 3:4), from that moment, we have carried with us an ancient, dark and irresistible instinct to become "gods" and claim all adoration for ourselves.

We violently subject, pressure, and obligate all people and all creatures to "worship" us. The values and realities within our reach are appropriated: money, beauty, sympathy, intellect, sex... Everything is subjected to our service and adoration. "Creation was made subject to your vanity" (Rom 8:20). We use and abuse what we consider to be "ours," like some despot.

If we could dominate the world, it would be done. If we could appropriate all creatures, we would do it. If we could oppress all of humanity, we would do it. We feel an insane and insatiable thirst for honor, applause, and adoration. Our life is a competitive battle to see who can capture the most attention. Sin resides within us and the sin *is* to pretend *to be like God.*

Everything that threatens to eclipse our power or lessen our honor is classified as an enemy; the dark seed of enmity is planted within us and war is unleashed to defeat any competitor.

We live full of delusions, hallucinations, and lies. For example, when we love, we think that we love but we almost always only love ourselves; the more we have, the more we think we are free, but in reality we are more slaves than ever before; the more people we dominate the more we believe we are in control, when in reality we are more dependent than ever before.

"Man's enemy is his own flesh," Saint Francis said. As a

result, because of our delusions of being first and rising above all others, we punish ourselves with envy, powerlessness, jealousy, worries, impossible anxiety, becoming victims by creating empires, kingdoms, and dictatorships, and then feeling trapped by our creations.

We exploit the weak. We pass up justice and mercy in order to amass more fortunes. We are insensitive to the cry of the poor. We amass fortunes with the blood and sweat of the workers. Often, when the poor become rich, they become the greatest exploiters of the poor.

In a word, we are slaves to ourselves. We need liberation. Down deep, and above all, we are idolators. We need redemption.

Making room for God

If this slavery consists of idolatry, the whole problem of liberation lies in displacing the "god of self" and replacing it with the true God. Salvation is that God is *my* God. For this to be so, that world of desires, dreams, and castles in the air that have sprouted from the idol of the self must be blown up. It is necessary to wipe out, to clean and empty our interior of all "appropriations" which have been absolutized and divinized, and, in its place, let God take possession and unfold, there, His holy Kingdom.

The path of liberation passes, then, by way of the poverty and humility of our Lord Jesus Christ (St. Francis). The *Maxims and Counsels* of John of the Cross contains this sentence:

The poor man who is naked will be clothed and the soul that is naked of desires and whims will be clothed by God with his purity, satisfaction, and will.

Only the way of the "nothings" (absolute liberation, total nakedness) takes us to the peak of the all that is God. As the Mystical Doctor says in his *Ascent of Mount Carmel,* "the soul must empty itself of all that is not God in order to go to God."

In the Sinai desert, the formula of the covenant sounded like this: Israel, there is no other god than God (Ex 20:2-4). With the savage force of a primitive desert formula, the Bible gives us the final secret of salvation: that God be God *within us*.

That simple formula is expressed in the biblical scene when Mordecai could have saved his people by bowing down before the proud Haman:

> But what I have done, I have done,
> rather than place the glory of a man
> above the glory of a God;
> and I shall not prostrate myself to anyone
> except, Lord, to you. (Est 4:17e)

Now then, the only "god" who can compete with God for kingship over our heart is ourselves.

Down deep there runs a tragic mystery: our "I" tends to become "god." That is to say, our "I" claims and demands worship, love, admiration, dedication, and adoration on all levels, something that belongs to God alone. The idols of stone, gold, and wood that appear in the Bible as competing with God (the golden calf, statue of Baal) are not real; they were and are purely symbolic.

The only idol which can do hand-to-hand combat with God over our heart is our self. In the end, one or the other gives up because the two cannot rule the same territory at the same time. "No one can be the slave of two masters" (Mt 6:24).

If liberation means that God is God *within us*, and the only "god" that gets in the way of that kingship is the "god of self," then we come to the conclusion that the kingdom, throughout the Bible, is a complete disjunction: God or us; it is understood that by *us* we mean the "old man," turned in on ourselves, with our insane desires for domination, of

241

owning everything and of demanding all honor and all adoration for ourselves.

When our interior is liberated from interests, ownership, and desires, God can become present there without trouble. On the other hand, as long as our interior is occupied by selfishness and egotism, then there is no place for God. It is occupied territory.

So we come to understand that the first commandment is identical to the first Beatitude: the more we are poor, detached, and disinterested, the "more" God is God within us. The more we are "gods" to ourselves, the "less" God is God within us. The plan, then, is very clear: "He must grow greater, I must grow less" (Jn 3:30).

"Blessed are the poor in spirit; the reign of God is theirs" (Mt 5:3). In the measure in which we make ourselves poor, letting go of every internal and external appropriation, and when this is done with God in mind, the kingdom of God automatically and simultaneously begins to unfold within us. If Jesus says that the first commandment contains and sums up the whole of Scripture (Mt 22:40), we can add, in a similar vein, that the first Beatitude contains and sums up the whole of the Gospel of Christ.

Liberation advances, then, along the royal road of poverty. The kingdom is like an extraordinarily simple axis that crosses the whole Bible supported by two points: the first commandment and the first Beatitude. That God is truly God (first commandment) is verified in the poor and humble (first Beatitude). This is where the biblical tradition has its origin, according to which, the poor and humble are the *heirs* of God and God is the *inheritance* of the poor. Only they will possess the kingdom.

Salvation is equivalent to love. But the quantity of love is equivalent to the quantity of liberated energy in our interior; that is to say, love is proportional to poverty. Because of this, Saint Francis said, "Poverty is the root of all sanctity."

Prayer ought to be the time and the means for liberating the energies tied to our own self-centeredness, making them available for service to our brothers and sisters.

Free to love

Being poor (total liberation) is also an indispensable condition for creating a joyful *community*.

Saint Francis of Assisi, who did not try to found an order but rather an itinerant fraternity of penitents and witnesses, placed evangelical poverty-humility as the only condition and possibility for there to be true community among his followers.

Francis clearly realized that all property is potential violence. Bishop Guido asked him, "Why do you not allow some property to the brothers?" Francis replied, "If we had property we would need arms to protect it." An answer of enormous wisdom.

If people are full of themselves, full of personal interest, the interests of some will clash with the interests of others, and the community will soon fall to pieces. It may be that where there are possessions, violence becomes present. When they feel their personal ambition or prestige is threatened, they jump to the defense of that ambition, and defense soon becomes offense, and very soon there are "arms to protect the property," such as rivalries, envy, intrigue, cliques, accusations — in a word, violence — that rips apart the common tunic of communal unity.

Because of this, Francis asks his brothers to make an effort to have patience, moderation, gentleness, and humility when they go preaching throughout the world (II Rule 3). He also pleads with them to have "humility, patience, pure simplicity, and true peace of soul" (I Rule, 17). It is evident that if the brothers are impregnated with this typical tone of the Sermon on the Mount, they will be men filled with meekness and gentleness, quick to respect, accept, understand, attract, stimulate, and love the rest of the brothers.

He counsels them to struggle against "pride, vainglory, envy, avarice, care, and solicitude of this world" (Rule, 10). If the brothers are found to be dominated by these attitudes, it will be a joke to call them *brothers*; community will be a torn, bloody, stepped-on banner lying in the middle of them all.

To be a good *brother*, one has to begin by being a good "minor." First and foremost, we must be liberated from all appropriation and ambition. Then we will arrive, by the path of this liberation, at community.

Poor to be mature

Liberation from ourselves is also a condition for *human maturity*, for *emotional stability*. To see this, we need do nothing but analyze the origins of overreactions and childish attitudes.

When we live full of ourselves, dragging ourselves around asking for public recognition, always seeking to look good in public, worried about our appearance... When our unlimited desires are met at any given time, we will have an overreaction. Our emotions will be so overwhelming that we will lose our balance, falling over.

But, oh, the day others cast us aside, forget us, or criticize us! That day, too, we will completely fall apart, this time because of bitterness. Others will see us "throw ourselves on the ground," becoming a "victim": they will see us destroyed, blown over by a reaction completely out of proportion with what actually happened. What is the profound explanation for all of this?

Let us suppose that what they criticized us for or cast us aside for was objectively just. Nevertheless, we consider it to be a monstrous injustice. There is, then, a problem of objectivity. We have an inflated image of ourselves, a sainted and idealized "I"; and our reaction was not according to objective reality, but rather according to the "I," divinized and falsely clothed by our dreams and desires. It is necessary to liberate ourselves from those dreams that falsify reality; otherwise, we will always be childish and bitter.

During the four centuries that followed the empires of David and Solomon, Israel's life with God fell to its lowest levels. Why? Because they lived resting on their laurels; they lived on two unreal dreams: on the past memory of the Solomon empire, dreaming that that empire would return one day (they lived in the past); and, second, they lived looking toward the future, to the nonexistent deeds of a messiah who would make them rulers of the Earth.

These delirious projections completely alienated them from the real, present situation (in which they were a divided and conquered people). And they were alienated from their fidelity to their covenant with God, in spite of the fact that the Lord had sent to them, during the whole of this time, a most impressive group of prophets.

God saw that the only solution was some catastrophe that would awaken them from the dreaming. And so it was. Deported to Babylonia, they realized that they had nothing in the world, not even the hope of having anything; that all of their dreams were lies, those about the past and those about the future; that they were no more than a handful of weak and defeated people. Waking from the false and inflated images they had of themselves and their history, realizing this, recognizing (and accepting) objective reality as it was, there and then did the great turning to God take place.

This is the terrible and endless history of every nation and of each person. It is necessary to be liberated from the false fronts with which we cover ourselves, and to accept the reality of our dependence, precariousness, indigence, and limitations. Only then will we have wisdom, maturity, and salvation.

Spiritual aristocracy

However, let us imagine the opposite case. There are people who have worked for many years to liberate themselves from their self-interests and "property," and have advanced in the "poverty and humility of our Lord Jesus Christ."

The first thing they acquire is objectivity. Flowers do not overexcite them, stones do not bother them much. If they rise to the throne, they do not die of joy; if they fall from the throne, they do not die of pain. Their mood remains stable before applause and before criticism, and the more liberated from themselves they are, the more unbreakable they feel. And if liberation from themselves is total, we find ourselves faced with people who feel the imperturbable serenity of one who is above the ups and downs of life.

We find ourselves before admirable and enviable figures, figures sculpted by the spirit of the Beatitudes, full of softness, strength, patience, sweetness, and balance. The poor one of the Gospel is an aristocrat of the spirit.

Nothing nor anyone can disturb the serene peace of their souls because they have nothing to lose, because they have not "appropriated" anything. What can disturb the person who has nothing and wants nothing? There will be nothing in this world that can exasperate or depress that person.

Liberation from oneself has given us a mature, balanced, extraordinarily stable person in his reactions and emotions, a human example of high caliber.

Vital circle

This whole process of liberation will carry us to the Kingdom of God, to the kingdom of community and to personal maturity, it will take place in the encounter with

God, in a circle that runs from life to God and from God to life.

Today, there is the common opinion that the place for the encounter with God is in humanity, in the world. Theologically, this principle has no answer. But it is an undeniable fact that the hardest fighting and most committed liberators of enslaved peoples — Moses and Elijah — did not meet God in the heat of military or social battles. Rather, they retreated to complete solitude and there found the courage and strength for the coming battles. The same was true of Jesus.

I have to bring to the presence of God my entire load of troubles and problems... It will be there (in the time and place of prayer) where I will have to ventilate my questions, crises, and pending projects to God.

That God with whom I have "communicated" in prayer, whom I have "seen," that most loving Father who must "come down" with me into life; that state of penetration and intimacy which I have lived with the Lord, that atmosphere (spirit of prayer, presence of God), ought to last and color my life, and "with him at my right hand," I have to fight the great battle of liberation.

The encounter with God is like a generator. But if the power of that motor is not transmitted by means of shafts and other gears that put machines in motion, the power is useless.

We have been with God. We have felt Him so vividly that His presence accompanies us wherever we go. A great difficulty arises: how to pardon an offense, feeling a great dislike for someone. For love of that God whom we feel is present, we face the situation and overcome our distaste. Conquering this, the love for God grows (I would say that God "grows": His presence is greater within me). This love pushes us to a new encounter with Him. This is the vital circle.

Not only that. The repugnant situation, overcome with love, has been transformed into sweetness, as happened to Saint Francis with the leper. And God said to him, "Francis,

247

you must renounce everything you have loved up until now, and everything which seemed bitter to you will be changed into sweetness and joy for you."

Any bit of selfishness (irritability, fantasy, envy, revenge, thirst for honor and pleasure) which is overcome (which we are liberated from) with God and through God makes love grow; and just as love is unifying ("my love, my strength," said Saint Augustine), attraction (strength) for Him grows; and it will carry us to a new encounter with Him.

In the encounter, we see that during the day we will have to do battle in the land of gentleness, patience, and acceptance, and "carry" God to the battle, and "with him at my right hand," we will have a series of conquests, at a high cost, of course, each conquest being rewarded by happiness and an increase of love.

There will be many who will say that this is masochism. Those who do, say so because they have never witnessed, even from a distance, the experience of God. Those who *live* for God, however, see this process as a joyful liberation.

When we find ourselves in a profound encounter with God, we feel as if the Thou "takes," "pulls out," absorbs the "I"; and then we experience the absolute freedom in which shyness, insecurity, ridiculousness, and all complexes disappear. No one will ever feel such an intense fullness of personalization, in spite of the fact that those who "know" nothing of God may speak of masochism. This feeling is exactly the same as that inebriating and powerful omnipotence that Paul felt when he said, "If God is for us, who can be against us?" (Rom 8:31). The problem is in experiencing that God is with me. Whoever has really felt it will *know* that it is total liberation.

We return again to life. We find ourselves faced with unfavorable comments about our behavior. Our desire is to look good, our natural thirst for esteem pushes us to justify ourselves. We remember the silence of Jesus before Caiaphas and Pilate and, without offering any explanation, we are quiet. We lose prestige but gain freedom. Liberation advances.

With the "Lord at my right" we return to life. There is a conflicting situation in which human prudence advises that we keep quiet; that way we are not involved. But we remember the sincerity and truthfulness of Jesus, and we say what we have to say. We get involved, but we feel free inside.

We go down to the burning sands of the struggle for justice. We become a voice for those who have no voice. Love carries us to the forgotten of this world. We are present among those whom no one sees, whom no one wants.

Soon, we see the reason why there are hungry and naked people, and we have to draw the sharpened sword to point it out and denounce it. War answered with war. And soon we feel the machines of the powerful at our side, with their intrigues, with their lies and provocations.

This is a very dangerous time for us. During the night (without our realizing it) the weed of hate against the oppressors may sprout in our heart. Our spirit may become poisoned, and the poison of hate may "kill" God Himself, and it may make the best plans sterile.

At such a delicate time, we need a strong tea in order to discern, among our feelings, those which sprout from below and those which emanate from God; we have to suffocate the first.

Although, at times, our actions may be the same as those involved in politics, we have an ever-present preoccupation with being a witness and not a politician. To keep our identity and to remain faithful to our mission, more than ever before, we need the "vision" of the Face of God so that, in its light, we may distinguish between pure and impure attitudes. We come down often from the "mountain of the Lord" with the "Lord at our right" (Ps 15) to remain at the side of the poor, to defend the oppressed and to liberate those in captivity, but at the same time not to be wrapped up in motives that are not those of a witness.

249

We live wrapped in God and pushed by love; we look for new opportunities and invent new forms of expressing love. We have found ourselves amid conflicts; in danger of breaking, we have remembered the wholeness of Jesus in his difficult moments, and we have remained whole. Last week we were upset and frantic; nevertheless, at the sight of the Lord, we balanced ourselves with serenity among the crashing waves.

Our daily liberation consists in accepting ourselves as we are, without bitterness, avoiding comments and reactions that bother others; we free ourselves to forgive and forget many details; to accept difficult things as they are; to share often with people whose presence alone disagrees with us; to avoid temptations, overcome sensitivities, and to have each time more lordship over ourselves.

While this is going on, faith and love grow; God becomes Prize and Gift, and life acquires new meaning, happiness, and splendor. In God and through God, the renunciations become liberations, privations become plenty and distastes, sweetness.

2. STEP FROM SELFISHNESS TO LOVE

Rectification

According to the Bible, what is the original plan of God in creating humanity? God wants to enter into communion with us. This is the ultimate goal of God's intervention in salvation history and, above all, it is the final objective of the Covenants.

In other words, having created us in His image (Gn 1:26), God wants to make humanity more like Himself. That is to say, first He wants to form a family with us, to make us more like Himself, making His children share in His own nature.

Before sin, this communion-likeness was an easy and

natural thing because we, according to the Bible, had been designed in such a way that we were a perfect echo of God Himself. Speaking with a certain clumsiness, we could say that God and we corresponded exactly, we were in harmony.

But sin came and disfigured our face. From that moment, harmony was impossible, communion was impossible for two beings so vastly different. There would have to be a profound purification through penance of our inner structure in order to re-establish harmony, unity, and likeness.

The Bible presents sin as the tragic reality that sinks its roots into our very essence: "I was born guilty, a sinner from the moment of conception" (Ps 51). Saint Paul says much more: "I do not understand my own behavior... it is not myself acting, but the sin which lives in me" (Rom 7:14ff). We are sinners, then, by birth and by personal guilt.

God, in the beginning, put order within us. This order was unbalanced by the eruption of sin-selfishness. Now it will be necessary to re-establish the original order by means of the re-ordering of penance. We would define Gospel penance as a re-establishment of that initial order established by God within us. In other words, a *rectification.*

A path of love

Penance also means conversion. And conversion means a difficult moving from ourselves to God. That is to say, an endless "passing" from the psychic structures of the "old man" (Rom 6:6; Eph 4:22; Col 3:9) toward the "structures" of God. What are these? They are the structures of love, because God is essentially Love (1 Jn 4:16).

In the Gospel, Jesus points out to us the route for this "step" with the penitential formula "Repent" (Mk 1:15; Mt 4:17). But the Sermon on the Mount is the most profound strategy of liberation from the slavery and demands of selfishness.

It is a program dictated on the top of the Mount, spoken to the winds, recorded by his listeners many years later, proclaimed in a style free of explanations. All of this makes it difficult to capture the exact meaning of his liberating message. But even so, we see that in the Sermon on the Mount the process of liberation, and its final goal – which is Love – is outlined perfectly. Essentially, in the first part, we are told of poverty of spirit, of humility of heart, of patience, of meekness, of forgiveness...

All of this signifies that the idolatrous demands of the "I" have been denied (Mt 16:24), even repressed (Mt 11:12), and, in this way, inner violences have been calmed.

And once these forces have been liberated, detached and unleashed from that "I," inflated by illusions and dreams, they are automatically turned into Love. Now, in the second part of the Sermon on the Mount, we will be able to use these forces, already transformed into loving ones, for the service to others:

to do good to those who wrong us (Mt 5:38-42)
to pardon those who offend us (Mt 6:12)
to make peace before offering gifts at the altar (Mt 5:23-25)
to correct our brothers and sisters (Mt 18:15)
to do good without seeking thanks or recompense
   (Lk 6:35)
to turn the other cheek (Lk 6:29)
to love universally, and not only those who love us.
   (Lk 6:32)

In summary, penance is an unending "step" from self-ishness to love.

Climb to the peak

But the secret strategy for conversion is found in the Gospel, in a series of successive scenes, antithetical and contradictory, that, like true psychological shocks, were at the point of stunning the Twelve.

Jesus accepts the "confession" of Peter. Essentially, he is the long-awaited Messiah (Mt 16:17). As a result of this unmasking, the "old man" awakens in the soul of the Twelve like a delirious fever. They begin to imagine their Master like a commander-in-chief above the Roman eagles, and they themselves (naturally!) sharing and enjoying the sweetness of power and glory.

Jesus, knowing how dangerous it was to leave them at the mercy of those dreams of glory, confronts them and says to them, Boys, get up! Let's go to Jerusalem, but — don't be mistaken — not to be crowned Messiah and King, but so they will take me, whip me, spit on me, crucify me, and kill me. Then on the third day, I will rise (Mt 20:17; Mk 8:31; Lk 9:22).

These words, which were like a pail of cold water thrown on their dreams, provoked the typical reaction of the "old man": "They did not understand what he was telling them" (Lk 18:34). That is, they turned away and did not want to know anything. It is the disgust that we feel when we see the Cross.

Then Peter, echoing this disgust, is ready to launch the final battle in favor of the old man and his dreams: Taking Jesus aside, he begins to "reprimand him": What do you mean? Go to Jerusalem? And what's more, to be executed? No way! The Messiah cannot fail, the Messiah is invincible and immortal (Mt 16:23; Lk 9:24).

We have the impression that this is an important time for Jesus. He rises to a doctrinal level, raises the torch high, and shows them the absolute conditions, saying to them, Friends, you still have time to stay or leave. You still have time to choose. But from now on, know that the one who chooses to follow me will have to abide by the following conditions: he will have to deny himself; he will have to take up his cross daily; he who looks after himself is lost, he is not worthy to follow me. He who denies himself is saved, he is worthy of my program. The grain of wheat will only be brought to life if it fulfills the condition of dying. So then, whoever wants to live has to die (Mt 16:24-27; Mk 8:34-38; Lk 9:23-27; Jn 12:25).

Jesus realizes that this rough program of penance has crumbled the strength of the Twelve, has become a stumbling block for their faith and hope. In light of this, Jesus takes the leaders of the group, leads them to the top of the mountain, and, to reassure them, is transfigured before their eyes.

In these contrasting scenes, we see the secret means of conversion as if we were looking at a "repressed subconscious." We see, in the first place, the resistance and disgust of the illusory "I" that cannot bear looking at itself or dying to self.

There is, in these scenes, a strange mixture of cross, death, and transfiguration. It appears at first glance to be a confused mix of success and failure, light and darkness, Tabor and Calvary. However, in spite of this apparent confusion, we see the faultless logic of the Gospel. It is a new logic for a new order:

to live, one has to die;
resurrection and crucifixion are the same thing;
Calvary and Tabor are the same thing;
resurrection is not a sequence but a consequence of
   Christ's death;
only penance leads to transfiguration.

Self-mortification, what for?

It is a historical fact, beyond any discussion, that men of God of great human stature, such as Saint Francis or John of the Cross, realized their transformation in Jesus Christ *in the measure and at the same time* that they subjected themselves to bodily penances.

A contemporary biographer says of Saint Francis that he "lived crucified," to the point of having to ask pardon from "Brother Ass" for having treated him so badly. And this seems even stranger to us when we consider the fact that Francis was a man who marveled at the beauty of creation.

It is true that penance does not only mean self-mortification, but, in the context of the Bible, mortification is included in the general concept of penance. In the Alexandrian translation of the Bible, there are two verbs: *metanoein*, which means a mental change, inner conversion; and *epistrefein*, which could be translated as self-mortification, meaning the external acts of penance which set the stage for and aid conversion.

Mortification, understood in its ascetic sense, has received quite a beating recently, and, of course, all in the name of new "theological" currents. Today, even the word *mortification* sounds bad and distasteful. And the term that it instantly calls to mind is this — masochism. I agree with a greater number of objections voiced against voluntary mortifications; however, the branches should have been trimmed without hurting the trunk. They have been struck blindly.

Starting from the theology of human values, these critics of mortification say that we should love life; that God has created all things that we might be happy and we should use these things to our advantage; that no one is happy by denying himself; that the verb *renounce* has no meaning anymore... I know that these ideas, understood rightly, are correct.

But then they are indiscriminately applied to the universality of life, even consecrated life — you should see what they mean for the three vows, for community...! And all in the name of these theories understood superficially and applied irresponsibly. The impression that one gets from these theories (so explained and applied) is not far from the pagan cry recorded in the Scriptures: "Let us eat and drink, for tomorrow we shall be dead" (Is 22:13).

We do not need to theorize. It is enough to touch our own skin a little so as to experience the fact that to deprive ourselves of something *for love* leads to the characteristic satisfaction of someone who has loved. In love, needs are filled or met. The more rewards we are given, the emptier we feel. The people of our consumer society have never had so many things as they have today, and never before have they felt so dissatisfied.

If Saint Teresa says that "whoever has God lacks nothing," any one of us can see that whoever does not "have" God has nothing, though he may have the whole world in hand. In this sense, the statistics about suicide speak loudly. Who are the ones who take their own lives? Primarily, they are the bored rich who need nothing, and yet, the emptiness of their lives oppresses them like an unbearable weight.

These are real experiences. All we need to do is dig down to the eternal roots of humanity and any one of us will see that each person is an infinite well. And an infinite well cannot be filled by an infinite number of finites; only one Infinite can fill it. Only God can fill the human heart and quiet its deep longings. The words of Saint Teresa sum up a great anthropological dimension: *God alone is enough.*

How can Jesus say that the poor, those who cry, the persecuted, the unwanted are happy, when common sense tells us that the happy are the millionaires, those who laugh, those who enjoy prestige and freedom? It is understood that if we have no money, freedom, prestige, etc., but do have God, then we have everything, we are blessed, filled with all good, because "whoever has God lacks nothing."

These things, intellectually understood, are unsupportable and even absurd. But, what does the head know? We only know what we have experienced. To understand the Gospel, we have to live it. To understand God, we have to "live" Him. Yes, the things of God are only understood by living them, and it is only then that they cease to be paradoxical.

When we enter deeply into the living stream of God, we immediately feel the need to externalize our answer of love with concrete actions in life. This would seem to say that love would be channeled in the area of community, in attention to the poor, in the acceptance of the sick... in that we are agreed. But what life demonstrates is the following: if we do not train ourselves in love with voluntary self-denials, we will not normally be capable of sacrificial love but will only love ourselves in a direct, indirect, or transferred manner. What happens today is that, to form value judgments, we stick to the human sciences and we avoid, in fact, God — at least the living and true God. Then, yes, when God is not the living source of experience, any mortification is masochism, celibacy is repression, obedience is childish dependence, self-denials are mutilations or death wishes, and life itself ends up being a mass of maladjustments, compensations, and misguided ways. For one who has no experience of faith, what meaning, for example, does marital fidelity or love of neighbor have?

We will never fully understand that self-denial is love, and that love matures and develops our personality, and those who are incapable of denying themselves anything are so because they are incapable of loving.

Victim souls: substitution or solidarity

Throughout the history of humanity, from the earliest centuries, these questions have been formulated:

- If God exists and is good and powerful, why does He not bury all the evils His children suffer once and for all?
- If God exists and is good and just, why does evil triumph and good fail?
- If the evil we suffer is the result of sin, why do the just live in disgrace and the sinners bathe in health, prosperity and happiness?

There are formidable problems which have tormented the age-old heart of humanity. They are the questions that are dragged across the pages of the Bible and which, even today, in the mouths of many, are true arrows launched against heaven.

The problem of evil takes to the road from these questions, a very complex problem from the philosophical, theological, and humanistic point of view. We are not interested in delving deeply into the problem of evil except only by taking these questions and letting them direct us right to the area we want to explore, the land of the "victim souls." The observation of these lives has left me with a number of impressions.

There are persons, it would seem, who were born to suffer. They have had an unbreakable chain of limitations, bad luck, biological or psychological faults, and suffering has been their daily bread. At times, evils arrive singly; at other times they come all at once. I have heard many people in the last years of their lives say, In my whole life I have not had a single happy day.

It seems to me that the principal source of suffering lies in the individual's personal makeup, beginning with the genetic code and the laws of heredity. There are persons who were born with an insatiable desire for esteem and a noticeable lack of qualities, giving rise to a highly conflicting personality. Others come into the world with manic-depressive tendencies and other obsessions that they cannot control. There are those who are always dominated by depression. They find themselves unhappy and do not know why. They were born bitter and they suffer. They are shy and always afraid. Why go on? It is a bottomless well.

Many others are unhappy because of their limiting illnesses, which take the feeling of well-being and the joy of living away from them. We all know our own clinical history: certain organic deficiencies that are with us until the end, temporary pain, serious emergencies...

For others, it is bad luck — as they say — which is playing a fixed game with them. Everything turns out badly for them. No one knows by what mystery some people continually live amid misunderstandings, persecutions, envy...

Faced with this general reality, we react differently according to our own criteria and mental categories. There are those who limit themselves, simply and passively, to complaining: We only live once, and with such bad luck!

There is, nevertheless, an almost universal way of reacting, though difficult to name, which almost always comes to the surface, although in different forms. It is a mysterious *constant* of the human heart.

What is it? What do we call it? The fact is that we find in the human heart — above all, in those who suffer — something like an innate vocation for expiation. Alienation? Masochism? People who live on the surface are always in a hurry to label it without bothering to analyze what it involves.

What is it? I would say that it deals with a need for transcendence, for openness. In the ancestral roots of humanity, there is a vocation (need?) for deep and transcendent *solidarity* with humanity, above all, with painful and sinful humanity. Could it be that we find, on this path, the means of relieving and liberating ourselves from the terrible weight of suffering? Or could it be that the need for redemption and solidarity existed even before we experienced suffering? Could it not be that within each of us, like a hidden shadow, there exists a "redeemer"?

Soloviev, Dostoyevski, Tolstoy in part, and Berdyayev reflected upon the messianism of the Soviet people. They spoke of the many ways in which humanity would be saved by the sufferings of the Russian people, sufferings accepted in silence and peace. Alienating consolation or messianic solidarity?

I remember having met persons who fervently adhered to the doctrine of reincarnation. They calmly suffered all the misfortunes of their lives, and many thought that they were expiating the sins of their past lives. And that gave them great relief and was the only thing that consoled them in the midst of their troubles.

I have known countless persons, downtrodden by illness and degradation, who felt peace and serenity only by believing that they were collaborating with Jesus in the redemption of the world. This gave them great relief, the offering of their pains in redemptive solidarity. In many terminally ill patients, lying in hospitals, looking at the crucifix, and believing that they are sharing His suffering for the salvation of the world, I have seen in their eyes a profound peace and a strange joy. A way of freeing themselves from suffering, or of fulfilling their vocation of solidarity?

The tragic thing is not suffering, but suffering uselessly. When there is a reason for it, suffering not only loses its virulence, but can be transformed into a noble cause and a transcendent "mission."

We are never isolated before God or before humanity. In the Bible, sin as well as salvation has a social dimension. We have a common destiny: the evil deed harms everyone, just as the good deed benefits everyone.

The prophet Isaiah was the first in the Bible to uncover one of the most mysterious recesses of the human heart, and to point out the role of substitution or solidarity on the part of the Just One, through his sufferings.

Ours were the sufferings he was bearing, ours the sorrows he was carrying... he was being wounded for our rebellions, crushed because of our guilt... we have been healed by his bruises. (Is 53:4-6)

The importance of the suffering and death of the just man for the redemption of others crystallized in the time of the Maccabees. The undeserved suffering and death of the just man represent not only satisfaction for his own sins, but even more so for the sins of others.

In place of...

The great French thinker Georges Bernanos treats these questions, from the perspective of *fear*, in his famous work *The Carmelites*.

At the beginning of his work, he speaks of the last days of the Prioress, a woman of God, admired in every way, who has exercised her duty for many years. The hour of death arrives and fear wraps itself around her like a serpent; she tries to hide this fear from the other sisters, but she cannot do it. She is overcome by the situation, which is very similar to Jesus' crisis in Gethsemane: panic, fear, sadness, anxiety. The only thing she is able to say in her final moment is some disjointed words: "I beg pardon... death... fear... fear of death." And, thus terrified, she dies.

A month later, while two young sisters are gathering flowers for her grave, this dialogue takes place between them:

Constance: I may be young, but I have already learned that good and bad fortune are more a matter of chance than logic. Yet, may not what we call chance, perhaps, be the logic of God? Take the death of our dear Mother, for example, Sister Blanche. Who would ever have thought she would have found it so difficult to die, and that she would have such a bad end! It is almost as though, when God gave her a death, he made a mistake about the kind of death he meant for her, just as the woman who looks after the cloakroom at a party or a theatre sometimes gives you, not your own things, but somebody else's. Yes, it must have been somebody else's death, a death not made to the measure of our Prioress, a death too small for her, so that she couldn't even get her arms into the sleeves...

Blanche: Somebody else's death — what does that mean, Sister Constance?

Constance: It means that when death comes, that person will be surprised to find how easy it is to die, and will feel at ease and comfortable. She may even boast about it and say, "See how easily death sits on me, what beautiful folds it makes." (Silence) Who knows if each one dies for himself, or some for others, or even *some in place of others?* (Silence)

Blanche (in a rather shaky voice): Our bouquet is finished now...

And so, simply by relating the incident of a candid novice, the author presents a tremendous dilemma, but at the same time he puts us on the track of, and insinuates, the solution to certain enigmas that have always tormented the human heart. He treats absurd events, without sense or logic, that happen before our eyes every day.

We see people who are actually very good, and we see them surrounded by misfortune and failure. And a little further, we see oppressors under a shower of triumphs, health, and honor.

Who understands this? What has happened? God has crisscrossed the roles: that which corresponds to one, He has given to another. As Bernanos says, some are suffering and dying in place of others. But, is this not evident injustice? Is this not an absolute lack of logic and common sense?

Why does God do these things?

We are timidly going to try to put forth an explanation. God needs to balance the wins and losses, balance the quantity of good and evil. We live in a unique society in which *we win in common and we lose in common.* Yes, the Church is like an anonymous society of common interests, in which there is an ebb and flow of goods, in which we all participate fully in the gains and losses.

And, because this "society" suffers from such a waste or loss of vitality on the part of those nameless baptized people, the losses will have to be balanced by the gains of others. Now then, those Christians who have lost vitality would not be capable of giving life to the crosses, and because of this God is forced to place the good in painful situations so that they can give merit and life to them. In this way, God achieves the balance between the wins and losses.

In order to understand this mystery better and so that this "explanation" may be convincing, we need to explore two other mysteries.

The "body" of the church

We are not associates but members of a special society, one which is like a body with many members, but all of the members together form one entity. Each member has its specific function, but all of the members work together toward the general functioning of the whole organism (1 Cor 12:12).

When our foot hurts us, do we let it bleed, saying, What does my foot have to do with my head? When our ear aches, does the eye say, I am not the ear, what do I have to do with you? No, each member helps the others, because all together they make up the organism. What would the arm be if it were not joined to the body? Of what value would the eyes be without the ears, or the ears without the feet? (1 Cor 12:14-22).

But there is more: If one member suffers, all suffer together; if one member is honored, all rejoice together (1 Cor 12:26).

And here is precisely the essence of the question. If we are hurting because of our tiny finger, it is possible that the fever can overpower the whole organism: all of the members suffer the consequences. Why should the knees suffer the consequences of the little finger? Why do we win in common and lose in common? Lose the little finger? All of the members lose. The finger is cured? All of the members are cured.

There exists, then, in the interior of that Organism, that we call the Church, an intercommunication of health and illness, of well-being and discomfort, of grace and sin.

Then, it does make a difference whether I am a saint or just lukewarm. If I win, the whole Church wins. If I love much, love grows in the living stream of the Church. If I am a "corpse," then it is the entire Church that has to drag this death along. There is, then, interdependence.

With this explanation, the mystery and the spirituality of the "victim souls" is clarified.

3. IN THE LIKENESS OF JESUS CHRIST

The night-time battle of Jacob

There is in the Bible a mysterious event, loaded with primitive and savage force. It is the battle that Jacob had with God.

> That same night he got up and, taking his two wives, his two slave girls and his eleven children, crossed the ford of the Jabbok. After he had taken them across the stream, he sent all his possessions over too. And Jacob was left alone.
> Then someone wrestled with him until daybreak who, seeing that he could not master him, struck him on the hip socket, and Jacob's hip was dislocated as he wrestled with him. He said, "Let me go, for day is breaking." Jacob replied, "I will not let you go unless you bless me." The other said, "What is your name?" "Jacob," he replied. He said, "No longer are you to be called Jacob, since you have shown your strength against God and men and have prevailed." Then Jacob asked, "Please tell me your name." He replied, "Why do you ask my name?" With that, he blessed him there.
> Jacob named the place Peniel, "Because I have seen God face to face," he said, "and have survived." (Gn 32:23-31)

"Israel," then, is the proper name of a person; Jacob was given this surname for having kept up a fierce battle with God.

This story is filled with awe-inspiring symbolism: the man who embraces God, who is overpowered in some way by His divine strength and whose shield is broken; the one who engages in battle with God and accepts being "attacked" by Him, is shaken and transformed by God, sharing His being and power to a high degree.

That sciatic nerve where Jacob was wounded is selfishness, axle wheel and main gear of all sin. God attacks his neurological center, all strength comes from this. Vulnerable at this point, the individual becomes transformed into God and shares in the maturity and greatness of Jesus.

The profound reason for all that has been said is this: Upon experiencing God as a loving Father, upon "knowing" of His beauty and power, there is born in us a pulsating love for Him. Now then, love is a unifying force and produces a strong desire to be *one* with Him.

But it is impossible that two so very different beings be one in everything unless one of them loses its own resistance: as sap is transformed into a plant, a drop of alcohol is dissolved in water, iron is converted into fire.

In a struggle, in an encounter between God and us, the Strong One — who is God — overpowers and transforms the weak one — who is each one of us — as long as we stop resisting. Because of this, we always insist on the attitude of surrender as an indispensable condition for all transformation.

With less resistance and greater surrender, we can become truly *one* with God in the union of wills. And so, the image and likeness can be so noticeable, the participation on our part so strong that, in this way, we go through the world as living reflections of God, living witnesses.

To be and to live like Jesus

We have repeated over and over that the final goal of all prayer is our transformation into Jesus Christ. Any relationship with God that does not lead to this end is, without a doubt, an alienating escape. We never arrive at the goal, that is certain. But life should be a process of transfiguration: the change from one figure to another.

We are a hard stone that the Father has taken from the quarry of life. From this stone, the Holy Spirit must carve the unveiled figure of Jesus Christ. All of life with God is directed toward this; and this means reproducing in us the feelings, attitudes, reactions, mental reflexes, and general conduct of Jesus.

Merciful and sensitive. The Gospel expressedly states many times that "he felt sorry for them" (Mt 9:36; 14:14; Mk 1:41; Lk 7:13). His face was changed, he identified with the unfortunate, his inner emotion was reflected in his words and in his eyes.

Jesus could never look at an affliction without being moved: he never lived "for himself," he always went out "with" and "for" others. This living "for" the other, suffering "with" the one who suffers was something so novel, so impressive, that witnesses could never forget it and they often commented upon it: "Feeling sorry for him, Jesus stretched out his hand, touched him and said to him, I am willing. Be cleansed" (Mk 1:41); "He took pity on them and healed their sick" (Mt 14:14); "Jesus made a tour through all the towns and villages... curing all kinds of sickness, and all kinds of disease" (Mt 9:35); He could not eat until he had cured the man suffering from dropsy (Lk 14:2-4); in the synagogue, he interrupts his teaching to cure the man with the withered hand (Mk 3:16) and the possessed woman (Lk 13:11-12).

Jesus invited the weary and those who find life burdensome, because he had a message for them that would give them peace (Mt 11:28ff). He came to cure the wounded heart, to announce liberty to captives, sight to the blind and liberation to the oppressed (Lk 4:18ff).

Jesus gave himself to the abandoned and forgotten with all that he was: his thoughts, his prayer, his work, his word, his hand (Mt 8:3), his spittle (Jn9:6), the hem of his tunic (Mt 9:20). He made works of mercy the final test for entrance into the kingdom (Mt 25:34ff).

Meek and patient. Jesus breathed peace, calm, sweetness, and dominion even when they "pressed," "assaulted," "implored" him (Mk 3:10; Lk 5:1). He offered every blessing and gift to those who are meek, calm, to those who suffer persecution patiently (Mt 5:5ff).

Jesus was humble, silent, patient, before his accusers and judges. He did not defend or justify himself. He did not respond to the rude slander of Caiaphas (Mk 14:56), or Pilate (Mt 27:13), or Herod (Lk 23:8), causing admiration in the one and disgust in the other.

Jesus, at the denial of Peter, "turned and looked at him" (Lk 26:69): a look of accusation but with love and forgiveness.

Jesus' patience, the night of His Passion, was submitted to severe tests when they whipped Him, dressed Him as a king, forced a crown of thorns on His head and a scepter into His hand; they hit Him about the head, ridiculed Him. As an answer to all of that, He suffered in silence. We should not forget that Jesus was very sensitive.

Jesus, up to the last moment on the cross, put up with insults. As an answer, He asked forgiveness for them (Lk 23:24). This meekness and patience on the part of Jesus must have impressed the witnesses so much that Paul swears to the Corinthians, "By the meekness and goodness of Christ" (2 Cor 10:1), and Peter, after many years, stirs with emotion when he remembers that "when he was insulted, he returned no insult, when he was made to suffer he did not counter with threats" (1 Pt 2:23).

Preference for the poor. With heart and hands open to the crowds (Mt 9:36; Mk 6:34), Jesus not only felt pity for the hungry crowds but worried about giving them something to eat (Mt 15:32; Mk 8:2). For Jesus, whose favorites were always the poor (Lk 6:21), the kingdom is for them (Lk 6:20). The sign that the kingdom has come is that the poor are taken care of. It has come expressly and almost exclusively for them (Mt 11:5; Lk 4:18).

Jesus looked sympathetically at the poor widow who gave a few coins (Lk 21:3). That same sympathy was demonstrated when poor Lazarus was placed in the arms of Abraham, while the rich man sank into the abyss of hell.

Jesus not only dedicated Himself to a preference for the poor, but also shared their social condition.

Understanding and attentive. The first to enter Paradise is a thief. The Father sent the Son to give preferential treatment to the weak and lost (Mk 2:17).

Jesus shared His kindness indiscriminately with sinners, so that they called Him "friend of tax collectors and sinners (Mt 11:19).

Jesus' tender and preferential relationship with publicans like Levi, Zacchaeus, and others who sat with Him at table outraged the Pharisees (Mt 9:9; Lk 19:1ff).

Jesus' principle was, It is not the healthy who need a doctor. And He cried, I want mercy, not sacrifice (Mt 9:13). One single sinner who returns to the Father causes more joy in heaven than all the just together (Lk 15:7).

Jesus was not afraid of the intentions of a mistress, but defended her publicly (Lk 7:36ff). To that adulteress, condemned to be stoned to death, He tenderly says, Go in peace! (Jn 8:1ff).

Jesus poured out His exquisite human sympathy and described Himself in beautiful parables (Lk 15:11ff).

Jesus paid special attention to Nicodemus, maintained a friendship with Joseph of Arimathea, honored many Pharisees and rich publicans with His presence, ran to Jairus and the Syro-Phoenician. He even related to the centurion from Capernaum, one of the Roman "oppressors" (Mt 15:21; Mk 7:24).

Jesus had preferences, but He was not exclusive.

Sincere and truthful. Jesus spoke clearly and directly; "Yes, yes; no, no," (Mt 5:37), without speaking one way to some and another way to others.

Jesus was courageous when they tried to trip Him up by surprise: "Hypocrites, why do you tempt me?" (Mt 16:21); give to Caesar what is Caesar's, and to God what is God's.

Jesus was magnificent when some friends came to tell Him that His life was in danger because Herod was seeking to kill Him: "Go and tell that wolf" that I will act when and where I think I should (Lk 13:32).

Jesus defended the truth at all costs, even of His life: "As it is, you want to kill me, a man who has told you the truth" (Jn 8:40ff). Even at the risk of losing disciples (Jn 6:66); even at the cost of causing scandal and persecution (Mt 7:3; Lk 7:39). Nothing disgusted Him more than hypocrisy, lies, and rationalizations. One of the most beautiful expressions in the Gospel: "The truth will set you free" (Jn 8:32).

Jesus, already within sight of eternity, summed up the purpose of His life: "I was born for this, I came into the world for this, to bear witness to the truth" (Jn 18:37).

Many years later, remembering the life of Jesus, Peter testifies, "He had done nothing wrong, and had spoken no deceit" (1 Pt 2:22).

Ever-loving. His own disciples had the most vivid impression: the Master, above all else, had *loved.* Because of this, they understood perfectly when He told them to love because He had loved them (Jn 13:34). He loved the little children with tenderness and simplicity (Mt 19:14), and He took one of them in His arms (Mt 9:36ff).

Jesus was affectionate with Martha, Mary, and Lazarus (Jn 11:1ff); before dying, He treated His own as "friends" (Jn 20:17). He received His own betrayer with a kiss and a word of friendship (Mt 26:50).

Jesus called an unknown paralytic "my child" (Mk 2:5),

and the hemorrhaging woman "my daughter" (Mt 9:22). He loved His people so deeply that, seeing them lost, He saw no other solution than to cry and weep (Lk 13:34).

Jesus invented a thousand forms and ways of expressing His love because love is ingenious (Mk 10:45; Mt 20:28). In that brutal irony, there is an enormous depth of truth: "He saved others; he cannot save himself" (Mk 15:31). He brought from the Father only one thing: "I have loved you, just as the Father has loved me. Remain in my love" (Jn 15:9).

This love of Jesus must have so impressed His witnesses that they give us this memory, recorded in priceless words: "God so loved the world: he gave his only son" (Jn 3:16); "[He] loved me and gave himself for me" (Gal 2:20); "... the kindness and love of God our savior" (Ti 3:4).

Humble and gentle. Jesus fled publicity to heal the sick, to multiply the loaves, to come down from the Mount of Transfiguration. When Jesus was ridiculed before Pilate and Caiaphas, He did not answer them on a single count (Mt 27:14). Jesus let Himself be "manipulated" by the Tempter without complaining (Mt 4:1-11). Jesus did not argue or raise His voice; no one heard His cries in the marketplace (Mt 12:15).

Worrying about others without worrying about himself. Jesus attended the hungry crowds (Jn 6, 1-16), the Apostles in the Garden, Peter (Lk 22:51), the pious women, the thief (Lk 23:39), His mother at the foot of the cross (Jn 19:25). He never worried about Himself, took no time to eat, sleep, or rest (Mk 1:35; 3:7).

Chapter 6

JESUS AT PRAYER

Your face is my only homeland. (St. Thérèse of Lisieux)

To be a Christian is to feel as Jesus felt and to live as He lived. This "mind" (Phil 2:5), however, can be taken wrongly. There is a more adequate expression: *disposition.* Disposition is woven with emotion, conviction, and decision. So, then, in other words, the Christian experience is one of reproducing in our own life the emotions, inner attitudes, and general behavior of the Lord.

In trying to live this disposition, it is relatively easy to know what were the preferences of Jesus, His lifestyle and spirituality, the main purpose of His life.

But there is another thing, as difficult to discover as it is to live, and it is this: how to capture the inner harmony of the Lord? In my opinion, this is the basic quest. Is the conduct of the individual the total person? No, of course not, because Jesus' conduct, in the end, is nothing more than a distant echo of impulses, fed by ancient ideals and a remote living situation.

We need to get to the roots, because the essential is always beneath the surface. To discover, then, Jesus' inner atmosphere, we need to descend to the primordial and original springs of the person where impulses, decisions, and life are born. In short, we need to discover and participate in the inner life of the Lord.

How do we do this? The "soul" of Jesus appears — is made transparent — in His words and deeds. We have to begin by leaning on the *whole Word* with a contemplative attitude in order to be rooted in the Lord.

Again, how do we do this?

Exercises for looking "within" Jesus

You should place yourself in an attitude of faith, asking for the assistance of the Holy Spirit and letting yourself be carried away by its inspiration.

Then, take an attitude similar to that of a person who holds his breath in a state of admiration: like the suspense of someone at the bottom of the sea, or of someone with a powerful telescope, who has the world of the stars opened up to him.

Then, with all of your faculties recollected, in faith and peace, let yourself be taken, with a contemplative gaze and infinite reverence, into the intimacy of Jesus, and "remain" there, letting yourself be surprised and sensing everything that is happening there in the depths. And, once submerged in that environment, quiet and motionless, let yourself be impregnated by those various existential and living harmonies, sharing in the profound experience of Jesus in this way.

This is the knowledge "beyond knowledge" (Eph 3:18), the "supreme advantage of knowing Christ Jesus my Lord" (Phil 3:8), the beginning of all wisdom, the reactor that generates all energy and apostolic greatness.

To advance through the dark corridors of faith, in the tiring and divinizing ascent, we must take only one path: the path of Jesus Himself. So as not to lose our way on this venture, we must walk firmly upon this ground.

Here is the method upon which there can never be too much insistence: place yourself, contemplatively, *within* Jesus, for any fruitful meditation.

Once "there," try to "know" in the Spirit what the Lord *felt* when He said "May your name be held holy" (Mt 6:9).

Look within Jesus and try to "know" (and share) what waves of tenderness rose within Him, from the deepest parts of Him, when He repeated so many times: *Abba* (O beloved Father!)

Look attentively and contemplatively, and try to "know" what "happened" in the distant and strange depths of the Lord when He said, My God, why have You abandoned me? (Mt 27:46). What happened in those moments of desolation? Was the light extinguished? Did extreme pressure or emptiness fall upon His soul? What was it?

Let us look within Jesus, and let us try to "know," in the Spirit, what rustled within Him, giving off perfumed sweetness, when He said, I am sorry for these people (Mt 9:36). What did Jesus want at that time: to suffer what they were suffering? To carry all of the crosses of the world?

What was that flock of white birds that suddenly took flight and crossed the sky above Jesus when, full of joy and happiness, He said, Thank You Father for hearing my prayer (Jn 11:41)?

What happened within Jesus when He took pity on the crowds (Mk 1:41; Lk 7:13; Mt 14:14)? What windows were shattered in His interior room? What sudden desires fell on His ground? What did He feel?

What was His feeling when He said to them: Come to me, the destroyed, the ones thrown upon the banks of the river by the rushing stream, the least and the forgotten; come to Me and you will see consolation spread its shade across your deserts (Mt 11:28)? How did Jesus feel in that moment?

* * *

This exercise of placing yourself *in Jesus' place* has a reverse side to it (if it is the same coin) and it is described in this way: What would Jesus do if He were in my place?

273

What would the Lord feel were He in the heart of this black night where I am now? Indignation? Compassion? Desire to tear down? Desire to console? What would Jesus' reaction be if they did to Him what they did to me?

Speaking from within Jesus

Those who *sense* this, will have to go out from the valley of contemplation to communicate something of what they "saw and heard." This is the essential task of true worshippers: to speak (or write) as someone who speaks from within Jesus, after having participated, in spirit and faith, in the profound experience of the Lord. It is an extraordinarily difficult but necessary task.

Among all human experience, prayer is the most profound and far-reaching. And now that we want to speak of Jesus' prayer, I am aware that we cannot utter a single word without the aid of the Holy Spirit, which we here ardently request.

* * *

The path is riddled with difficulties. First, there comes to us that eternal enigma of the human person, the "unknown": I "am" *me*, a singular and unrepeatable mystery. Everybody else is "other"; each one, a unique experience. They will not "enter" my experience nor will I "enter" theirs. No one will *experience themselves* as I do. I will never *experience myself* as they do.

Now then, does it not seem foolish to try to "enter" the experience of Jesus? Without even touching His person, remaining on the outskirts, the scriptural sciences are full of questions. What words did Jesus actually speak? Although some words may not actually be His, what words express the real thinking of Jesus? In which of the parables,

274

allegories, or sermons is there "something" of the vast interior richness of Jesus?

The Gospels are feeble attempts at making "transparent" and transmitting Jesus Christ to us. The attempt is, in itself, disproportionate. The Gospels have been "cut off"; Jesus Christ is immensely greater and more brilliant than He appears in the Gospels; the Gospel glimpses are shadows, nothing more than crumbs, tiny bits of a Being whose greatness is beyond us.

Paul is, among the "witnesses," a contemplative who has been blinded by the infinite richness of Christ, and who invites believers to plunge into the mystery of Christ in order to be able to "understand":

> the breadth and the length, the height and the depth [of Christ's love] so that knowing the love of Christ, which is beyond knowledge, you may be filled with the utter fullness of God (Eph 3:18).

Perspective

Jesus Christ is both Son of God and Son of Man, without confusion or division: two natures forming one unique *I*. Who is able to decipher such a formidable mystery?

If each person is a closed circuit, a unique reality, original and ineffable, what will we say about this infinite well that is the person of Jesus Christ? Where do the boundaries begin and end between what is divine and what is human in Christ? What reciprocal relationship is to be found between them? Do they cancel each other out? Do they interfere? Do they enrich each other? How inaccessible and puzzling for us is this unique I of Jesus Christ!

What was His prayer like? An ecstatic and silent gaze? A wordless intimacy like that of one person at the feet of another? An imperturbable peace? Burning words "with loud cries and with tears" (Heb 5:7)? Exaltation with a gift of tears? A pure and dry faith? Simply being? "How rich and deep are the wisdom and knowledge of God!" (Rom 11:33). The profound psychology of Jesus escapes us, because of the mystery of two natures in one person.

But we, in the reflection of the following pages, are going to leave to one side, for purposes of *methodology*, the fact that Jesus is Son of God, and we will center our contemplative focus on the *Son of Man*. We will use this perspective.

We are seeking the One who is our Brother. He is our *guide*. A guide is that person who travels alone along unexplored paths in the mountains or forests. Then the guide takes the others and leads them along the path that is no longer unexplored. We are seeking that Brother who has already taken the path that leads to the Father.

1. PERSONAL RELATIONSHIP
WITH THE ABSOLUTE

On the journey of Jesus' soul, in His religious experience as Son of Man, I would timidly venture to distinguish two (how should I call them?) chronological stages.

First, Jesus appears to have lived with a radicalness and unequalled strength what we call the *absoluteness* of God, according to the monotheistic tradition in which he was born and grew up. And, secondly, He appears to have "discovered" and lived the experience of the *Abba*, the great novelty of the Gospel.

Naturally, there is a permanent interrelation between both experiences. If we look at the parables, allegories, or sermons in which the interior life of Jesus is revealed during His days of preaching, both experiences seem to be intermixed, confused, and sometimes identical. However, we, by reason of method and the search for clarity, are going to study the two levels separately.

In order to understand well what I am going to explain, we must take into account the following information.

Jesus' gradual growth in human and divine experiences (Lk 2:52). Still a youth of fifteen or twenty years, Jesus was advancing at high speed into the depths of God. This youth, made of mystery and dreams, in prayer on the naked hills on starry nights; sailing through the immensities to touch the poles of the earth; exploring unmapped regions to discover the other side of the mystery; Jesus, a twenty-year-old man, each time more interior, each time farther out in total presence... The human mind is lost... What can we say?

Jesus' sensitive temperament. Essentially, Jesus was knit from very sensitive fibers. The Gospels reveal many occasions that filled Him with compassion upon seeing so many people hungry and without a shepherd (Mk 1:41; Lk 7:13).

One day, tired from walking along dusty roads beneath the sun, He wanted to rest. He took a boat and guided it to a place where there were no people. But the crowds guessed where He was going and went by land, arriving at the place before He did. Getting out of the boat and seeing the people, He felt pity for them and, instead of resting, stayed with them the whole day (Mk 6:32-35).

Another time, arriving at the gates of the city, Jesus met a funeral procession. The situation caught His interest and they told Him that the deceased was a boy, the only son of a widowed mother. Hearing this, the Lord was moved with pity, almost to the point of tears (Lk 7:11-14).

One day, hearing of the death of His friend Lazarus, Jesus wept openly. The Jews, seeing Him from a distance, admiring His sensitivity, said: How this man feels! What a good friend He was! (Jn 11:34-38).

After the solemn entrance into Jerusalem, saddened by the stubborn resistance of the theocratic capital, Jesus could not avoid tears of helplessness (Lk 19:41). He felt saddened by the ingratitude of the lepers (Lk 17:12), disillusioned by the laziness of the disciples as they slept in the Garden.

He was attentive to friends, courteous with women,

277

loving with children. He always showed a preference for invalids. In a word, He was very sensitive.

He was deeply pious. The human constitution is made of qualities and defects, possibilities and limitations, all of which are substantially rooted in the vital depths of each person.

There are those who have a gift for studies and none for sports, and vice versa. There are those who have a talent for the arts and none for the hard sciences. There are those who have no gift for painting but who are marvelous in the field of music. Each individual, then, is born with certain predetermined dispositions, or gifts of the Holy Spirit, that are called charisms.

Among these predispositions there is a *sensitivity* for the things of God. There are persons who were born with a tendency so strong for God that they cannot live without Him. I do not know if this is grace or if it is natural. In either case it is a gift from God. This sensitivity or tendency is called *piety.*

In this sense, we find Jesus very pious, a personality trait that He definitely inherited from His mother.

The religious context within which Jesus was born and grew up. Israel had struggled for many centuries against all idolatry, which came from the great empires and from the surrounding tribes. Always in contact with other peoples and their gods, Israel felt drawn to the strange cults which were in vogue at the time. Many times they gave in to the temptation. They returned to God under the watchful eyes of the zealous guardians, the prophets, who paid for their zeal with their lives. So, with blood, death, and tears, Israel forged a monotheism that was radical and somewhat fanatical. Jesus was born and grew up in this atmosphere.

This monotheistic history had shaped a very concise "creed" called the *Sh'ma,* which every Israelite had to recite several times a day. The *Sh'ma* was not only the foundation for all Jewish prayer but it was also the soul of that culture, the national anthem, the national flag, the ultimate *raison d'être* of Israel. It says:

> Listen, Israel: Yahweh our God is the one, the only Yahweh. You must love Yahweh your God with all your heart, with all your soul, with all your strength. Let the words I enjoin on you today stay in your heart. You shall tell them to your children, and keep on telling them, when you are sitting at home, when you are out and about, when you are lying down and when you are standing up; you must fasten them on your hand as a sign and on your forehead as a headband; you must write them on the doorposts of your house and on your gates. (Dt 6:4-9)

Jesus, from the time He was able to utter His first words in Aramaic, learned these words by memory. Josephus tells us that it was a matter of great pride for every mother in Israel that the first words which her child learned should be the words of the *Sh'ma*.

If this was the case for every mother in Israel, how much more so for the mother named Mary of Nazareth: she was a normally quiet and reserved woman, but God plucked the chord and the world saw that she sounded like a vibrant harp. In the words of the *Sh'ma* that His mother said, that He repeated (what an indescribable scene!), we sense a great profundity. Jesus was nourished with this strong food from the very first years of His life.

Jesus repeated these words thousands of times: while He was still on His mother's lap; as a child of eight, when He would go to the pump for a pail of water, or collect firewood in the nearby hills; as an adolescent of fifteen, when He went out on those starry nights, or while fashioning a yoke in the carpenter's shop, or maybe a donkey cart; while in the synagogue...

This is a fact of utmost importance for unveiling the interior life of Jesus and for affirming, in the form of a conjecture, that the basic religious life of Jesus was an experience of the *absoluteness* of God.

At about five years of age, Jesus began going to school, a school not at all like our schools today. That school was the "house of the book" *(beth a safer)*, for learning by memory the book, that is, the Law and the Prophets.

There, Jesus learned to cover His face with His hands when the divine tetragram appeared, the four consonants of the name of Yahweh.

This, then, was the religious context in which Jesus' spirit was opened up to life. His first religious experiences were a living of the Absolute.

God alone

Taking into consideration His gradual growth in divine experience and His sensitive and pious temperament, Jesus passed the spring of His childhood and adolescence wrapped in the mantle of the Admirable. By the attitudes and expressions which appear later, in the days of the Gospel, we feel right in thinking that now, as in the days of His childhood and youth, the Incomparable completely occupied His person.

At twelve years of age, He had already felt the burning closeness of the Formidable and the One. His words, answering the grief of His mother (Lk 2:49) indicate that at that age, the bottomless and boundless ocean which is the Absolute had completely taken possession of this little boy. From then on, God alone would be His occupation and preoccupation.

And so, we discover in Jesus a profound and extensive "region of solitude" that no one, not even His mother, can enter, no one but God alone. My mother? Who is my mother? You are my mother. Anyone who takes the Admirable seriously, anyone who declares and makes God the Only One in life, this is my mother, my father, my sister, and brother (Mk 3:35). Wife? Not five wives nor all of the lovers in the world are able to quench the eternal thirst of His heart. God Alone is fresh water; whoever drinks of it will never be thirsty (Jn 4:11-19). If you only knew what God is like, if you only tasted the water...

Karl Adam, author of *The Son of God*, states:

> The Father was his world, his reality, his life. Only through the Father does his solitude become a communing, the most fruitful of communings.

This child, who knew that on Sinai, Moses alone was able to approach the presence of the Formidable, while the others could only look on from a distance; who knew that the Holy and Terrible resided in the "holy of holies" where only once a year a single person could enter; this child was entering deeply into the closeness of the One who is beyond all Time and all Space. His sensitive soul was marked by the impression that God is All. He took this *absoluteness* of God and carried it to its final consequences.

Scattered experiences

We are now going to see how these powerful experiences appear, scattered like gold nuggets, in the pages of the Gospel. Jesus speaks of God and, behind His words, the echo of passion is heard. They stand out like a peak in a mountain range to declare, God is All. In this sense, Jesus gathers together all of the ways and voices of the great prophets, but their voices do not even reach the height of His sandals.

God alone is the Lord of the universe and author of the Kingdom. He goes out to look for workers in the vineyard. There is no need to inquire about the salary, because even the last worker is paid the same as the first. There is no payment, everything is gift (Mt 20:1-20). He organizes weddings, and He Himself goes to the streets and market-places to look for guests (Mt 22:1-14). Yes, He Himself sends the invitations (Lk 15:3-7).

There are some who like to read Tarot cards, for

example, to know and be ready for the future, and to know when the end will come. It is useless. Not even the Son of Man knows. God alone knows the exact hour (Mk 13:32; Mt 24:36, 25:13). God is All.

Ridiculous vanities? Who will occupy the first place? Are you able to pass the test? Even if you are able, know that not even I, the Son, can give it to you. God alone gives it. He appoints each one their place. Everything is grace. No one deserves anything. Here everything is received, just as in the case of a child. Only those who make themselves "little" can receive the Kingdom, life, food, dress, education, love. The Kingdom is a gift, a present (Lk 12:32). Jesus "knew" God in His long encounters with Him and there "discovered" All-is-Grace.

Very good, Simon, son of Jonah, how well you have spoken! But what you have just said has not been told you by instinct, intuition or any other form of wisdom. God alone has inspired you. How happily Jesus looks at him, how happy He feels that God be All! How He would like to pray these words:

You are great and do marvelous deeds,
you, God, and none other. (Ps 86:10)

Because of this, He wanted nothing for Himself, neither applause nor recognition nor gratitude. To *God alone* give glory. You are already healed, but say nothing to anyone, go to the temple and give thanks to God (Mk 1:44). The young girl was healed, the deaf had their ears opened, but without anyone knowing (Mk 5:43; 7:36). You have been cleansed of leprosy, but do not bow down in the dust before me; go to the temple to give thanks to *God alone*.

Satisfied by what they had eaten in the desert, delirious by what had happened, they look for Him with the intention of crowning Him king. The thought of this seemed to Him like an overthrow and He escapes to the mountain because God alone is King, and all glory belongs to Him. In the solitude of that hill, that night (Jn 6:15) how well would these words have sounded:

Not to us, Yahweh, not to us,
but to your name give the glory. (Ps 115:1)

You call me good? Who is good? God alone is good (Lk 18:19). We see Him as a Son awed by the infinite purity and holiness of God. He does not put up with anyone who takes away the absolute attributes that belong to God alone.

In the years of His youth, perhaps when He goes out in the countryside, gathering wood and tree trunks, designing the yokes for the mules, coming to the spring with its fresh water, seeing the vines grow and the wheat mature... His soul, lost in the immensities of the Eternal, understands that God dresses the land, feeds the birds, makes sprigs blossom. We see Jesus as a child awed by the infinite power of God.

God, who is like you? (Ps 71)

With surety and joy, He assured those who think about the difficulties of salvation: "By human resources it is impossible, but not for God: because for God everything is possible" (Mk 10:27).

Jesus sees each and every thing coming directly from the hands of the Father. He shudders with the magnificent power of God. "How great are your works, Yahweh, immensely deep your thoughts!" (Ps 92:5). He does not think in terms of secondary causes, He does not think about a universal order designed by a genius and functioning by mechanisms of causalities and cosmic laws, like a piloted spaceship. Beyond appearances and events, Jesus contemplates with joy the Creator, a Person full of freedom, power, spontaneity, and goodness (Mt 6:26).

If you "knew" what God is like, who God is, you could say to that mountain: Move from there (Mk 11:22) and throw yourself into the sea; and the hill would fly like a bird to the water. And to this sycamore tree that is in front of you, you would say: Be uprooted and transplanted in the sea; and it would humbly obey you (Lk 17:6).

How much you have done,
Yahweh, my God
— your wonders and your plans for us —
  you have no equal.
I will proclaim and speak of them;
  they are beyond number. (Ps 40:6)

Remembering the frequency during His preaching days with which He retreated from the sight of the crowds to be alone with God, preferring the night, we can envision the state of adoration and awe in which Jesus' spirit permanently lived. This was so from His early days, as much during work and traveling as at the synagogue.

Above all, we are right in imagining what His intense moments with God were like, in His younger days, in the nearby hills of Nazareth at night. His sensitive soul would have been swept over and over again, like a wave sweeping over a beach, by the presence of the Without-Name, in a wrenching closeness, being able to say with the psalmist:

All your waves and breakers
have rolled over me. (Ps 42)

This is what happened — allow me to conjecture — in the event of the Transfiguration. In his narrative, Luke says, "As he was praying, the aspect of his face was changed..." (Lk 9:29). We may conclude, from the context of the story, that the intensity, the possessiveness, and the concentration of Jesus' spirit was such that, with the strength of spiritual energies, physical laws were broken, producing a change — how, we don't know — in the appearance of Jesus, the same as in the case of Moses at another time. In a word, Jesus was "made" a living reflection of God, radiating the brightness of God in His robes, in His face, in His body.

In those encounters, He was experiencing that the Admirable is the only Good on whom it is worth betting everything. If you knew how much God is the Great Treasure, you would sell your land and your houses, abandon your profession in order to "possess" that Treasure (Mt 13:44).

The birds have their nests and the foxes their lairs in which to sleep. The Son of Man does not know what He will eat tomorrow or where He will sleep the day after tomorrow. He has renounced all security and has depended on God as His only Refuge and Safety (Mt 8:20).

The Kingdom of the Eternal is of such magnificence that its "conquest" is an heroic deed that demands courage, "violence" and perseverance (Mt 11:12; Lk 13:24).

* * *

We ask what the beauty and magnificence of the Admirable will be like, to what point the Incomparable will be inebriating wine for someone who has intimately "known" Jesus, who proposes a radicalness that is frightening.

Your father has died? Let the dead bury the dead. That is not important (Mt 8:22). You want to take God seriously? You want to declare Him to be the Only One? Go home. Break ties with everyone and everything. The Only One is worth the trouble (Mk 10:21). The game we try to learn is called *all or nothing*. Before choosing to play, think about it. But once you put your hand to the plow, there is no turning back, you must play to the end (Lk 9:21). Why so many desires, Martha? Why so many preparations for the banquet? Few things are necessary. Better yet, only one thing is necessary: God (Lk 10:42). I have not come to bring tranquillity and peace, but the sword (Lk 12:51).

In His days of preaching we see Him acting with joy and dedication. His life for the people has no possible human explanation. The source of so much energy and joy has to be found in a hidden and underground spring in His inner depths. All of His words and actions arise from an emotional depth that, without a doubt, comes from His encounters with the Lord from His earliest days.

Again quoting Karl Adam,

If we ask what in all the manifold thoughts and acts of Jesus was the most inward and enduring and immutable, was, as it were, the abiding golden background to his words and actions, the answer must be his intimate sense of union with the Father. It is the essence of his life. We here draw near to the very center of his will, and we might already conjecture that here the holy spring has its rise, whence flows both the loneliness of his heroism and his all-embracing, all compassionate love for mankind, and where they attain unity.

Dizziness

Certain perspectives of Jesus, even in the realm of conjecture, escape us without fail. We see that the great contemplatives, upon delving into the mystery of God, are first struck by the distance between them and God. We call that sensation vertigo, or dizziness, because it has to do with a mixture of fascination and fright, dread and surprise.

This sensation appears very vividly in the Psalms. For example, in Psalm 8, after expressing "how majestic is your name throughout the world," the psalmist measures the distance and asks, "What are human beings that you spare a thought for them?"

What is typical of spiritual dizziness is that it deals with a terribly present distance, a vertigo made at the same time, of closeness and distance, of transcendence and immanence.

In this area, with respect to Jesus, I feel lost and can only venture to ask, From His human experience, from His position as a man, how did Jesus see, how did He measure, how did He sense God? In what way did He measure the distance between God and humanity? Did He experience the dizziness of the psalmist when he said that "they pass away but you remain" (Ps 102)? This will never be answered satisfactorily. If it is true that Jesus was the Son of Man, He was also Son of God.

Nevertheless, I am impressed by the infinite reverence with which He spoke to God on the night of His departure: "Holy Father!," "Just Father!" This entire final prayer is filled with profound veneration, reflecting the feeling of admiration and awe that Jesus felt before the Most Holy. It seems to me that Jesus felt that same reverence, that is a child of distance and veneration every time He raised His eyes to heaven (Jn 11:41, 17:1).

2. THE FATHER'S FACE APPEARS

Everything that has been said up to this point is not qualitatively different from the concept of God which was lived in Judaism at the time of Jesus. Many prophets lived in intimate communication with the transcendent and personal God, although not to the extent to which Jesus lived it. The prophet Jeremiah seems to us to be very close to the religious experience of God-Father. The psalmists speak at times of a state of peace, surrender, and confidence of the soul in God, like a child in the arms of its mother (Ps 131). The prophet Hosea, that we might sense the tenderness of God, uses expressions that could be attributed perfectly to the religious experience of the *Abba*.

When Israel was a child I loved him,
and I called my son out of Egypt.
But the more I called, the further they went away from me;
they offered sacrifice to Baal
and burnt incense to idols.
I myself taught Ephraim to walk,
I myself took them by the arm,

but they did not know that I was the one caring for them,
that I was leading them with human ties,
with leading-strings of love,
that, with them, I was like someone lifting an infant to his cheek,
and that I bent down to feed him. (Hos 11:3-6)

In spite of these sparks of inspiration, getting close to the idea of God as *Abba*, there was no real advancement in the theology of earlier Judaism. The God of Sinai ruled the individual and the collective religious life of Israel.

The new name for God

During His early childhood and adolescence, Jesus lived a relationship with the Lord God according to the theology of the people among whom He was born and grew up.

But beginning at some age (fifteen? twenty?), the young Jesus, in a gradual process of interiorization, began to experience, to relate to God in an *essentially different* manner; in a manner that, outside of a few fleeting glimpses, no other prophet in Israel had dreamed or lived. The young Jesus passed beyond the stage of awe and adoration. He entered completely into that area of trust that belongs to the most loving Father in the world.

There was, then, a gradual transformation in the soul of the young Jesus.

What happened in the soul of the young Jesus?

With fear and reverence, we are going to enter the sacred precinct of this youth, at age fifteen, twenty, or twenty-five, and we are going to attend a spectacle: before our eyes will rise a kingdom without swords or scepters, without crowns or thrones; sadness will be buried and anguish will be destroyed; and above the horizon, the day without end will dawn. A youth will rise above the highest peak in the world to proclaim: we have a Father, we are brothers and sisters, we are saved, alleluia.

To understand this, we have to take the following into consideration: Mark tells us that Jesus retreated for forty days to a mountain so inaccessible that only the wild beasts dwelled there (Mk 1:13). From this fact, the following psychological conclusion emerges: An individual, if not familiar with the silence and solitude of the mountains, does not, on a whim, spend so many days in such an inhuman place. If, in fact, He went there, it is a sign that He was already accustomed to the solitude of the mountains.

In addition, there are many Gospel passages that state that Jesus used to retreat at night to the hills near Capharnaum or Jerusalem, to be alone with the Father.

This, together with our previous observations, brings us reasonably, and by means of psychological premises, to believe that Jesus, while a youth in Nazareth, was used to going away often and for long periods of time to the hills near Nazareth to be with his Father, and that during the days of His preaching, He maintained the habit.

* * *

The childhood of Jesus was completely occupied by the Admirable (Lk 2:49). That presence illuminated everything in this youth: what was above and below and what was on the other side of things. It was like when the sun's rays warm the earth, give it light, and make it fertile.

Jesus was a normal boy, but He was not like the others: His eyes were always bathed in a strange splendor and He looked a great deal within Himself, like someone who looks at a companion; and it seemed that He was not alone but that *he was he-and-Other*.

Yes. Someone was with Him, and He was with Someone, as if all distance had disappeared. But here, there was the sense that there were no bridges because, it seems, the two had been united by intimacy. And, in this case, intimacy was total presence, made of two presences. In other words, the intimacy was the meeting, crossing, and fruit of two infinite interiorities.

The young Jesus (seventeen? twenty?) advanced from day to day, from night to night, deeper within, to the most remote recesses of the Lord God; and so, there came the time in which intimacy and love set up within the youth a tension, in the sense that the stronger the intimacy with God was, the greater the love; and the greater the love, the stronger the intimacy. In this way, interior velocity was gradually accelerating until all distance had been devoured.

> Love is born of a look,
> a moment of forgetting oneself.
> It grows with the desires of giving oneself
> supported in hope.
> It is consummated in the total forgetting
> of a reciprocal joy.

Summer was fading over the orchards of Jesus. The apples were ripening. The beehives were filling with tenderness and sweetness.

Bringing to fruition the tension between intimacy and love, and with the disappearance of distance, trust was growing in Jesus' soul, like a wide oak tree covering His deep desires with its shadow. The boy felt total openness-trust-tenderness toward His Lord and God.

Oh, those nights Jesus spent in the lonely mountains, blanketed by the mantle of His Lord God in the most absolute closeness and in the most absolute presence as well: there were so many stars on those nights!...

The boy (twenty? twenty-two?) with such sensitivity, with that strong predisposition to be with God, takes one step and then another, gradually experiencing different sensations and each time perceiving more clearly that God is not exactly the Feared nor the Inaccessible.

And so, a time came when the youth began gradually to feel like a beach washed by a wave of tenderness coming from the most profound depths of the ocean. Ten thousand worlds came down upon Him, loving Him, covering Him, assuring Him, as if God were a widening ocean and Jesus were sailing upon its waters; as if the world were (What? Cradle? Arms? Sheltering wings?), everything was security, certainty, jubilation, freedom... He came to have a definite, certain, and unforgettable sensation: feeling that the Lord God is like the most loving Father in the world.

> O God, your love reaches to the heavens,
> and your faithfulness to the clouds.
> Your justice is like God's mountain,
> your judgments like the deep.
> O Lord how precious is your love.
> My God, the sons of men
> find refuge in the shadow of your wings,
> They feast on the riches of your house;
> they drink from the stream of your delight.
> In you is the source of life
> and in your light we see light. (Ps 36)

During the years of Jesus' youth, the most revolutionary interior transformation of all times takes place. Jesus experienced in His own flesh that the Father is not primarily Fear, but Love; that the Father is not above all Justice, but Mercy; that the Father is not even, first of all, Holiness, the Most Holy, as the prophet Isaiah explains, but He is kindness, forgiveness, care, tenderness... And the young Jesus came to the conviction that the first Commandment no longer had meaning, had been replaced forever: from then on, the first Commandment would consist in *letting oneself be loved* by the Father.

It was a new world, a world of surprise and ecstasy, of happiness and drunkenness, a world "discovered" and lived by this normal yet different youth, a world that could be expressed by these words: All-is-Love. Jesus felt really loved and completely liberated. Love liberates from fear. One who feels loved does not know fear.

The Father took the initiative; he opened Himself and sent Himself completely to Jesus; Jesus responded, opened Himself, and surrendered Himself completely to the Father. The two gazed at each other with a look of love. This gaze was like a clear lake in which the two lost themselves, an embrace in which everything was common and shared, everything was given and everything was received, all was communicated wordlessly... It was something indescribable, like music coming from another world.

In light of this experience, Jesus analyzed His surroundings and found that the most beautiful things of the world, such as spring, childhood, motherhood — in short, everything that signifies love and life — is nothing more than the overflow of the inexhaustible vitality of the One who is not Father but Fatherhood, an unstoppable cascade of all life and all love. All-is-Love. All-is-Grace.

God already has a new name. From now on He will not be called Yahweh. He will be called Father because He is so close, protects, cares for, understands, forgives, worries... From now on, adoration does not consist in covering one's eyes and face with one's hands but in surrendering one's self with unconditional and infinite trust into the all-powerful and tender hands of He who, forever, is and will be called our *dear Father*.

> Father:
> You who live in love and happiness
> while on the earth the storms shout
> and the passions cry.
> You who say that I should share everything,
> feeling completely the suffering of your children,
> show me your peace.
> Guide me to that deepest area
> where pain cannot enter,

where words, smiles and peace bud forth,
where everything is happiness
because everything is happiness.
O Love, from which I was born! (Bergson)

Jesus now possesses the maturity of the golden wheat. We can imagine Him as an adult man of twenty-eight years of age. He is a fountain of peace. A filled abyss. The presence of the Most High appears through His hands, His eyes, His mouth...

The "growth" of Jesus does not end here. In the Spirit, there are no boundaries. Better, Jesus broke all boundaries.

With His sensitive temperament and His predilection for the things of God, submerged each time more frequently and more deeply in His solitary encounters with the Father, Jesus continues sailing at full sail in the waters of tenderness and love. Confident in the Father, boundaries and control are lost. One step and then another toward total surrender.

And so, one day — I do not know if it was at night — carried away by the dizziness, in the fullness of the drunkenness from the "stream of delight"... a completely strange word escaped His mouth, scandalizing the theology and public opinion of Israel: *Abba*, which means: O dear Father.

With this, we have reached the highest peak of religious experience. Joachim Jeremias, writing in *The Central Message of the New Testament*, comments on this:

It was something new, something unique and unheard of, that Jesus dared to take this step and to speak with God as a child speaks with his father, simply, intimately, securely. There is no doubt then that the *Abba* which Jesus uses to address God reveals the very basis of his communion with God... *Abba* as an address to God is *ipsissima vox*, an authentic and original utterance of Jesus, implies the claim of a unique revelation and a unique authority... We are confronted with something new and unheard of which breaks through the limits of Judaism. Here we see who the historical Jesus was: the man who had the power to address God as *Abba* and who included sinners and the publicans in the kingdom by authorizing them to repeat this one word, *Abba*, dear Father.

The Father loves me

And now, yes. Now Jesus can strike out on the roads and mountains, to proclaim and announce the *latest bulletin*, news that He "*discovered*" and lived in the silent years of His youth: *God-is-Father*. If God is all-powerful, He is also all-loving. If with His hands He holds the world, with those same hands He takes and protects me.

By night, He watches over my sleep and, by day, He accompanies me wherever I go. When people complain saying "I am alone in the world," the Father responds "Do not be afraid, for I am with you" (Is 41:10). When individuals lament, saying "No one loves me," the Father answers "I love you" (Is 43:4). He is closer to me than my own shadow. He takes better care of me than the most loving mother. There is nowhere I can become lost, for wherever I go, He goes with me.

Furthermore, it is a freely given love. The fact that He loves me does not depend on whether or not I deserve it, whether I am just or unjust. The Father loves me freely. He understands me because He knows very well of what soil I am made, and He forgives me much more easily than I forgive myself. He has no reasons for loving me. "I am gracious to whom I am gracious and I take pity on those on whom I take pity" (Ex 33:19). He loves me because He loves me; He is simply my Father. Does a mother look for *reasons* for loving her child?

I am not, then, the product of an assembly line. I am the carefully designed work of an artisan. I was conceived in eternity by Love and I was *born* in time through Love. From the beginning and forever, I am freely loved by my Father. "Blessed be the God and Father of our Lord Jesus Christ, the merciful Father and the God who gives every possible encouragement" (2 Cor 1:3).

To love and be loved

I never tire of repeating: to love God is difficult, almost impossible. To love our neighbor is even more difficult. But when we are won over by the love of the Father, there is the uncontainable desire to "reach out" *to love.* At this time, to love God will not only be easy but almost inevitable. Even more, we will feel the insane desire to meet someone, anyone, along the innumerable roads of the world, to treat them as the Father has treated us, and to make others happy as the Father has made us happy.

Only those who are loved are able to love. Only the free are able to liberate. Only the pure purify, and the only ones who can sow peace are those who have it.

Someone who is loved is not told to love. Without anyone telling that person, an inescapable force brings him to understand, forgive, accept, gather, and take care of all the orphans who walk the earth in need of happiness and love.

For me, here is the mystery of Jesus: Jesus was that one who, in His youth, lived an intense experience of the Father.

During those years He felt drunk with the warm and infinite tenderness of the Father. On the outskirts of Nazareth, in the hills surrounding the village, the son of Mary felt, a thousand and one times, loved, enveloped, and penetrated by a loving Presence, and as a result of this, He experienced vividly what it means to be free and happy.

After that, he could not be contained. It was impossible for Him to remain in Nazareth. He needed to leave and to go out into the world to reveal the Father, to shout to the four winds the great news of love, and to make all people happy.

And He went everywhere, liberated and liberator,

loved and lover, to relate with others as the Father had related to Him.

I have loved you
just as the Father has loved me. (Jn 15:9)

How does one reconcile all that has been said here with the fact that Jesus is also Son of God? I ask myself: Will anyone ever be able to know that? The Mystery is completely beyond us. We only know that He was also, completely, the son of Mary.

The One who reveals the Father

Now Jesus begins to lift the veil and reveal the face of the Father. We have the impression that the Revealer feels incapable of transmitting what He "knows." Like a popular narrator who dresses great truths in simple clothing, Jesus uses fantasy, invents parables and comparisons, giving explanations from natural phenomena and ways of life. But after all this, we are left with the idea that the reality is something else, that Jesus has cut Himself short. His experience was so long and wide, and the human word is so short.

Have you ever seen a hungry child ask his father for a piece of bread and be given a stone instead? Or, if he should ask for a piece of cooked fish, will his father give him a snake instead, which will bite him, poison him and kill him? You, with each other, are capable of anything. But with your children you are always kind and generous. I tell you: If you, in spite of the bad leaven within you, treat your little ones with such tenderness, how much more tenderly will your Father treat you? If you only knew...

I "know" him well, and so I can guarantee: Ask, seek, knock at the door. I assure you that the door will be opened to you, you will find what you seek, you will receive what you need. Yes. Before you even open your mouth, He already knows what you need. Before you have gone to meet Him, He has spent a long time in coming to meet you. If you only knew...

Why do you look ahead with anxious eyes and heavy heart? Why do you shout, What will we eat? Where will we sleep? Where shall we live? How will the business we have just taken on go for us? Take care, yes; worry, what for? Struggle, but not anxiously. Risk yourselves, organize, work, but in peace. Preoccupations? Deposit them into the hands of the Father. Security for tomorrow? Be careful! Don't place your trust in money, which is a false god. Let the Father be your only security.

Look at the birds: with what joy and abandon do they fly through the sky. I assure you that not one of these birds falls to the ground hungry. Yet, they are not like us who, to eat a piece of bread, have to sow, reap, and grind. Those birds do not work and yet they eat. Who gives them food every day? The Father. And how much are those birds worth? About twelve cents. And you, are you not worth more than they? Are you not immortal children of Love? Why worry yourselves?

And what shall we say about clothing? Lift your eyes and look at the lilies now that it is springtime. Not even Solomon, the elegant king, was dressed in such splendor as are these flowers. They do not sew or knit. Who clothes them so beautifully each morning? The Father. If the Father cares so much for these lilies, which one day blossom and wither away the next, what will He not do for you, His children? What is more important, clothes or the body? Oh, if you only knew the Father...

They say that the daughter of the chief priest of the synagogue had died; they say not to bother the Master because it is useless: the girl was already dead. What? It is useless? Only the Son "knows" the Father. And Jesus says to the chief priest: Look, it would be enough for you to believe in the goodness and power of the Father, and your daughter, under the resurrecting hand of love, would come back to life like a flower that awakens from a dream (Mk 5:35-42).

* * *

There was once a son who was as insane as he was insolent. He went before his father and said, "Father, working like a fool for so many years on this land, you have increased your lands, you have built castles, you are practically the king of this region. But you have never enjoyed a single day as we are meant to do. I do not want the same thing to happen to me. While I am still young I want to enjoy life. Give me, then, the part of the inheritance that belongs to me."

And he went away to a far land and pilfered his riches on riotous living.

When the son realized that beneath the surface of so much satisfaction there was a well of infinite dissatisfaction, that nothing could take the place of his father's house, and when homesickness and poverty fell upon him, do you know what that ingrate did? He memorized a list of justifications and returned peacefully to his father's house. Do you know why? Because he knew his father well.

And he was not wrong. That venerable man, when he was told of his son's return, jumped up from his chair, ran down the stairs, got on his fastest horse, went out to meet the boy, hugged him, kissed him, gathered the workers of the fields, and said to them, "Faithful servants of my land, prepare a banquet more splendid than any this house has seen, because this is the happiest day of my life; bring a gold ring for his finger and the clothes of a prince for his body..."

Ah, if you knew the Father. He is like that: understanding, forgiving, kind... Look at that sun. Do you think that the king of the sky shines only on the land of the just? That ball of fire also gives life and splendor to the fields of the traitors, liars, and blasphemers. The Father is like that.

And the rain? Thanks to her the deserts are green and the trees are laden with golden fruit. Do you think that there is discrimination and that the rain falls softly only on the land of the elect? You are mistaken. It also falls on the land of those who bribe, pillage, and take advantage of others. The Father is like that: He returns good for evil. If you only knew Him...

* * *

One day they will raise me up on a cross, between heaven and earth. The sun will abandon me. All else will also abandon me: personal prestige, friends, the results of my efforts. I will be exiled from every land and from all good things. But it does not matter. I will not be alone because "the Father is always with me" (cf. Jn 8:29).

The hour has come, for which I have been long waiting. I see the scene that is going to take place: like a flock of frightened doves, all of you will disappear, scattering in a thousand directions, each one trying to save his own skin; you will all abandon me and I will be left at the mercy of the wolves. "And yet I am not alone, because the Father is with me" (Jn 16:32).

This is the continual inner state of Jesus: always face to face with His Father. The Son looks at the Father and the Father looks at the Son, and that mutual gaze is transformed into a mantle of tenderness that wraps the two in infinite joy. Failure? Agony? Calvary? The storms may clamor outside. Their winds will not reach the inner lake, except for a few gusts like the one in Gethsemane.

This is, it seems to me, the reason why Jesus crossed the stage of His Passion with such dignity and peace. Throughout His life, Jesus did nothing but dig an infinite well which His loving Father would fill completely.

Brilliant light

In the upper room, on the night of His departure, Jesus was more inspired than ever before. It was as if a river had run over its banks; everything was flooded with emotion. It was a brilliant night: the Lord opened wide the doors of His intimacy, and nothing was seen except an infinite dwelling of solitude, inhabited by only one Person: the Father.

That was the reason why He said to them, From now on, I call you "friends." Do you know why? Because a friend is the friend of another when the first one shows the second the secrets of His heart. I have shown you the innermost parts of me and you have seen what is the single greatest secret of my life: the Father.

And just as when a person is overpowered by a sacred obsession, the Master endlessly repeats the name of *Father*:

In my *Father's* house there are many rooms.
I am going to the *Father*.
No one goes to the *Father* except through me.
The *Father* is greater than I.
I am the vine, the *Father* is the vinedresser.
I came from the *Father* and I return to the *Father*.
My *Father*, the hour has come.
Holy *Father*, I come to nou now.
Just *Father*, glorify your Son...

Never has anyone said or will say that name with such veneration, such tenderness, such admiration, and so much love. Will there ever be a contemplative in the world who will be able to tell us what stirred in the heart of Jesus when He repeated that name so many times that night? Who will be able to describe the expressiveness of that gaze, full of admiration and love, when, in chapter 17 of John's Gospel, Jesus lifts His eyes to say His final prayer?

The Apostles must have seen Him in that moment so radiant, so brilliant, so inebriating. Philip, summing up the feelings of the rest, was brought to say, Master, enough of words, you have lit a burning fire within us and we are dying of homesickness. Lift the veil and show us the Father in person because we want to embrace Him.

During the days of evangelization, speaking with such inspiration, a deep desire arose from the heart of the world up to the Father. Because of this, the brothers in the first communities felt like pilgrims weighed down by homesickness for the paternal home, "far from the Lord," like outcasts who dream of their homeland (2 Cor 5:1-10; 1 Pt 2:11) until, on *the great day of liberation* which is death, that blessed Face appears in all its splendor.

Beneath all the metaphors, Jesus presents *salvation* to us as a perpetual living in the Father's house, while damnation is presented as being left outside of the golden walls of that house forever.

Hell? It is the absence of the Father: loneliness, emptiness, unending desire. These high and spiritual concepts would never have been understood by the disciples if they had not previously had a great desire for the Father.

Eternal life consists in that "they know You, the One True God" (Jn 17:3). The whole problem of salvation and damnation revolves around the absence or presence of the Father.

Sheol? Annihilation? Nothingness? No. Death is a "joining in your master's happiness" (Mt 25:21). Heaven? Heaven *is* the Father; the Father *is* heaven. The Father's House? The House is the Father; the Father is the House. The homeland? The Father is the entire homeland.

Jesus of Nazareth? He was the One sent to reveal the Father to us, and to relate to everyone as the Father related to Him.

3. JESUS SURRENDERS

If we go within Jesus, if we descend to the foundations of His person and explore the impulses that are the origin of His inclinations and aspirations, His intentions and desires, and, above all, if we begin to look for the secret key that explains His moral greatness, we will find nothing else but *surrender*, fulfilling the will of His Father.

This is His food and breath. The will of the Father sustains and gives meaning to His life. He lived like a small happy child, carried in the arms of His Father: "My delight is to do your will; your law, my God, is deep in my heart" (Ps 40).

Later we will see how this unconditional attitude of surrender is the origin of that energy, joy, and security with which we see Him living and acting. We will also have to see that this same surrender strongly enriched His personality, making Him a sound witness to God, full of grandeur and courage. Surrender, in the end, is the primary spiritual attitude of the Gospel.

An offering

For Jesus, surrender meant leaving His own interests aside and delivering Himself to the Other, confidently placing His head and His life in the hands of His beloved Father.

The act of surrender is, then, a transmission of domination, a giving of the "I" to a "Thou." It is an "active" gesture because there is a total offering of our own will to the will of the loved one.

It does not mean resigning ourselves to the fateful march of events. To surrender is to deliver ourselves with love to Someone who loves us and whom we love, and because we love that Someone, we surrender.

The first generation of Christians saw Jesus primarily as the Servant of God, that *poor one of God*, filled with the spirituality of the *anawim*,* who did not ask or question,

---

* Translator's note: *Anawim* is a Hebrew term referring to the widows, the orphans, the poor, and the homeless — all those who are in need.

who did not resist or complain but who surrendered, in silence and peace, to the plan of the Lord as manifested in the events of history. According to that statement, Jesus did not come primarily to evangelize, not even to redeem, but rather to bring the will of the Father to fulfillment. Renouncing His own will to take on the will of the Father, Jesus was liberated from Himself. Freed from Himself, He was made Liberator.

I am a Servant because, "By myself I can do nothing" (Jn 5:30). I am not a leader. I am Sent. I cannot take the initiative. I am not a prophet nor a messenger, nor even a redeemer; I am simply a submissive and obedient Son; I am an "alert," an "attention," permanently open to what my Father desires because for this alone have I been sent (Jn 6:38).

The Father loves me because I do His will (Jn 10:17). Here is the complete mystery of that *unifying relationship* between the Son and the Father: there exists between the two a total agreement of wills because they love each other so much; and they love each other so much because that agreement of wills exists. In a word, the sacrificial love and the emotional love meet and are equated.

And linked by the chain of one unified will, the two live love and tenderness reciprocally, not only in the sweetness of intimacy but also in times of fright and panic (Mt 26:37). And so, the sweet word *Abba* (O dear Father) was tirelessly repeated on the Mount of Olives, on the night of the great test, in a moment of terror and nausea: "Abba... for you everything is possible. Take this cup away from me. But let it be as you, not I, would have it" (Mk 14:36).

According to one school of Christology, the relationship of Jesus with His Father was carried on in a highly emotional state. This becomes evident if we look at the Gospel passages and the personality structure of this same Jesus. I will never tire of repeating: the capacity of believers for sacrificial love is in proportion to their emotional capacity, when this is properly channelled. If Jesus heroically took on His Father's will, it was due to that current of tenderness circulating between the two of them.

* * *

Master, eat something because surely you must be hungry. It is true that I am hungry; but I have food of which you do not know. My daily bread is the will of my Father (Jn 4:34). That bread sustains me.

And that will is manifested in small, everyday details. Today, Jesus attends a wedding party quite naturally. There, He mingles with simple people and shares the happiness of everyone. The next day, He spends the whole day walking to Capernaum. Along the road, He helps the fishermen, talks to the publicans, pardons the sinner, plays with the children. Today, He worries about those with hungry stomachs. Tomorrow, He will worry about those with hunger of heart. Always calm, trusting, tireless, completely surrendered into the loving and beloved hands of His Father, Jesus is a happy Son. I am free because I am open. Thy holy will be done, on earth, in heaven, and everywhere! Glorify your Name, O Father!

Rudolf Bultmann, the renowned Scripture scholar, wrote:

> For him, God is not an object of thought, of speculation. God is to him neither a metaphysical entity nor a cosmic power nor a law of the universe, but personal Will, holy and gracious Will.
>
> Jesus speaks of God only to affirm that man is claimed by the will of God and determined in his present existence through God's demand, his judgment, his grace.
>
> The distant God is at the same time the God near at hand, Whose reality is not grasped when a man seeks to escape from his own concrete existence, but precisely when He holds it fast...
>
> He brings the message of the coming Kingdom and of the will of God. He speaks of God in speaking of man and

showing him that He stands in the last hour of decision, that his will is claimed by God.

When the disciples who had gone to prepare the way for Jesus were expelled from Samaria, at that time, the red wall of resistance appeared, demanding revenge and fire. You do not know what you are saying. It is not the spirit of my Father that speaks from your mouths, but the evil spirit of bitterness. I did not come to destroy but to build. If my Father permits the resistance of Samaria, we cannot raise the sword of revenge. Resist? No. Surrender (Lk 9:55).

Jerusalem, Jerusalem, you who kill the prophets...! Jesus breaks down emotionally (Mt 23:27). Just as He appears in the Gospels, Jesus is the one who does not have the least consideration for Himself and is incapable of being easy on Himself. Essentially, He is poor of heart: He has no personal interests nor does He render homage to His own image. Because of this He was free, frightfully free. Because of this, too, He always proceeded without "political" motives and never acted out of calculations like someone looking for the support of the rest. He was unbeatable, because in the game of life He never bet anything — because He had nothing; He bet everything, that is, for the Other. He ended as was His lot: crucified and rejected. If He cries now, it is not for Himself but for the Father, before Whom the capital city had stubbornly closed its doors.

Well, then, weeping and sad, Jesus does not face it on clouds of anathemas and fire, but rather surrenders in tears like a frail child faced with the impotence of divine power.

What's that, Peter? Organizing an armed resistance against those attacking troops? If I wanted to, right now, I would have powerful legions of angels who, in an instant, would annihilate this handful of mercenaries. But how many times do I have to tell you that what is seen is one thing, and what is not seen is quite another! What you see here is a complicated religio-political-military mixture promoted by a frustrated and resentful person like Caiaphas. That is the surface, the appearance. The reality — which is always hidden behind what you see — is the will of my Father who permits this sequence of events that are already foretold in the Scriptures. Put away your sword, Peter. And we are going to surrender to the Father's plan (Mt 26:52).

And, turning to the assailants, He says, You are armed to the teeth, as if you were going to capture a world famous criminal. In the temple, when I was speaking, you were the most ardent listeners, and you never dared to touch me, even with a rose petal. Now, however, you dare. You do not know why things happen this way. I do know: from ancient times, my Father decided that everything would happen this way and it says so in the Scriptures. Put down your swords; there is no resistance here. I deliver myself to you voluntarily (Mt 26:55).

Teaching one day in Capharnaum, His relatives arrived and told Him, Listen, your mother and your brothers are outside asking for you. Jesus replied, My mother? Who is my mother? All of you are my mother. I tell you, all who take the will of my Father seriously realize in that the completeness of blood relations. The will of the Father is the common ground (Mk 3:31).

On the last day, old friends will come banging on the doors and shouting, Lord, Lord, open to us the gates of Paradise because we ate and drank with you. He will answer them, The gates of Paradise will not be opened to those who call out but only to those who quietly accept the will of my Father (Mt 7:21).

In *On Being A Christian*, Hans Küng states that:

This is the common denominator of the Sermon on the Mount: *God's will be done!* The time for relativizing God's will is past. What is required is not pious enthusiasm or pure interiority, but obedience in disposition and deed. Man himself must accept his responsibility in face of the closely approaching God. Only through resolutely, unreservedly doing God's will does man come to share the promises of the Kingdom of God.

Prelude

Thus did Jesus speak. And He lived that way, too. In His final days, however, Jesus suffered a crisis, a prelude to the great crisis He would have to experience on the dark night in Gethsemane. It was the day following the solemn entry into Jerusalem. The Greeks, from the Diaspora, wanted to interview Him. The Master went off into strange metaphors. He said, for example, that to live one had to die, that the life of the wheat is born from the death of the grain.

And suddenly, the shiver, like a death squad, overpowered His heart for a moment. He was scared. He wavered. For a moment He was taken aback. It was a momentary crisis.

This moment of confusion is reported in the Gospel of John (12:27-28). Probably, John — who does not record the crisis in Gethsemane — places here the synthesis of that bigger crisis. Be that as it may, in the two verses, four scenes are alternated, with four opposing reactions. The contradiction took possession of Jesus' spirit and disintegrated it. It was the crisis of contradiction.

> Now my soul is troubled.
> What shall I say:
> Father, save me from this hour?
> But it is for this very reason that I have come to this hour.
> Father, glorify your name! (Jn 12:27-28)

In the disturbance, the following takes place: Anything threatened pleads with its owner, saying, Defend me. Then the owner releases energies for the defense of the property. This is the disturbance. Our first and foremost property is life. Feeling His life threatened, Jesus is troubled.

In the second scene, the face of fear appears among the clouds: to have to die. The unknown. The absurd: a life ended in such a way, almost without meaning, before His time. It was too much! Is there no other way for salvation?

307

Why does it have to be this particular cup? Free me from this hour; at least, postpone it.

Then, like someone waking from a nightmare, bathed in perspiration, Jesus opens His eyes, shakes His head as if to wipe out the bad dream, and that word falls which echoes in His innermost depths: Remember, son of Mary, for this I came, now is my hour.

And, freed from fear and breathing calmly, He lifted His eyes to say, Yes, Father! Thy will be done. May your Name be glorified.

No one takes my life from me

What happened in Jesus' soul during the time of His Passion? As the scenes unfolded, would Jesus have suffered some dismay as He was taken from tribunal to tribunal? When the sentence was pronounced — You will be crucified — would Jesus have had some "remorse," like someone who says: What a shame! If I had not committed that foolish act, if I had not hurled those curses, would I be in this situation right now?...

Humanly speaking, could Jesus have avoided death? Could He have interrupted the chain of events? When He felt the approach of His persecutors, why did He not escape to the Golan Heights or to the mountains of Samaria? Did Jesus lack a defense strategy, retreat tactics, sense of direction, or maybe a certain counsel? Is it that, maybe, they used a surprise tactic on Him and, when He realized it, they were already near, leaving Him no chance for escape?

Bethany, a few kilometers from the capital, was it a place of rest or a refuge from the detectives of the Sanhedrin? Why did He not stay quiet during those last few weeks? Sensing the bitterness of the Sanhedrin against Him, why did He not go to Galilee for a while, until feelings calmed down? Why did He continue to antagonize and defy the authorities, right up to the last minute? When

Caiaphas and Pilate both invited Him to defend Himself, why did He remain silent?

* * *

What really happened? Was it a normal and fatal development of historical events, or a free and voluntary decision on the part of Jesus? Did they get Him or did He let Himself be gotten?

Let me explain. The river of history falls from far above, from the time of Jesus' birth, carrying with it concrete factors: the ups and downs of Israel's political situation, Roman imperialism, the personalities of such people as Caiaphas and Judas, initiatives of the compromising politics of the Sanhedrin, etc. All of these factors, in a blind combination, were rolling along like the waters of a stream, carrying Jesus and dragging Him to His death. Was that it?

All of that certainly existed. But with this alone there would have been no redemption. It was necessary that Jesus accept, freely and voluntarily, all of this. Those events were *history*, but not *salvation history*. For there to be salvation, Jesus had to form a "soul" to fit those external events.

Either historical fatality and death destroyed Jesus, or Jesus destroyed death. Feeling closed in and lost, Jesus could have resisted, defending Himself. He could have died swearing against the Sanhedrin. In that case, there would have been no salvation. Jesus could have looked at the facts from a sociopolitical perspective, saying, Everything began with the jealous reaction of a frustrated man like Caiaphas, was completed by the cowardly reaction of a timid man like Pilate, and everything was combined by the fact that my death would bring good political benefits for a few people. If Jesus had "looked" at things this way, He would have felt wrapped up and destroyed by the blind fate of history and there would not have been the slightest bit of salvation in it at all.

But it was not so. Jesus did not fix His gaze on phenomena but on *reality*. He did not analyze facts superficially but, behind the stream of events, He saw the face of the Father. He did not give homage to the facts but only to the will of the Father. In absolute terms, the Father could have interrupted the chain of events and stopped the march of history. If He did not do so, it was because He wanted everything to follow its course and He wanted His Son to disappear, burned on the pyre of a disaster.

The difference between blind fate and redemptive death was that Jesus had to see (or not see) the will of the Father in everything and *accept it* (or not).

Faced with given facts or with inevitable situations in which human beings can do nothing, Jesus sees and accepts the will of the Father. With this attitude, Jesus is liberated from fear and is made Liberator. As Paul will tell us, Jesus delivered Himself, submissive and obedient unto death, death on a cross. Because of this, Jesus was not only liberated from death but received the title of Liberator of Humanity and Lord of the Universe. In this way, Jesus completed His mission and transformed historical events into a decisive stage for the kingdom of God.

* * *

The question — could Jesus have avoided death? — is not important to us. If He could have avoided death and did not, He let death overpower Him without even looking for it. There are many passages in the Gospel that confirm the impression that He did not want to avoid death, as we have said above. For example, the fact that He continued to defy authority to the end and, instead of turning His heels on the battle, fleeing to other provinces, He remained where He was, within the reach of His persecutors; He did not open His mouth to defend Himself at the two opportunities He was given to do so, giving the impression that it did not matter to Him that He was going to die.

However, that was not what was important. What was decisive was something else: He could, or could not, have avoided death, but He voluntarily dies anyway because He accepted all that happened, considering it to be an expression of the Father's will. The inevitable or given facts were not for Him as if He were a powerless victim; they had no effect on Him because He did not resist. He delivered Himself nonviolently to the violence of the events, giving Himself up peacefully and silently into the hands of the One who permitted everything to happen.

Because of this, Jesus crossed the stage of His Passion with dignity and peace. The four evangelists abound in details, confirming this impression. And if we were to synthesize all those details, and if this synthesis were to be expressed in a painting, we would have the famous painting of Velazquez's *Christ*.

That painting is the historical and pictorial answer to the question about the voluntary nature of the Passion on the part of Jesus: with open arms, delivered into the hands of the world, into the hands of humanity, into the hands of God, surrendered, asleep, dead — satisfied? Yes, with the satisfaction of having *given* His all. There is in that face, half covered with black hair, with eyes closed, an infinite peace, an imperturbable serenity, how do we say it? A strange sweetness. Certainly this dead man has not fought with death. Here there has been no struggle or resistance. Over the top of the cross, we could put the sign, "Mission Accomplished." And that other inscription, "No one takes [my life] from me; I lay it down of my own free will... this is the command I have received from my Father" (Jn 10:17).

311

The great crisis

In the attitude of surrender, maintained without fail by Jesus throughout His whole life, there was one powerful and emotional fall.

Throughout His life, Jesus had been the faithful and complete response of the Son to the Father. He was the "faithful" and "true witness" (Rv 3:14). I am always struck by the way the author of the Letter to the Hebrews presents Jesus as the model of fidelity in the midst of frailty and the temptations that surround Him, and that also surround us. He invites us to have "our eyes fixed on Jesus" (Heb 12:2). "Remember how He endured the opposition of sinners that you may not grow despondent or abandon the struggle" (Heb 12:3).

Jesus, then, began by traveling along all *human paths* to the end, except for the path of sin. He was "put to the test in the exact same way we are, apart from sin" (Heb 4:15). We have, then, a Brother to whom it cost a great deal to be completely faithful to the Father, and that is an enormous consolation for us.

Being more human, He deprived Himself of the divine glory, that glory which He had before the world existed (Jn 17:5). With the act of the Incarnation, He renounced all of the advantages of being God and submitted Himself to the disadvantage of being human. He experienced the same limitations such as the law of cause and effect, the laws of space, the law of mediocrity, the law of loneliness, and the law of death.

In short, He accepted Himself as a human being; and He accepted Himself without reservations or compensations, without recourse to His divinity in moments of need. He never took advantage of His divine power for His own use; He did, however, do so for the use of others. He was completely *faithful* to humanity. He never "betrayed" His human condition. All of this is reflected when the Scriptures say that Jesus "descended" to the condition of a slave, the same as any other human being (Phil 2:5ff).

But in this human experience, Jesus lacked the most bitter drink: death.

There is no grace in standing erect like a sapling on a calm afternoon. The merit in faithfulness lies in remaining standing when the winds blow violently. And it was at this time, in the hour of the Great Test, when Jesus surrendered to the will of the Father, purely and radically, without reservation or hesitation. It was the moment of utmost faithfulness.

In Gethsemane, Jesus was transformed into the *great miserable one*, not in the sense of one laden with every human misery, but in the sense of one who experienced the misery of *feeling human* to the point of the ultimate human weakness, to the point of feeling cowardice, nausea, and contradiction. He descended to the lowest levels of the human condition.

He distinguished between two wills that were violently opposed to each other. Jesus came to be, in that moment, a battlefield where two antagonizing forces carried out their final struggle: "what I want" and "what You want."

Before Jesus' vivid and sensitive imagination, there appeared the face of death, very close; better, the fear of death.

It is easy to theorize about death and to construct beautiful philosophies when it is not within sight. It might also be that death itself is a vacuum, something without substance, like the word *nothing*. But we are the ones who give "life" to death, filling this emptiness with our fears and fantasies. Yes. We are "living" death. In Gethsemane, Jesus "lived" death.

All that lives — vegetable, animal, human being — has mechanisms of self-preservation. It is an instinct of preservation, powerful defensive forces, stronger in the animal than in the plant, and much stronger in humans than in animals. An animal, once it has begun the process of death, lets itself die, it does not resist, it is snuffed out like a candle: death is "realized" in that animal.

Agony exists only in human beings, because we are conscious of death and resist it. (Only humans *die*. Animals *are killed*.) For many, life is a slow agony, especially in the later years, because they live dominated by fear.

On the other hand, death is an unknown and the mind always fears what is not known. Death cuts off for good certain nice things: to be able to enjoy the joy of this sunshine, of this spring ("now that spring has come, I must die" one person said to me), of this friendship, of the appreciation of so many friends; to be able to dream, to be able to make others happy, to be able to see or relate to family, friends... In short, it is the Great Good-bye: I am leaving, and no one can "come" with me.

Once dead, the individual suffers nothing of this good-bye. It is while the person lives that we continue to "live" the uprooting of every good-bye. And just as fear is a defense of property, and death causes all property to escape our grasp, it is natural that the nearness of death should be the cause of the greatest fear, which is nothing more than the maximum release of energy to defend the general ownership of life.

Jesus lived all of this in Gethsemane; but He lived it in *high gear* because there were other circumstances that came together to make this departure even more heartrending.

Whoever faces the closeness of death, as Jesus did, must create the consolation that many people are going to be affected by that death, that they will lament it and that they will cry over it. The loneliness of death may be partially relieved by this sense of solidarity with others.

But in Jesus' case there was no solidarity, but rather hostility and indifference. In His case, the majority were happy or remained indifferent. As an example of the latter group, there were His disciples, peacefully asleep as He went through His tragic agony. Anyone, in these circumstances, must feel completely unhappy and miserable. How could one not feel disgust and nausea?

314

Furthermore, this whole thing appears absurd. If I take this bitter cup, with sweat and blood, to save them, and if salvation means nothing to them, if they do not even recognize it or feel thankful for it, then we are at the height of the ridiculous. It is a useless sacrifice!

* * *

The New Testament presents us with that battle enclosed in a living context that is extremely frightening. The physician-evangelist tells us of the sweating of blood, a phenomenon which science tells us is called *hematidrosis*. The heart is a powerful muscle that has as its function the pumping of blood. It is covered with fibrous motor nerves just to keep it in constant motion. When we reach a highly emotional situation, that noble muscle may begin to pump so violently and rapidly that it can break capillaries, producing the sweating of blood. This, then, is a physical phenomenon that is nothing more than a distant echo of an elevated interior state.

The Letter to the Hebrews gathers, preserves, and records a very emotional account of Jesus pleading with the Father on that night, "with loud cries and with tears" (Heb 5:7). Mark informs us that He invoked God with the word Abba, the most tender of expressions (Mk 14:36). And Matthew adds that He "fell on his face and prayed" (Mt 26:39). This is strange, because the Jews always stood while praying. This position could be interpreted as meaning that He had been struck down as if by a strong wind. Who understands this mysterious combination: crying and wailing like a child, but with words of tenderness, shaken and struck down by fright?

The synoptic Gospels give us all the characteristics of agony. Jesus says He feels "sorrow" (Mt 26:37). One who does not want to die is, above all, in agony; He is in terror of death. The evangelists use the word *distress* (Mk 14:33; Mt 26:37), which means the same thing. At the same time,

315

one who is in agony feels so bad physically and psychologically that the desire to go on living is lost. He is tired of life. Sick or nauseated, we commonly say. If He does not want to live, if He does not want to die, the one in agony is a disintegrated being, pulled by opposing forces in opposite directions.

Simply — and essentially — this was the case of Jesus on that night; a being brutally pulled in two directions by contradictory forces: "what I want" and "what You want."

At first, "what I want" was winning. All of the questions rose up in the name of reason, piety, and common sense. The voice of Jesus came from the deepest part of Him. It came from His youth when so many hopes shined before Him... Why, Holy Father, a useless and meaningless end? Why? Life was so nice, Father, I felt so happy making others happy, and now You take away the joy of sharing happiness. Why? We may lose battles and still win the war; we may also win battles and lose the war, and You put me in this corner with no alternatives. Why? Don't You love me? Are You not my Father? Is it not true that You can do anything? Can't You replace this cup with another one? Why does it have to be *this* one?

And so the voices of protest emerged, but in the end, I do not know where Jesus found the strength to do away with all of those voices, He said, My Father, up to now I have spoken only foolish words. Better yet, it was not I who spoke; it was the "flesh." But now, yes; now I am going to speak *my* word: *No, to what I want! Yes, to what You want!*

The synoptic Gospels make a point of the fact that Jesus repeated the same words many times. We may have beliefs; but what is important is that these reach the emotional depths where decisions are born. It is also possible that Jesus was experiencing complete aridity on that night and so He needed to repeat the same words many times.

Jesus never reached as great a stature as in that moment, "accepting death, death on a cross (Phil 2:8). And, identified with "what the Father wants," He delivers Himself, peacefully, into the hands of His executioners.

316

* * *

What counsel did the angel give (Lk 22:43)? I would venture to interpret that scene in its psychospiritual sense. Jesus resisted the Father's proposition with "sweat and blood." It is even possible that at some point He thought that He had foolishly risked His life, for example, with His criticisms against the Sanhedrin or with His intervention in the Temple. But that was over. There was no escape.

Finally, Jesus abandoned His resistance and surrendered Himself, like an obedient child, with the "let it be done as You will." And His surrender was liberation from "sadness and anguish" (Mt 26:37) that produced in His soul the normal fruits of every surrender: peace, consolation, calm, and above all, an infinite satisfaction of having done the supreme act of Love.

We also see that, having been a coward in the preceding scenes, from the moment He surrenders to the will of the Father, He rises strengthened, courageous, serene, available to the others in the difficult time to come. He alone is calm when He is confronted by the troops armed with sticks, swords, and spears (Jn 18:3). Such serenity left the troops astounded (Jn 18:6).

From this moment until He dies on the cross, Jesus is, in the annals of human history, a unique case of grandeur: He appears as a total offering of love. We find no traces of bitterness, no complaint; he crosses the stage without resistance, with infinite peace, with an unbeatable serenity, surrendered like a humble child into the hands of His beloved Father in the midst of a storm of slaps, insults, and whippings.

They swear at Him: He does not defend Himself. They insult Him: He does not respond. They hit Him: He does not protest. Faced with such majesty, the judges appear to be the accused and His silence appears as their judge. Like a lamb before the slaughter, like a sheep carried away to be killed, Jesus is "carried" by the storm, unconditionally and confidently surrendered to the plan of His beloved Father until, like the symbol of surrender that was His whole life, He ends by saying, "Father, into your hands I commit my spirit" (Lk 23:46).

Joy and happiness

Surrendered into the hands of His Father, His life continues to be happy and joyful, in spite of the hostilities and failures. Amid great difficulties, He lives a profound and infectious peace.

In peace I lie down and at once fall asleep
for it is you and none other, Yahweh, who make my rest secure. (Ps 4:9)

If by happiness we understand the unperturbable serenity of someone who is above all the changes in life, we can affirm that Jesus was happy, joyful.

One of His constant themes, when He spoke privately with the disciples, is the joy that filled His heart as a result of the willingness and trust with which He surrendered to His Father's will.

Do not be afraid, do not let your hearts be troubled, live content and happy for I am going to my beloved Father (Jn 14:28). I want you to share my joy and happiness; just as the Father is always with me and because of this I live happily, I would like you to share that same happiness (Jn 16:12-24).

Shalom — a type of total blessing — is what He leaves them as their inheritance. "Peace I bequeath to you, my own peace I give you" (Jn 14:27). He had always lived surrounded by that peace (happiness). Leaving it like the greatest treasure means that His own had seen (with admiration?) Him live in that serene joy, and it is given to them as an inheritance, but on condition that they also live in that same state of faith and trusting surrender in the hands of the Father. Only once does Mark record a gesture of impatience: "How long?" (Mk 9:19).

Here is the particular greatness of Jesus and of all Christians: the ability to live in the midst of trial and failure with a spirit filled with serenity and calm, the ability to be profoundly happy living in the face of adversity. This is the most delicious fruit of sensing that God is Father and of living surrendered in His blessed hands.

Remain in my love as I remain in the care of my Father, that my joy may be in you and that your joy may be complete. Now I come to You, my Father, and I say these things to them that they may also have my joy within them (Jn 17:13): that is to say that the purpose of His life has been to make all share in His profound happiness.

* * *

Letting Himself be carried by the Father, Jesus of Nazareth has acquired a unique moral stature, becoming an incorruptible witness to the Father, full of inner freedom.

By the authority with which He teaches, by the frankness with which He speaks with friends and enemies alike, by His actions at all times without regard for personal acceptance, without fear of losing His life, without desiring personal honor, Jesus is a valiant man.

We act with sovereignty when we are free. When we are full of self-interest, then insecurity and fears take hold and make of our life a begging for prestige and honor from others, depriving us of freedom.

We see Jesus profoundly free because we do not see Him anxious. There is no need for establishing or declaring His identity or status. He simply presents Himself, nothing more and nothing less, as the Servant of the Father and of humanity. He is free because He has no personal interests. He has not come to dominate but to serve and to do the will of His beloved Father.

Trusting, loving, surrendered into the hands of His Father, He outshines them all. He delivers Himself without regard for His own person and with regard for everyone else.

He feels free to serve everyone without moralistic prejudices, be they pagans or prostitutes, sitting at the table of publicans and sinners. He feels free to serve everyone without nationalistic prejudices, the Romans as well as the centurions, the Samaritans who were considered to be "heretics," the pagans of Tyre and Sidon and Caesarea Philippi. He was decidedly for the poor, but free also to be with the rich. He was decidedly for the humble, but He was free to attend to the Pharisees and the Sanhedrin like Nicodemus and Joseph of Arimathea.

Jesus was not a "politician," much less a diplomat. He never worked with a "bias," with "prudence," or by human calculations. Otherwise He would have died in bed instead of on a cross. His honor and His life did not matter –only the glory of His beloved Father. He played to the hilt and He was consistent.

His own adversaries took a perfect psychological photograph of Him: "Master, we know that you are truthful and that you are not afraid of anyone, not acting out of human respect, but teach God's way of life sincerely" (Mk 12:14).

Spiritual childhood

When Miguel de Unamuno died, among the manuscripts found on his desk were these verses:

Widen the door, Father,
for I cannot enter.
You made it for children,
and I have grown up.
If you do not widen the door,
have pity and make me smaller.
Take me back to that age
in which to live was to dream.

Nicodemus, a sincere man but committed to his caste, asks Jesus for a secret nighttime appointment. "Master, we know that you have come from God." As a good Pharisee, he was a specialist in the Scriptures, but he sees in Jesus someone who "knows" things in another way, and he asks Him for something like a secret recipe, a basic and complete attitude for entering the Kingdom.

We speak of what we "know" (Jn 3:11), says Jesus. Essentially, Jesus teaches what He has previously experienced, the living and revealing of the *Abba*, making ourselves little and returning to the Father's arms: *one has to be born again* (Jn 3:7). We have to return to childhood, feeling small and helpless, depending on an Other for everything and courageously trusting in the infinite love of the most-loving Father. This is what the first Beatitude says and only to such as these is the kingdom promised.

— What is that? Return to the mother's womb? asks Nicodemus.

— What? You are a doctor and you don't know those things?

Irony has a certain strangeness about it. Jesus is playing with the word "know," and that is the key. The things of the spirit cannot be "known" if they have not been "experienced." Saint Francis said, "One only knows what one has experienced." And the strange recipe for salvation that Jesus reveals to Nicodemus — rebirth — is only "known" if it has been experienced in the intimacy of the beloved Father. Otherwise, it is nothing more than an unbearable paradox.

* * *

To be saved, according to Jesus, is to *gradually become a child*. To the wisdom of the world, this is something completely strange because it implies an inversion of values and judgments. In human life, according to psychology, the secret of maturity (salvation) is in gradually getting away from maternal dependence and any other attachment, until we arrive at complete independence and the ability to stand on our own two feet.

However, in Jesus' plan, a veritable Copernican revolution, salvation consists in becoming more and more dependent, not standing alone but supported by the Other, in working not on our own initiative but on that of the Other, and in a gradual progression toward an identification, until — if it can be done — we cease to be ourselves and are *one* with God, because love is unifying and identifying; in short, to live the Other's life and the Other's spirit. This dependence, of course, is utmost liberty, as will be seen shortly.

Thérèse of Lisieux says:

> When we keep little we recognize our own nothingness and expect everything from the goodness of God, exactly as a little child expects everything from its father. Nothing worries us, not even the amassing of spiritual riches...
>
> Being as a little child with God means that we do not attribute to ourselves the virtues we may possess, in the belief that we are capable of something. It implies, on the contrary, our recognition of the fact that God places the treasure of virtue in the hand of his little child for him to use as He needs it, though all the while it is God's treasure.

We find ourselves in the very center of the revelation brought by Jesus, the revelation of God the Father (*Abba*). The kingdom is given only to those who trust, to those who hope, to those who surrender in the hands of the Father. All is Grace. Pure Gift. Everything is received. To receive, we have to surrender. Those who surrender are only those who are "small." It is necessary to become small, like a child, a "minor." But once we have placed ourselves in the orbit of God, surrendering ourselves, then all barriers are broken and we share in the infinite power of the loving Father, in His eternity and immensity.

If you do not become like a child, you will not enter the

kingdom of heaven (Mt 18:1-4). Become a child! Children are essentially poor and trusting, trusting because they know that their weakness needs someone else's strength; in other words, the poverty of the child is wealth. By themselves, children are neither strong nor virtuous nor secure. They are like the sunflower that is always open to the sun; from there, all hope comes, everything is received from it: heat, light, strength, life...

To become a child, to live the experience of the Abba (dear Father) not only in prayer but most of all in the circumstances of life, confidently surrendering to what the Father wills, all of this seems to be an easy and simple thing to do. But in reality it means the most fantastic change, a real revolution within the old castle built up in self-sufficiency, self-centeredness, and delusions of grandeur.

As one of the Carmelite sisters says in Georges Bernanos' *The Carmelites*:

> Whatever happens, do not shed simplicity. To judge from our good books, one might suppose that God tests his saints as a blacksmith does a bar of iron, to try its strength. It does, however, sometimes happen that a tanner tests a piece of doeskin between his hands, to appraise its softness. Oh! my daughter, be you always soft and yielding in his hands.

Technology has conquered and transformed matter. Psychology seems to have dominated us. A vain illusion. At the time of diagnosis, psychoanalysis achieves good results; but at the time of healing (salvation), the individual, in his profound complexity, is an ever-fleeing and unreachable shadow. We are daily witnesses to the powerlessness of psychiatric therapy for any interior liberation.

No other "science" has been invented nor any other plan for the transformation of humanity than that revelation brought by Jesus: to renounce dreams of omnipotence, to recognize the impossibility of salvation by purely human means, to be conscious of our smallness and fragility, to surrender confidently and unconditionally into the powerful hands of God, and allow ourselves, day after day, completely passive in His hands, to be transformed from the very roots of our being. God alone is Power, Love, and Change.

In ecclesiastical circles, there has been the obsession — almost a mania — for interior liberation through the psychological sciences, a fact that reflects a deep lack of faith. Although these sciences are a great help, if we do not begin by recognizing Jesus Christ as the only Savior and the surrender to His grace as the only salvation, we will tumble down the path of frustration.

* * *

After giving an emotional description of how humanity and the universe are in the hands of God, and after telling them not to worry about anything except the support of the Father, Jesus, full of joy, ends by telling them, "There is no need to be afraid, little flock, for it has pleased your Father to give you the kingdom" (Lk 12:32).

That simplicity of spirit, that sweet surrender to the Divine Majesty is the goal of our lives; we want to acquire or to find it again, for it is one of the gifts of childhood which, as often as not, does not survive the years of childhood...

This spirit of childhood has subtle enemies, difficult to discern because they are wrapped in sheep's clothing. Various name tags have been invented which threatened this spirit that is so fragile and vulnerable... These dangers are called self-realization, personalization, independence, liberty, respect for individuality... It is necessary to safeguard against all appropriation, power, sufficiency, attitudes that apparently "save" and mature but which, in reality, enslave and burden.

This surrender into the Father's hands is a seemingly passive attitude. But whoever begins to live it will realize that all the Beatitudes are contained in it. I would say that this spirit of childhood is the synthesis of all of the active virtues. It is as if someone had conquered all of the castles of the soul and, once taken, they were surrendered to the Lord of the castle, as sole owner.

* * *

The seventy-two returned from their first apostolic journey. They were happy and told of their "exploits." They were almost illiterate. There was not a doctor, scribe, or rabbi among them. Hearing these stories, Jesus, always so sensitive, felt immense joy and said: Praise to you, loving Father, Lord of heaven and earth, for what you have hidden from the learned and clever you have revealed to these children. Thank you again, my Father, for having willed it so (Mt 11:25; Lk 10:21).

The line of salvation is drawn by the poor in spirit and the humble, those who are conscious of their weakness and are convinced of their need to be saved by an Other, in Whose hands they are held like small children.

Sanctity is not such and such a practice but consists in a disposition of the heart which makes us humble and small in the arms of God, conscious of our weakness and trusting to the point of audacity in his goodness as Father. (St. Thérèse of Lisieux)

Conclusion

STRUGGLE BETWEEN DISCOURAGEMENT AND HOPE

Discouragement speaks

I am a man bent over by the weight of disillusion and the experience of life. I have lived fifty or sixty years. I am an old seawolf. Nothing inspires me and nothing saddens me, everything trips me up; I am burned by life and immune to it.

I was young once. I dreamed; but only those who have not lived dream. My trees, back then, blossomed with illusions. Every afternoon, however, there was a gust of wind and the illusions flew away. I stood up and fell down. I got up again, and fell down again. On my horizons I hung the flags of combat: Obedience, Humility, Purity, Contemplation, Love...

I saw that those dreams and reality were very far apart, as far as east is from west. I heard them say: "You still can," and again I embarked on the golden ship of illusion. Shipwrecks took place. Again, I heard: "There is still time," and, though bent over by the weight of so much disaster, I climbed the pinnacle of illusion again. The fall was worse.

Today I am a deceived man.

I was not born to be a man of God. I took the wrong route. But it is not possible to return to happy childhood or to the mother's womb to begin again.

I look back and everything is in ruins. I look at my feet and everything is a disaster. I do not know if I am guilty or not, I am not even interested in knowing. I do not know if I fought with everything I had or if I held something back. Is something the matter? No one can go back.

What I do know with certainty is one thing: there is no hope for me. What I was until today and what I am now, I will be to the end. My grave will rise upon the ruins of my own castle.

Hope speaks

On the cloud of illusions you have built your house. Because of this, it has fallen a thousand and one times, at the whim of the waves. The sand of the beaches was the foundation of your building, and ruin was inevitable.

The rules of your game were probability and psychology, and the end results were clearly in sight. But I have a final word to say to you this morning: You still can; hope is still possible; tomorrow will be better.

Let us begin again.

If, up until now, there were ruins, from now on there will be castles of light pointing their towers to the heights. If, until now, you have harvested disasters, remember: spring showers are coming.

Behind the closed night there are high mountains, and behind the mountains of night the dawn is coming. It is beautiful to believe in the light when it is night.

Behind the silence breathes the Father. The solitude is inhabited by a presence, and above us waits rest and liberation.

Come. Let us begin again.

I, hope, was born on a dark afternoon, on a barren hill, covered with blood, when everyone repeated, All is lost; there is nothing left to do; the dreamer has died; the dreams are over.

I was born in the womb of death. Because of this, death cannot destroy me. I am immortal because I am the only child of the immortal God. Although you may tell me a thousand and one times that all is lost, a thousand and one times I will answer you that we still have time.

If up until now success and failure were alternating like day and night, from now on Jesus will be resurrected in you each morning, and He will blossom on the dead leaves of your autumn. He will conquer selfishness in you, and death. Yes, the Brother will take you by the hand and lead you to the transforming hills of contemplation. Your old banners will fly again: Strength, Love, Patience...

Purity will raise her naked head of silver among your orange trees, and beneath the flowers of your garden will blossom, invisibly, Humility.

You will shine with the brightness of the ancient prophets before the peoples. And, seeing you, all will say, That one is a child of our God.

Come. Let us begin again.

Look: those stars, blue or red, sparkle from eternity to eternity. Be like them: never grow tired of shining. On dry land and arid mountains, plant the seeds of mercy, hope, and peace. Do not grow tired of planting, though your eyes never see the golden shafts. One day the poor will see them.

Walk. The Lord God will be light for your eyes, breath for your lungs, ointment for your wounds, goal for your path, reward for your effort.

Come. Let us begin again.

...eran Kavanaugh, OCD and Otilio Rodriguez, OCD. ...ington, D.C.: Institute of Carmelite Studies, 1973.

...Walter. *Jesus the Christ.* New York: Paulist Press, 1977.

...akis, Nikos. *Saint Francis.* New York: Touchstone ..., Simon & Schuster, 1971.

...Hans. *On Being a Christian.* New York: Image Books, ...leday, 1976.

...he, Friedrich. *Thus Spoke Zarathustra.* Translated by ...r Kauffmann. New York: Viking Penguin, 1978.

...Rev. Thomas N. *Saint Thérèse of Lisieux: The Little Flower* ...s. New York: P.J. Kenedy, 1926.

...of Avila. *The Interior Castle.* Translated by E. Allison ...New York: Image Books, Doubleday, 1972.

...Way of Perfection.* Translated by E. Allison Peers. New ...Image Books, Doubleday, 1972.

BOOKS FOR ALL SEASONS

The works of Ignacio Larrañaga provide analysis and solutions, doctrines and orientations for the needs and problems of the person, as a whole. They are a summary of the total mystery of man and his needs. A summary that has helped millions and millions of people to experience the joy of interior liberation and the joy to live. Now, the message of Father Larrañaga is becoming available to the English speaking readers.

A) For the relationship with God, we have SENSING YOUR HIDDEN PRESENCE, where is described and practically analyzed man's scheme from his first steps to the heights of contemplation; ENCOUNTER (forthcoming), a simplified and practical manual of prayer; PSALMS FOR LIFE (forthcoming), a practical manual to learn how to pray the Psalms.

B) For man's relationship with himself, FROM SUFFERING TO PEACE (forthcoming) shows the way man, by means of practical orientations and exercises can "save himself" freeing himself from anguish, obsessions, depressions, sadness, anxieties and fears. THE UNAVOIDABLE FORCE OF AGING (being written), explains what to do, how to face and solve all the forces which make man feeble, such as uselessness, impotence, solitude, sickness, old age and death.

C) For man's relationship with others, in the midst of any community, be it matrimony, family, work or any other group, the book entitled COME WITH ME (forthcoming) deals with respect, understanding, forgiveness, communication, acceptance, dialogue and what to do with difficult persons.

In addition to these, Ignacio Larrañaga wrote three other books: THE POOR MAN OF NAZARETH (forthcoming), THE SILENCE OF MARY and THE BROTHER OF ASSISI (forthcoming). These books offer totally original and appealing points of view on three outstanding figures of christian tradition: Jesus, the Savior, the Virgin Mary and Saint Francis of Assisi.

Although the author is a Catholic writer, his message is valid for any Christian, any believer and simply, for any man and woman as proved in many countries. As a matter of fact, many psychologists recommend Ignacio Larrañaga's books to their patients.

A testimony about SENSING YOUR HIDDEN PRESENCE:

"An electrifying book from the first line. No one interested in Christian spirituality and its relation to contemporary problems can afford to miss this witness to the power of living faith in Christ founded on an intense life of prayer." (Benedict J. Groeschel, O.F.M. Cap).

by
Was

Kasper

Kazan
Boo

Küng,
Dou

Nietzs
Wa

Taylor
of Je

Teresa
Pee

—. The
Yor

Selected Bibliog

Adam, Karl. *The Son of God.* New Yo bleday, 1960.

Bernanos, Georges. *The Carmelites.* 1965.

Bonhoeffer, Dietrich. *Letters and Paper* Eberhard Bethage. New York: Maci

Bultmann, Rudolf. *Jesus and the Wor* Pettibone Smith. New York: Scribne

Catherine of Siena. *The Dialogues of* Translated by Algar Thorold. R Books, 1976.

Dechanet, J.M. *Christian Yoga.* Trans marsh. New York: Harper & Row, 1

Flannery, Rev. Austin, General Editor *Conciliar and Post Conciliar Documen Spes* and *Perfectæ Caritatis*). Northp lishing Co., 1975.

Francis of Assisi. *Saint Francis of As Biographies: English Omnibus of the Francis.* Edited by Marion A. Hab Herald Press, 1973.

Fromm, Erich. *The Art of Loving.* New 1956.

Jeremias, Joachim. *The Central Messag* New York: Scribner's, 1965.

John of the Cross. *The Collected Works* (including *Ascent of Mount Carmel*).

BOOKS FOR ALL SEASONS

The works of Ignacio Larrañaga provide analysis and solutions, doctrines and orientations for the needs and problems of the person, as a whole. They are a summary of the total mystery of man and his needs. A summary that has helped millions and millions of people to experience the joy of interior liberation and the joy to live. Now, the message of Father Larrañaga is becoming available to the English speaking readers.

A) For the relationship with God, we have SENSING YOUR HIDDEN PRESENCE, where is described and practically analyzed man's scheme from his first steps to the heights of contemplation; ENCOUNTER (forthcoming), a simplified and practical manual of prayer; PSALMS FOR LIFE (forthcoming), a practical manual to learn how to pray the Psalms.

B) For man's relationship with himself, FROM SUFFERING TO PEACE (forthcoming) shows the way man, by means of practical orientations and exercises can "save himself" freeing himself from anguish, obsessions, depressions, sadness, anxieties and fears. THE UNAVOIDABLE FORCE OF AGING (being written), explains what to do, how to face and solve all the forces which make man feeble, such as uselessness, impotence, solitude, sickness, old age and death.

C) For man's relationship with others, in the midst of any community, be it matrimony, family, work or any other group, the book entitled COME WITH ME (forthcoming) deals with respect, understanding, forgiveness, com-

331

munication, acceptance, dialogue and what to do with difficult persons.

In addition to these, Ignacio Larrañaga wrote three other books: THE POOR MAN OF NAZARETH (forthcoming), THE SILENCE OF MARY and THE BROTHER OF ASSISI (forthcoming). These books offer totally original and appealing points of view on three outstanding figures of christian tradition: Jesus, the Savior, the Virgin Mary and Saint Francis of Assisi.

Although the author is a Catholic writer, his message is valid for any Christian, any believer and simply, for any man and woman as proved in many countries. As a matter of fact, many psychologists recommend Ignacio Larrañaga's books to their patients.

A testimony about SENSING YOUR HIDDEN PRESENCE:

"An electrifying book from the first line. No one interested in Christian spirituality and its relation to contemporary problems can afford to miss this witness to the power of living faith in Christ founded on an intense life of prayer." (Benedict J. Groeschel, O.F.M. Cap).

Selected Bibliography

Adam, Karl. *The Son of God.* New York: Image Books, Doubleday, 1960.

Bernanos, Georges. *The Carmelites.* New York: Macmillan, 1965.

Bonhoeffer, Dietrich. *Letters and Papers from Prison.* Edited by Eberhard Bethage. New York: Macmillan, 1953.

Bultmann, Rudolf. *Jesus and the Word.* Translated by Louise Pettibone Smith. New York: Scribner's, 1958.

Catherine of Siena. *The Dialogues of St. Catherine of Siena.* Translated by Algar Thorold. Rockford, Illinois: TAN Books, 1976.

Dechanet, J.M. *Christian Yoga.* Translated by Roland Hindmarsh. New York: Harper & Row, 1960.

Flannery, Rev. Austin, General Editor. *Vatican Council II: The Conciliar and Post Conciliar Documents* (including *Gaudium et Spes* and *Perfectæ Caritatis*). Northport, NY: Costello Publishing Co., 1975.

Francis of Assisi. *Saint Francis of Assisi, Writings and Early Biographies: English Omnibus of the Sources for the Life of St. Francis.* Edited by Marion A. Habig. Chicago: Franciscan Herald Press, 1973.

Fromm, Erich. *The Art of Loving.* New York: Harper & Row, 1956.

Jeremias, Joachim. *The Central Message of the New Testament.* New York: Scribner's, 1965.

John of the Cross. *The Collected Works of St. John of the Cross* (including *Ascent of Mount Carmel*). Translated and edited by Kieran Kavanaugh, OCD and Otilio Rodriguez, OCD. Washington, D.C.: Institute of Carmelite Studies, 1973.

Kasper, Walter. *Jesus the Christ*. New York: Paulist Press, 1977.

Kazantzakis, Nikos. *Saint Francis*. New York: Touchstone Books, Simon & Schuster, 1971.

Küng, Hans. *On Being a Christian*. New York: Image Books, Doubleday, 1976.

Nietzsche, Friedrich. *Thus Spoke Zarathustra*. Translated by Walter Kauffmann. New York: Viking Penguin, 1978.

Taylor, Rev. Thomas N. *Saint Thérèse of Lisieux: The Little Flower of Jesus*. New York: P.J. Kenedy, 1926.

Teresa of Avila. *The Interior Castle*. Translated by E. Allison Peers. New York: Image Books, Doubleday, 1972.

—. *The Way of Perfection*. Translated by E. Allison Peers. New York: Image Books, Doubleday, 1972.